i what i said

AN ANTHOLOGY OF BLACK WOMEN IN NONPROFIT

The Black Women in Nonprofit Leadership Cohort

GATHERED BY ERRIKA Y. FLOOD-MOULTRIE

I Said What I Said

An Anthology of Black Women in Nonprofit

The Black Women in Nonprofit Leadership Cohort

Copyright © 2023 Errika Y. Flood-Moultrie

All rights reserved First edition 2023.

ISBN: 9798394376528

ACKNOWLEDGEMENTS

Errika would like to take the time to acknowledge the women who authored the transformational chapters to follow. There is so much gratitude to be extended to each woman who has shared her personal experience, perspective, insights, and journeys in this anthology. Every journey is different, but every journey is important.

Additionally, it is important to mention and recognize the support of Dallas Truth, Racial Healing and Transformation and the initial funders of the pilot cohort because without their support the group would not have been able to complete this project.

Errika Y. Flood-Moultrie is to be honored and celebrated for her visionary leadership, passion for helping women thrive, and bold stance for speaking truth to power with fierceness, unwavering love, and commitment. This book is a reality because of Errika's obedient heart and courageous spirit of supporting Black women in expressing their unique truths clearly, boldly, and freely. May you see yourself in these pages and be inspired to own and stand in your greatness. Enjoy!

TABLE OF CONTENTS

INTRODUCTION

Errika Y. Flood-Moultrie

"I am not free while any woman is unfree, even when her shackles are very different from my own."

– Audre Lorde

It's hard to believe this book is here. I remember when the vision of Black Women in Nonprofit Leadership became a piece of my soul; it was a part that became obsessed with ensuring that Black women would have a safe space to empower their full and authentic selves. A place of no judgment. A place to release and to turn off. This was about and for them ONLY. A place where their skin color and gender were not a hindrance and where curly hair and all the colors of brown were fit for society.

As a Black woman, I was made to realize the notion of white supremacy and norms. My childhood was built on the perception that my curly hair and brown skin were unfit for society.

Battling these disparities, I stepped into the nonprofit sector where the missions focus on uplifting others, yet, even still, racism found a way to meet me there. The greatest disparity and lesson was when I was told to enter an event through the "Help's" doors.

I thought I would put so much into this introduction. There is

1

the story and really the start of Black Women in Nonprofit Leadership about the first time I invited Black women in the sector and how I thought no one would show up, and EVERYONE attended. It is the story of the growth from one peer group to five to quarterly lunches where Black women in the sector would show up to network, connect, and grow professionally. However, I don't want you to focus on that story. I want you to focus on the journeys of the women of the inaugural Black Women in Nonprofit Leadership cohort and the lessons they want you to learn from them as they did in real-time.

The book *I Said What I Said* is dedicated to women of color struggling through the racial disparities in nonprofit and for-profit workplaces and how they champion being phenomenal executives. This dedication is further exemplified through the commitment of the women of BWNPL Cohort One (or the OGs as they prefer to be called), through their insistence that all proceeds from sales of this book will benefit Black Women in Nonprofit Leadership future cohorts and Black women leading in the nonprofit sector through leadership development support.

The hope is that readers will learn, from real-life experiences of Black women, that their voices matter, their truth is to be appreciated and valued, and their lives are valuable and worthy of recognition and celebration. Throughout this book, you will live various women's lives and experience their frustrations in the nonprofit sector. Each contains an inspiring lesson for many to overcome hurdles and find ways to uncover and address racial issues.

The book's authors are women who are or have been directly involved in nonprofit organizations.

Some stories are about their journeys to leadership in nonprofits, how racial disparities stopped them from achieving their goals, the marginalization they felt by white hegemony, and finally, how they learned to stand and succeed in the face of opposition.

Finding "your calling" - the purpose of your existence - is the first step to combating obstacles as a Black female nonprofit executive.

CHAPTER ONE

Alana Pierre

"I embrace mistakes. They make you who you are."

- Beyoncé Knowles

When I started my journey with this group of wonderful women, I felt like I was carrying the weight of the world on my shoulders, more so personally than professionally in the beginning.

My personal relationship began to crumble on the very first day we all met virtually in January, and quickly a great day turned into something bleak. By our next meeting in February, the relationship was over. I remember thinking … how can I do this? How can I be fully present with this cohort while maintaining my work responsibilities and dealing with the emotional stress and pain from the loss of someone I thought would be in my life until the end? It ended with such little regard for me and everything we said we would share together. Drowning is a good word to describe how I was feeling at the time while trying to appear like I was completely together, happy, and at peace. I thought I had to appear okay, not realizing this was an opportunity for me to show I was not okay and be supported in that feeling of not being okay. So again, when I started this journey, I had no clue what I needed. I did not know I needed a village because I had not felt that level of comfort since spending childhood summers with my grandparents in Louisiana, but that is what was presented to me, a village of women who knew versions of my pain and struggles on so many levels.

A village that provided healing even in moments of silence during our first yoga and meditation sessions as we all placed our hands on our hearts and breathed in and out in unison. Never underestimate the importance of a supportive group, especially a group of women, in full support of everyone being connected, feeling empowered, encouraging growth, and embracing the strength within each of us.

This cohort, these wonderful ladies, supported me through my struggles and such deep sadness, even though they did not specifically know what I was trying to overcome. I welcomed the opportunity to stop and breathe and soak in the peace of it all, allowing my brain to move beyond the worries of the day and focus on what could be for me.

On day one of the cohort, our wonderful benefactor, Errika Flood-Moultrie, shared so many incredible things she had in store for us along the way, and I remember crying at the thought of such amazing opportunities. I allowed myself to cry happy tears for these opportunities and sad tears about how that day was going for me personally. After that day, the relationship unraveled more and more, and by the time I met with my executive coach provided by the cohort in February, the relationship was physically over but still emotionally overwhelming, weighing me down and really making me wonder again if I could make it through the cohort.

With my emotions still very raw, I met with my executive coach, and she asked me how I was doing. My mind scrambled a bit because, in my wildest dreams, I never imagined I would ever share anything regarding my personal life and what I was going through with her, but when someone asks how you are doing, and you are drowning on the inside, the overflow begins. It all came out ... how our relationship started, how it went over the years, how he finally committed, how he left, how it ended, and how I pretty much felt broken at that point. While I spoke, I was screaming at myself in my head to please just stop, but I kept talking. I apologized to her, and she calmly said, "I cannot help you professionally if you are struggling personally." Wow, I thought, that rings so true.

This opportunity to speak freely to her and, most importantly, that she heard me and validated my feelings was the first key to unlocking a door that had held all this anxiety, hurt feelings, terrifying thoughts, regrets, self-doubt, childhood trauma, and uncertainty surrounding my life choices. She had joined the village!!! Now, this did not resolve everything overnight, but it opened the door for me to begin facing all those things and start healing.

That honest conversation that, also admittedly, had plenty of tears shed, began clearing a path for me to own the fact that I needed healing and deserved healing. I deserved to be heard.

This newfound energy and respect for myself fit right in with what we first discussed in the group. We started with addressing mental health. Many of us need mental health resources but rarely stop to take care of ourselves and allow ourselves to receive support in that space. Somewhere in our minds, when we think of mental health and equate it to being taboo or something to keep hidden, I was making it day-to-day, trying to push any stressors unrelated to work to the background while focusing on what I convinced myself was most important, but you cannot fool your body into thinking everything will be okay if you just kept going and pushing through, without stopping to think about how if I was not well, everything I was paying more attention to over myself would land at someone's feet anyway.

At some point, I would have hit that wall and shut down. However, it was like Errika had a crystal ball, and I suppose in some ways she did because while our struggles may not be the same, they are often similar for Black women striving to be successful not just in work but also in life. The insights were eye-opening and doubled down on what my current employer's wellness team had been sharing throughout the pandemic, that we deserve to give ourselves attention, which in turn allows us to be present with our family, friends, coworkers, and even strangers.

Connecting with each other outside of our monthly meetings was encouraged. Honestly, part of my mind said yes, I want to be connected … I want to meet up with my cohort members and enjoy, but the other part, and more so my body, said no, sit here on the couch and wallow some more in this house. From January through March, getting through my workday efficiently was my focus, and after the workday ended, I then had to appear okay to my son until I would retire to my room for a bath and then bed. Usually, I only got a few hours of interrupted sleep; yes, interrupted. I had my routine of falling asleep to *Friends* and then waking up in the wee hours to *watch* Reba, which I had never watched before, by the way, until *The Golden Girls* came on. Before I knew it, daylight had come without having gone back to sleep, and it was time to get up and start another workday.

Sometimes, my Life 360 app mocked me when it showed my car literally had not moved in two weeks or more unless I had to go to the office. I had moved to Rockwall, known as the island in the Dallas/Fort Worth metroplex, which was a compromise with my significant other at the time since it was on "his" list of acceptable cities to move to. So, here I was in Rockwall, knowing close to nothing about the city, far away from my former life of places and people that gave me comfort and peace, which I had convinced myself would be okay because we were starting our life together in a new home. Not caring to know anything about Rockwall after the way it all ended, who would have thought a cohort connection would be the second key to unlocking a door keeping me confined to my couch and inside my house, shades closed, of course. She said, "I live in Rockwall, and we should meet for brunch one day." Of course, I happily accepted, but Lord knows I almost canceled that Sunday morning, not because of her, but because of me. I managed to drag myself out of bed, get ready, and head to Gloria's Restaurant at the Rockwall Harbor, which I wasn't even entirely sure how to get to. I laughed because when I entered the address into my GPS, it was less than ten minutes from my house, but I did not have a clue how to get there. I know … sad … but remember, I had pretty much shut down for social fun at that point. To say I had a good time is an understatement! We had so much in common and talked so effortlessly like we knew each other already, and a new friendship was born. Suddenly, I did not feel so isolated anymore, and I realized how much I missed people and something other than my weekly TV lineup on repeat.

Please know I was blessed many times over before this cohort too. The road has not been easy, but I would be remiss for not sharing how I could have been homeless more times than I care to admit, but I have never been.

I have come full circle in a way because, at one point, during a layoff, I had to seek assistance from a nonprofit organization. I went there three days in a row, waiting in line before I got an appointment for them to do the intake. They made sure I was helped and provided me with more resources than I anticipated, showing me kindness and giving me hope the entire time. I left there feeling blessed once more.

Three years later, I started with the North Texas Food Bank.

This was the first agency that I was assigned to help people in crisis. The lady who helped me was still there, and I went to her and said I know you do not remember me but thank you for what you did for my children and me. I am now here to serve others. I have been blessed to be able to work hard and learn skills that benefit my current career, where I feel valued, and which partly led me to be eligible to receive the benefits of being a part of this cohort. I have learned I am not an imposter who happened upon my current career but someone completely deserving of everything God has in store for me because I will always give my best when advocating for the people we serve, honored to serve with compassion.

My story is not unique as a struggling young Black woman, and many of those struggles molded me into who I am today. BUT what I am learning through this cohort will yield so many blessings. I have learned I am worthy of great relationships and opportunities, and it is okay to ask questions about everything I am curious about because there may be opportunities for growth that I am unaware of but can learn about through believing in myself and speaking up versus staying quiet.

I do not have to lock myself in a box, limiting myself because I allow fear of the unknown to occupy every part of my mind to where I just stand still in the comfort of what I already know and do well. I need to open myself up to new opportunities and be willing to step outside my comfort zone, recognizing that seeking a hand-up does not automatically result in closed doors or unwelcomed

10

consequences, leading to a setback versus a step up.

The hustle I had to learn as a young, single mom, often carrying the bulk of the work while some made six times my salary just for showing up at 10 am and occupying their desk until they walked out at 3 pm having done ten percent of what I had accomplished for the day, does not have to be my life for the rest of my life. Who knew anything about negotiating a fair salary or not selling yourself short just to be considered? That inner doubt would creep in, saying, "Am I asking for too much here, or maybe if I ask for too much, I will lose this opportunity altogether." I did not allow what I brought to the table to speak for itself, and I handicapped myself by being afraid to leave the table even when it did not respect what I brought to it.

What did I say earlier? Blessed! To be supported in this experience through the cohort and my work leadership has been amazing. I thought, for the most part, everything was under control, but really, I had been settling for existing, thinking this life was as smooth and under control as it was ever going to be. I glossed over things to keep everything going, not realizing there was rarely an off button for myself, neither personally nor professionally. I was giving others the power to cripple my spirit when they should never have been allowed such power over something as sacred as my peace of mind.

When you have the support of a village, it breathes life into your soul, whether with you physically or not. The spirit of that village is always there, driving you to keep moving forward. If you must stop and reset, the village does not judge you for recognizing that you need a reset, but they will not let you pause for too long. I have learned to appreciate the nudging and sometimes not-so-subtle push forward through stern but encouraging words meant to lift you up versus tear you down.

Abundant opportunities and new beginnings are things I now have available to me due to this wonderful experience.

I never thought about writing a Ted Talk, prioritizing self-care for myself and not just for my team, developing my personal brand outside of my employer, not only recognizing my value but believing in my value, and having an opportunity to write a chapter in a book to share all these experiences swirling through my head with others in hopes they will get a glimpse into this journey the cohort has afforded me.

I want you to know there will be times when you are broken, and everything seems like a never-ending ball of pain and uncertainty, but you must not stay in that space. Find yourself a village, and if you cannot find one, sometimes you must create one. I feel the Black Women in Nonprofit Leadership cohort was a vision first formed in Errika's heart and soul that took shape in her mind, and we are all honored to be a part of this great vision that I am happy to hear will live on for many more years. I started to say when I leave this cohort, but I do not ever want to lose the village. The journey will continue in me. I want to apply what I have learned from all the wonderful ladies in the cohort and all the phenomenal speakers who presented to us throughout this journey in my daily life. I will continue to walk in faith and lead by example for other women in my life and along my path to see what can be accomplished when you believe in yourself and seek to enhance your life spiritually, personally, and professionally.

Sincerely and grateful to be Blessed,

Alana Pierre

BWNPL Cohort Member

CHAPTER TWO

Ashley McIver

"Unity does not mean sameness. It means oneness of purpose."

- Priscilla Shirer

I grew up in Hope, Arkansas. A mighty town of 10,000 people. In Hope, my father was the principal at my school, one uncle was a teacher at the alternative school, and the other uncle was the superintendent. Yeah, I got away with NOTHING. Like most young children who know they are going to college but have to answer the annoying question, what do you want to be when you grow up? I didn't know. However, I did know I didn't want to be an educator. In high school, I was pretty involved in student organizations and loved working with children. From my limited worldview, I felt my only option was to become a doctor because education was out of the question.

I never envisioned myself working in nonprofit. The truth is, I didn't know the nonprofit sector existed when I was in high school. I was going to Baylor University to be a pediatrician. Why else would my parents send me to an expensive private school? Definitely not to work in a "not-for-profit."

Fortunately, my answer was wrong. I wake up every day and count myself blessed to be able to use my God-given gifts to help build a better community. I truly feel my work is my ministry, and that goes beyond a title or position. Purpose is bigger than all of that. It's my Guide. It's my Freedom. It's my Why. My purpose is why I ended up in nonprofit. It's why I am one of a few Black women working in philanthropy, especially in Texas. Paraphrasing from Madame Vice President Kamala Harris, I may be one of the first, but I won't be the last. My purpose is what gives me the confidence to walk boldly in spaces that weren't created for me. It's what makes me a kickass leader in this space. And so are you!

In the following pages, I seek to share the values that guide my everyday journey in the nonprofit world and ones I hope you can relate to because they have given you the same validation and purpose.

Purpose is rooted in values and is necessary for vision. I majored in biology pre-med in my first semester of college. What was I thinking? Baylor was very big on finding "your calling," but I wasn't sure what that was. However, it resonated enough to spark curiosity and led me to reflect on what it meant to me. I had a feeling it had something to do with living a fulfilling life. It seemed like something I should be interested in learning more about, right? As I got older, I realized it was another way of telling me to find my purpose.

I remember the most important class in my freshman year. It wasn't biology; it was a pass-or-fail class every freshman who

15

declared a pre-med major had to sit, which I imagine was about 70% of my class. One day, we gathered in a large auditorium to listen to two doctors who had gone through our program. One shared what I would call "the good news" that day. He encouraged us to major in something we were passionate about. He was trying to give us a heads-up because we were going to be taking the required courses to prepare us for the MCAT. That was his way of saying you will have enough hard classes. You don't have to make it harder on yourself; it's important to find balance and enjoy yourself. He continued to share that he enjoyed music, so he majored in music to create a balance for his rigorous pre-med courses. That was music to my ears, and I was listening on the highest volume.

Values. I remember coming home from the third grade and telling my mom that some of my friends, white friends, told me they were better than me. I can't remember why they said it. Was it my hair, my skin, both? I can't remember. But I remember my mom's response, one that I have used as a guide for how I view and treat others today. She said, "Ashley, no one is better than YOU! She paused to let me get my confidence back, almost instantly. She continued, saying, "but neither are you better than anyone else." I took that to heart, even in the third grade. My mom knew just what I needed to hear to feel empowered because she knew the power within me. She also wanted to make sure I knew I was supposed to use my power to influence and inspire others around me for good. That was one of my first lessons in humility.

Humility - Humility is necessary to serve. I'm sure you remember your first lesson in humility. Maybe it was from your parents or grandparents or not getting a job you thought you had. If you practice faith, maybe it was a lesson from God reminding you who He IS and who you are NOT! Humility helps us put ourselves and others in the right place in our minds and our hearts. It helps us not think of ourselves as too high or others as too low. I've found humility to be freeing. It also helps me not carry unnecessary burdens. It allows me to live in the moment and appreciate and value what and who are around me.

Discipleship – Discipleship is necessary for growth. The goal is to be better regardless of whether you call it mentorship or discipleship. For me, being better means being more like Christ, which comes from spiritual reformation. I believe God's power working in us helps us grow. Being good doesn't come naturally, but it helps when you have someone to walk alongside you, serving as your personal truth-teller, wisdom bearer, and encourager. For others, mentorship may be your preference, and that's great. The point is to be personally connected to someone so they can share knowledge you can apply to improve whatever skill or area of life you seek to grow.

I have had the great fortune to walk alongside great women who have mentored and discipled me – a double blessing. Both types were needed, but only one was necessary. One of my life goals is to always have a mentee. I have been both a disciple and a mentor, and I cannot think of a more humbling and rewarding experience. Centering and serving others help you stay humble.

Listening - Listening is necessary to gain wisdom. I changed my major to psychology, pre-med after my first semester and got a work-study job at a local nonprofit afterschool program. This opportunity gave me the freedom to explore my true passions. My job at Mission Waco opened the door for me to discover how I could actually "help people." I've always learned from others. I don't have to go through hell to know that hell is real. That may be why one of my strengths on the strength finder test was faith. Now, don't get me wrong. I veered many times, but they were usually intentional choices because I knew the consequences. I remember always telling myself, "Now you know if you do this, that will happen." I would answer myself and say, "yes, and I am willing to suffer the consequences." Bold, I know. Now, to speak of God's mercy would require a whole book. Just know I am humbled by God's grace and thankful for His mercy. I am also thankful that I learned humility early in my life. It taught me to seek both Godly and elderly wisdom, which has guarded and protected me in many rooms and situations in which I have found myself while navigating the nonprofit space.

I completely dropped my pre-med major after my sophomore year. The feeling can be summed up as "free at last, free at last, thank God Almighty; I am free at last!"

Balance is necessary for sustainability. One lesson I took from the Covid pandemic was that being busy was overrated, unproductive, and distracting. Busy for what? Why do we allow ourselves to get so busy? Another book for another day, *Busy in America; a dream killer.* Rest and balance are countercultures; it's a good thing my purpose isn't given or driven by the culture. We don't have to do the most; our gifts will make room for us.

I was watching the Disney movie *Encanto* with my children for the tenth time in three days, and one song just hit me. It had a nice beat, and I felt it could have been a theme song for women of color. It's called *Surface Pressure.* It starts by saying:

I'm the strong one

I'm not nervous

I'm as tough as the crust of the earth is

I move mountains

I move churches

And I glow 'cause I know what my worth is

I know what you are thinking! Yes, women, we run the world; we do it all! This verse exudes confidence, but wait, it continues:

Under the surface

I'm pretty sure I'm worthless if I can't be of service ...

A flaw or a crack

The straw in the stack

That breaks the camel's back

What breaks the camel's back it's …?

Under the surface

I think about my purpose; can I somehow preserve this?

If I could shake the crushing weight of expectations

Would that free some room up for joy

Or relaxation, or simple pleasure?

Instead, we measure this growing pressure

Keeps growing, keep going

'Cause all we know is

Pressure like a drip, drip, drip that'll never stop

Pressure that'll tip, tip, tip 'til you just go pop

Give it to your sister, it doesn't hurt

And see if she can handle every family burden

Watch as she buckles and bends but never breaks

No mistakes …

As the song says, we keep succumbing to the weight of expectations, be it the world, work, or family. It keeps taking our peace, joy, and rest. What would happen if we all operated in our gifts? What if we all did our part to light up the piece of the world that God has given us responsibility over? Notice I said, "piece." We can't shoulder the whole world, nor can we save it, even if we work in nonprofit. The truth is, we aren't supposed to. So, be humble and sit down. When we operate within our purpose, the impact of our collective gifts is greater because we see the value of others' gifts and the critical, non-competing role they all play in helping the sum of us find peace, rest, balance, and purpose.

Sometimes, to create balance, you must say, "No." Many things compete for our time, and some are good things. It's easy to say no to the things you don't want to do. It takes more discipline to say no to the things you want to do but should not prioritize at the time. The deadline for this chapter was the week before Thanksgiving. At that time, our Black Women in Nonprofit Leadership (BWNPL) cohort was preparing for a big speech we all had to create. It was like a TED Talk without the TED stage. I remember feeling so much pressure and stress during that time. So many opportunities were presented to me at once it was overwhelming. I asked for an extension, which was graciously granted. After I didn't meet that deadline, I concluded that I wasn't meant to become a first-time author. I just didn't have the time or mental capacity to write a chapter.

What would I write about? I was once more overwhelmed by the pressures of expectations and feelings of disappointment. About a month after my extension deadline, I texted Errika, BWNL's fearless visionary leader, to ask if it was too late to submit. She texted back and said, "No!" I was relieved. I still had time. You would think I would have gone straight to my computer. I didn't. I was tired and needed a break. I took two weeks off to be with family. I didn't work; I took time just to be present. I spent those two weeks doing things that brought me joy. I took walks, I took a road trip with my family. I had a party for my daughter and celebrated Christmas with family and friends over a game night. I prioritized balance. If we want to sustain ourselves and our impact, we must be intentional about creating space for simple pleasures and relaxation. We should never sacrifice purpose for productivity.

Faith - Faith is necessary for transformation.

I mentioned earlier that one of my strengths is faith. There's a spectrum of faith spanning those who have none and those who have a lot. I believe you don't need much, but you do need some to navigate life because faith is power.

For me, my faith is in God. Faith does so much for me. Faith is what allows me to have and be all the things I listed in the previous paragraphs, namely humble, balanced, disciple, mentor, and listener. Faith gives me hope that I can always get back on track when I choose to go left instead of right. God is rich in love, mercy, and grace, and I need all three, especially when I find myself trying to control or fix things that are out of my control. Faith puts this fight called life in perspective when I slip into comparison and forget my divine uniqueness. Faith helps me wake up and fight when the world we live in seems to be against us women, no, me – a Black woman.

God is literally the reason you are reading this chapter today. After that two-week vacation, I quickly jumped back into the saddle of work and concluded that I wouldn't submit my chapter. But purpose had another plan. I got an email on my way to my nephew's third birthday party saying, "This could be a complete oversight on my end, but I am unable to locate your chapters. Can you please resend them to me ASAP?" So here you are, reading my chapter. My mom drove the two-hour trip back from the birthday party so that I could start writing. I hung out with my mom and dad all afternoon once we got home, and then around 11 o'clock at night, I started writing again. I submitted my chapter at 2:30 am. Faith is the action that unlocks God's provisions. Nothing is impossible with God. He had the final say. "Now faith is the substance of things hoped for, the evidence of things not seen." (Hebrews 11:1). Faith encourages me. As songwriter Danny Gokey sings:

He had the solution before you had the problem

He sees the best in you when you feel at your worst

So, in the questioning, don't ever doubt His love for you

Cause it's only in His love that you'll find a breakthrough

It's like the brightest sunrise

Waiting on the other side of the darkest night

Don't ever lose hope, hold on and believe

Maybe you just haven't seen it, just haven't seen it yet

You're closer than you think you are

Only moments from the break of dawn

All His promises are just up ahead

Maybe you just haven't seen it, just haven't seen it yet

The final value that keeps me grounded and contributes to an automatic increase of positive energy in the room, the reason things get done, the value that nurtures and heals communities as well as executes; that value is … BEING A BLACK WOMAN!

BLACK WOMEN are NECESSARY for the nonprofit sector. No other words are needed. PERIODT (*pronounced Peer-ee-uhd-Ta*)!

I hope this chapter affirms your role in the nonprofit space and beyond. Remember, we are bigger than our jobs and better than our problems. I hope you are inspired to operate within your gifts, thereby freeing your mind, body, and soul to live a life of Balance, Peace, and Purpose! You've got this!!

CHAPTER THREE

Benaye Wadkins Chambers

"I'm no longer accepting the things I cannot change ... I'm changing the things I cannot accept."

- Angela Davis

I needed a minute, so I took a minute.

I first heard this from a friend of mine and fellow Black woman CEO, Bianca Davis. She posted it on her Facebook page, and it was a picture of her with a champagne glass in a hotel room. It struck me as "wow, that's awesome" because I love the saying she included. I found myself jealous and honestly a little internally critical of the decision, the statement, and the post, so I had to check myself, and I mean honestly check myself. Then, I got it.

Bianca was taking a minute because, as a Black woman leader in the not-for-profit sector, she needed a minute, and not a minute to be at home where she might have to think about cleaning or where people might know where she was but a minute to just be away from everything that would cloud her mind. Yet, I still questioned the need for it. As a CEO, I know what it means to need a minute, but I also know that I long went without taking a minute and what it cost me, then in that moment, I was proud of her. I was proud of her and to be her friend. I was proud that she didn't let opinions keep her from doing what she needed to do to take care of her mind and body and restore her peace and energy.

Then I was suddenly even more jealous. I mean, not envy, but I was jealous of why I hadn't thought of it for myself. I would never take a minute, until recently. It took a long time for me to get to the point where I understood that when I need a minute, especially as a Black woman in leadership, I really needed to take a minute and, guess what? So do you, Black woman. So do you!

I've been in this field for about 20 years. I'm the kind of person that pushes myself to the utter brink. I once chose to do a bike ride of 355 miles over four days, and in doing so, I had to train for months. I remember training with a friend when my leg started cramping up. I just couldn't go anymore. I remember he walked up to me and said, "Benaye, today is not the day for you to shine. Today is the day for you to let your body rest. The race is coming, and then you'll need to push yourself but not today." I remember being so angry at him and disappointed in myself that I couldn't finish this ride. It wasn't even that long; it was only 40 miles. I had ridden twice that much in a day. Quit? Me? But I've only done 40 miles, never mind it's 100° outside with a leg cramp so bad I couldn't feel my foot, but I couldn't go any farther. I decided to sag in, depressed, disappointed, and feeling like a failure. One month later, it was race day, and I did it. I rode 88 miles on day one, 89 on day two, and on day three, I rode 103 miles. My best friend Errika was working the volunteer crew, and was there to meet me. My father had put together my tent, and there were flowers inside. I felt amazing. But then, that night, the rain came in. I mean pouring down rain. Not just the rain but the cold came in too, and when we woke up the next morning, it was freezing, dark, and still raining. Half of my 11-member team quit the day before, with only five of us remaining. I coached one of them at the first rest stop. "Kerry, you can do it; we have come this far!" Steely-eyed, wet blond hair sticking to her face, she said with emphasis, "Nope." She was done, my main riding partner. We were on our way up a two-mile hill, and her legs locked up; she just couldn't go any farther. As a nurse, she said, "I'm not gonna push my body past what I know I can do, and you shouldn't either!" I said to her, "but I'm good; I'm gonna keep going." Then, at some point, I'm going through this area headed to the third and final rest stop before the finish, and my father passes me! My dad!! The man who had ridden all this ride with me, bought me a bike instead of a car when I was 16; he was 24 years older than me! He had sagged in every day of this ride, and now he was passing me. He was going faster than me, but that's okay because I'm gonna get up here and finish. I reached the rest stop, racked my bike, and headed for the snack table.

I got my snack, and I remember it was peanut butter on apple slices with raisins. I'd never had it before, but it was the best-tasting snack I've ever had. I can still taste it! I climbed into the warming van

28

with 20 riders I didn't know, all wrapped in mylar blankets, and sure enough, I got warm enough to go back out. I climbed on my bike. I was headed to the finish, and then I looked up. There was a guy standing to my right, a woman on my left, and another person behind me I never saw. I remember asking, "how are you guys moving so fast?" because, in my head, I was moving fast. The man very gently said to me, "you're not going to finish today." I said, "of course I'm going to finish!" They said, "no, your legs are locked." I wasn't moving; they were holding me up. It was the only reason I was still on my bike. They literally had to clip my feet out for me. The defeat and depression of that day set in. I wasn't celebrating riding 340 miles from Dallas to Houston, or that I had ridden over 2,000 miles training for this bike ride, or that I had done something most people would never do in a lifetime or even attempt. All I could think about was failure. I had failed. Crazy, right?! To think that I had failed after doing something so amazing, but I did, and this wasn't the only time. As I continued through my life and career, I would push myself to breaking point. I would work 20 hours a day, not sleeping, not eating. I used to travel for my job, and I remember once when I was on nine planes in four days just because I could. I never took a break just because I needed one. Black women I knew didn't do that. Ever.

A few years later, I started in nonprofit leadership. Working for a nonprofit gave me the type of energy and impact that would change people's lives – literally change people's lives – yes, that's what I wanted for my life. I started out as a manager and went back to school for another degree focused on leading the sector. Once more, I would nearly break myself working 40 or 50 hours a week, attending graduate school, and caring for my sister and husband, who were out of work at the time, and my nephew. I was driving myself literally insane. I didn't just need a minute; I needed many minutes, but I never took one because somehow, I thought it wouldn't get done if I took a minute for myself. Who's going to do it if not me?

Then, my personal life took a turn. My high-risk pregnancy was the limelight of my life, except it was the most traumatic physical and emotional experience I've ever gone through. Once more, I would push myself, even though the doctors told me to rest because I was extremely high risk. I never did. I went into labor at home, losing a liter and a half of blood. It would take three days before I saw my son because I was in the ICU, literally dying. I distinctly remember that our organization needed resources from a particular funder. I was supposed to meet with them the next week; it was going to be a very important meeting. Of course, being in the ICU, I was going to miss it. The minute I was awake and alert enough, I ensured my son was okay, then pleaded with my sister, "You've got to call my office and talk to my financial manager. You've got to tell her and the board chair what needs to happen with this meeting. " and I went through all of this in front of the nurses and the doctors. They were all shocked, puzzled, and asking, "You kidding? We are about to put a pic line in your heart!" My sister, knowing me all too well, said, "just let her get it out, and then she can refocus on what's really important." I would go through traumatic experiences for the next year while raising my son, dealing with all these health issues, and running an organization that was coming out of some really challenging times. I would go to the ER numerous times over the next year and, once, had to be taken from my job by ambulance. I can't tell you what I was doing to myself, but I needed a minute, and I never took one.

Fast forward to a new job. I've now changed my life. I thought I could go hide in a job or maybe I could do less and there would be less stress. As soon as I arrived, God had a different plan because he would put me in charge of a $50 million campaign in South Dallas for a small private Black school. It had never been heard of before, let alone talked about; there I went again, pushing myself until I was sitting in the office with one of my staff members, and suddenly, she became very blurry, and there was a ringing in my ear. I could barely hear, my chest was pounding so hard, and she took me down to the school nurse's office, where my blood pressure was 222/185. I was rushed to hospital. They thought I was having a heart attack or a stroke; neither was the case. The cardiologist visited to say, "there's nothing wrong with your heart, and your blood pressure is a little elevated, but what I think happened here is you had a panic attack." I lamented out loud with great irritation, "Me? A panic attack? No. I don't have panic attacks; you have me confused with someone else, right? I don't have panic attacks." He said, "yes, the only explanation is that you had a panic attack and you're stressed out. I don't know what you're going to do about it, but you need to do something." I thought about that long and hard. I started thinking about how tired I was, how stressed I was, how broken I felt emotionally at home and at work, and there was nowhere in my life that I felt at peace.

So, I went back to counseling. I had gone for two years but stopped because I made some decisions and didn't feel like I needed to go any longer, but the fact was, I did. I decided to leave my marriage because it was one of the places I knew there was no peace for me, and that wasn't going to change. I decided to open myself up to the opportunity of other jobs, not because they were going to be less stressful but because I no longer had peace in my work. I was frustrated, depressed, angry, and disappointed in myself. It was time to take a minute, or several, for me.

I started making small changes, working out again, hell, working out a lot, eating better, taking time away with my friends, not just a few hours but real time away. I started taking mental health days, not because I was sick, but because I was tired. I told my boss as much, while he was not sure about it. Then, before I knew it, these small changes began to bring me peace. My blood pressure and my overall health improved, and people started to say, "you look younger" because, believe it or not, I had started graying early. Nobody in my family grays before the age of 50. I finally had peace. I adopted the mindset that I would take care of myself first because I needed to take care of myself before I could take care of anyone else.

Now, as a divorced, single mom, I was okay and going strong.

Then Covid hit. Even in that, I met somebody new who was amazing and treated me like I deserved to be treated. I was great with that, but the lesson of Covid would truly teach me to take a minute. Not just any minute, but I was forced, like so many others, to take many minutes and really take stock of my life and ask myself who I had become. What had I accomplished? What should I be proud of? To my surprise, that list was long, my friend, it was very long. I have done so much more than I have given myself credit for; I have worked so much harder than I realized; more significantly, I was everything everyone said I was. Brilliant, beautiful, bold, and amazing. Oh, I am amazing. Let me say it now ... so are you, Black Woman.

I started to "believe my own press." I believed what everyone said about me and began to step into my purpose. I began to own my place in this world, my position as a leader in the not-for-profit sector. I started answering the call to the request, "I wanna pick your brain; you're so amazing. I want to know more about what you know and how you can help me." I started making myself available to be the expert that I knew I was and still am. Then more than anything, I started to take a minute!

I started to be okay with "I'm tired, and I don't want to do it today. I am exhausted, and I need a nap, so I'm going to take one. I need to get away, so I am going to get away, even if it's just for the day or night or a weekend." I needed to be away from whatever was bothering me to focus only on me. As a new CEO of an emerging organization into the next transition of its lifecycle, I am committed to taking a minute when I need a minute. No apologies. I need a day, an afternoon. I need to take myself to lunch, not to be with my friends or colleagues or donors or board members but just to be with Benaye. Not to surf my phone or read a book but to sit quietly and allow myself a minute.

What am I saying to you, BWNPL? The road ahead is hard and long. If this is your desired journey, you better be ready. You better pack up all the tools you'll need, and so many of them are included in this book and hundreds of others. Put on that backpack and get walking, sometimes running, sometimes standing still but always in forward motion. This world has it out for you, and that's the truth. I'm not going to sugarcoat it. You are the epitome of what many fear. History tells us we have always been the go-to person to "get it done" as long as it was for someone else. The Black woman was brought here as a slave, rose early to feed her family and take care of her children and her husband, if she had one, or the community of people she was in, and then go pick the cotton, birth her own baby, and go back to work the next day. After a full day of field labor or housework, she would return home to care for her family, broken in every way at the end of the day, emotionally and physically, then, she would rest briefly to start all over again the next day, and that's what we were bred and trained to do. The sad part is the mindset of the hard-working Black woman has been passed down for generations. Just go until you can't go anymore. That's why Black women are leading in deaths by heart attack, stroke, high blood pressure, and diabetes; we take care of ourselves last and, sometimes, not at all.

Now, back to my friend whom I admire so much for posting her truth that she needed a minute, so she took a minute. Back to reminding myself how history trained me to push hard through this life to this moment, making that statement from her defining for me. I was starting a new role as CEO, as I mentioned. I saw the writing on the wall, "You are about to push yourself to breaking point," but I didn't want to say I committed in that moment when I read that post that I would take a minute whenever I needed a minute. So, what do you think happened? I didn't. What did happen? I bought and began renovating a house while planning a wedding with my child going from elementary to middle school. I could see it all ahead of me, all the crazy. Then, I snapped my ACL. What was I doing? Absolutely nothing. I was trying to get some gum out of my purse with my leg wedged between the seat in front of me and my seat, and it just snapped. A month later, I had surgery and had to sit down. I asked God, "What are you trying to say to me? Because clearly, I'm not getting the message." He said what he said when I broke my foot two years prior, what he had been saying every moment since, "Slow down, I've got you. You don't have to be more for anybody. You are enough for me." I've been driving around with a license plate that says "IAMENUF" with the wonder woman signal next to it. That's a whole chapter in another book. But I hadn't quite accepted it until I tore my ACL because it was then that it was clear that God spoke to me, so clearly, "You are enough for me," and that's where I want to take you, my friends. Stop trying to be enough for all the rest of the world and start with being enough first for the God you serve and second for you. When you are enough for God and for you, you are, by nature, enough for everybody else. Black woman, if you haven't been told, hear it today. You are more than enough for all who need you.

The moral of my life's stories is simply this: When you need a minute, take a minute. I know that sometimes, we don't know how to do that, but I want to take these next few pages and give you five major ways I believe are the outcomes and the benefits of you taking a minute.

Take a minute to BREATHE.

If you look up one of the reasons so many people are tired, it's because they don't actually breathe when they're under stress. Have you ever thought about how often you sigh deeply during the day? Most often, it's because you haven't been breathing at a regular rhythm. One thing that yogis or stress management experts will tell you is to breathe; the deeper, the better. We often do so much or run so hard that we don't realize we're not breathing. Worse, we are holding our breath, reducing the oxygen in our bodies that helps our brains function better. I have learned that when I'm really stressed out and things are making me feel crazy, I just stop and breathe deeply through my nose and out through my mouth, long, exaggerated deep breaths. Years of yoga have helped me learn to touch my belly to feel the breath coming in all the way until I can't hold it anymore. The key to the cleansing breath is to avoid just blowing it out hard rather than breathing out slow and steady. What I really love doing is whatever is stressing me, I think on it while I'm blowing it out with my breath. For example, I think about that staff member who can't follow instructions, breathe in, then blow out their name and the frustration. Try it. Breathe in as deeply as you can, then think of the matter that is causing you not to have peace. Is it your job, marriage, a family member or child, or the news of the day? Then let it out with a long, slow deep breath.

Just keep breathing until all those thoughts about how unhappy or frustrated you are, until your impulsive reactions are gone, and you feel like you are calmer with clearer thoughts. If you try now, then you will know the feeling of being more relaxed. However, if you did, I dare you to try it the next time you are in that moment. You know the one, the one only you understand, then start breathing long, deep breaths for five to 15 minutes. These exercises also work great just before bed. I am not telling you anything new; you probably teach this concept to people in your organization or to your children but aren't we the worst at following our own advice?!

It is the moments we take to focus our minds and spirits that allow us to lead better and stronger organizations and teams. Yes, I promise you will lead better through good breathing habits. So as a leader, do what we know works, put it on the calendar to take a minute and breathe. You set the time before meetings regardless of the news to be shared. The other gem of this simple activity is you can do it anywhere. Take a quick walk around your office or outside your building, turn off all devices, then sit silently and breathe in a closed office or your car. My best friend sits in her garage, and often I laugh at her, but the truth is, it's a very quiet place, and almost no one looks for you there. And let us not forget this exercise is good for everyday living even when you're excited; it's even more important. Sometimes, when we're excited, we let negative thoughts in. Take a minute, be excited, breathe in all the joy of the moment, and breathe out anything that might be negative. Use these breaths as opportunities to receive the good and release the bad, receive the air, and let out all the negative energy from things going on in your day and life. I guarantee these efforts will improve with regular breathing practice. Take a minute and breathe, my Black sister … breathe.

Take a minute to LAUGH

I firmly believe that laughter is medicine for the soul. TikTok drives me crazy, I mean, it really drives me crazy, but the one thing I love about TikTok is that some stupid people are doing some really stupid stuff that just happens to be gut-bustingly funny! Sometimes when I need a laugh, I watch a bunch of TikToks or turn on the comedy channel or my favorite funny show. I will laugh and immediately feel better. I will call that friend who I know always has something crazy to say because I know they're going to make me laugh. I'll even go back over silly things I've done or call a friend and say, "girl, you remember that time …" because I know we're going to laugh about it and hard. I encourage you, Black women, to find laughter, and if you can't remember the last time you laughed, I mean really laughed, then it's been too long. Life is too short, and too many funny things are happening around you. Find reasons to find laughter in your life and keep a smile on your face because it does really take fewer muscles to laugh than it does to frown. If you're not experiencing joy, you can't experience laughter, so if you can't remember the last time you laughed, take a good long look, my friend; find a reason to laugh, and, most of all, find a reason to re-discover your joy.

Take a minute to be ALONE and SILENT

This is not to be lonely but to be by yourself and okay with that. We are overstimulated with technology and noise, forgetting to just be alone and silent. We don't forget; we just don't want to because when we're silent, our minds start to speak to us. If you haven't done it in a long time, it might have some things to say that you really want to hear.

When we are alone and silent, we really hear our hearts' desires, the truth and joy, but we can't do that when there's always noise in the background, whether it's music, kids running around, work calling, or messages and notifications of many kinds.

I challenge you as a Black woman to find a moment in every day to be alone and silent, whether to wake up an extra five minutes or when out walking. Take time to listen to what your body has to say.

Where does it hurt that you hadn't noticed before because you are constantly moving, or where does it suddenly feel good where it hurt before, but you didn't notice it got better? What is your mind telling you is unhealthy that you need to check and check hard, then get rid of? What is your heart saying it needs from you? Does it need more time with your family? Does it need more time like this with you, just alone? Does it not need love from others but love from you to yourself? Does it need to rest? Whatever you need, you deserve that time.

Decide three things from your thoughts that you will address, whether physical, emotional, or spiritual. As a believer in God and His son, the Christ, it is in these quiet and alone moments that He speaks to me most clearly. God is not going to fight through your noise to talk to you, so if you never take time to be alone and silent, giving Him your undivided attention, you can miss hearing from God. Then you say, well, he doesn't talk to me. I never hear from Him, or I don't know what He wants from me, but the reality is you haven't given Him the space. Give yourself time to restore your mind, body, and spirit.

Take a minute to GET AWAY.

I remember several years back, I worked with a woman who said she goes on a trip every year and sometimes on two or three. I wasn't that impressed until she went on to share that these were not regular trips. "I'll take myself away sometimes, at least once a year, but sometimes more, depending on what's going on." Her family and coworkers love it when she goes away. "In fact, my husband books my trips for me," she said. "When I've been really stressed, I've taken a whole week!" What she and her family and friends had figured out was that she is a better person when she takes time away.

In my last CEO role, I really needed a break. I had been working myself to the bone, and my stress level was through the roof. I went to my board to request a sabbatical, and they said they couldn't approve one, but I had seven weeks' vacation, and if I wanted to take that, I could. And indeed, I did. As I was preparing to leave, one of my staff members came to me to share her appreciation for my time away." I'm so glad you're going away, Benaye. We need you to come back better and stronger. You are all over the place; you were having five conversations at once and don't know whether you're coming or going. You are amazing, and you're brilliant, but we are not getting that Benaye right now, and that's who we need."

I thought, wow. I was so proud of her for saying that to me, but I was also horrified that she had to. I was gone for a month, and when I came back, I had more clarity than I'd ever had in my life about so many things, and one was that I needed to do this more often. Now, that's not to say I did; I just knew I should.

We already talked about the fact that Black women are notoriously the people who take care of everybody else and take care of themselves last. Please be encouraged today if you want to be your best as a leader, learn how to take time away, and even if all you can manage is to drop the kids at school and see your husband off to work, the same if you're not married and don't have kids, go spend an entire day at the park. One of my standby favs is to pack a picnic lunch, a blanket, my favorite book, and my music and just be in a different environment to get a fresh perspective and a different view of the world. Take it all off, take off being the executive or other roles who everybody needs you to be, and just take a minute because the truth is, you need a minute; you need several minutes. If you don't take it, most people aren't going to give it to you, and when you take a minute, you will come back energized with new ideas and ready to take on the next phase. Take a minute to get away and take care of yourself.

Take a minute with REAL FRIENDS

Iron sharpens iron, my friends. If you don't have iron-sharpening friends, you will end up dull. Surround yourself with people who will sharpen you. I believe every Black woman and nonprofit leader needs these friends to sharpen her and keep her ready to lead.

First, you need an older, wiser woman who can tell you the ways of the journey, not because you must follow the same one but because she's wise and she's been down the road. She knows a bit about what you're going through and will have some great suggestions for how to get you there. These are the women you just listen to. Ask as many questions as you can because you want to understand how she became the best in her field or the most renowned by name, or how she didn't, and maybe why she chose not to. What failures did she encounter that she would impart upon you to avoid? There is wisdom in age and experience. One day you will be the wise woman a young Black woman in leadership seeks out. Be sure you are learning from one so you know how to be the teacher in the future.

Second, you need friends your age or one headed through this journey with you. There's nothing like camaraderie to understand, "Hey, this is a hot mess; what are you doing? How are you handling this?" And you'll have the same sage advice for her, or it will just be good to commiserate that it's hard and to be reminded you are not alone in this journey. They don't make it easy for us. We have to live and work by different standards of expectation, and there's nothing like a friend or partner in the space that you can sharpen yourself against just because they understand what you're going through or you get to be the person that understands what they're going through.

Third, you've heard it 1,000 times; every woman needs a mentor. It is equally important that you are mentoring. I don't care how old you are; if you are a Black woman and a nonprofit leader, you have something to teach about how you got there, your hopes, and what you've encountered thus far. Mentor a young woman on her way up through the ranks. Maybe you're early in your career, and this is a college or high school student, but always be willing to take that wisdom you have learned from that older woman in your life who is a seasoned expert you spend time with. Take that knowledge you're gaining in the camaraderie of your colleagues in the same space and impart that to a young woman who is seeking, yearning to be you one day. That's the first step you need to realize.

Someone out there is seeking to be you who is looking at you, watching you all the time, and just because you don't see it doesn't mean it's not happening. Be available to that young woman. Maybe you need to seek her out through a program or ask your mentor to recommend a young woman who needs you. She will find you someone. Join a cohort and reach out to the leaders in your sector or just look around your circle to see if there's some young woman who could do good for you. Take a minute to evaluate your opportunity to influence another Black woman in any kind of sector.

Lastly, but most importantly, I want you to take a minute with your girlfriends. These are the women (and maybe even a man or two) who know those secrets about you. They know the truth about you. There's no need to code-switch with them, you are exactly who you want to be and who you need to be, and they accept you for it always. There should be a standing time that you spend with them, whether on FaceTime because they're in another location or you just can't get together, over Zoom because that's the best you can do, brunch (with BACON), weekends away, walks in the park, etc. Where is your time with your friends? These "sistas" are here for you at the end of the day; they just get you and, most significantly, let you be you. These are your ride-or-die down for whatever friends. You know all there is to be said with a look or a nod.

I am there for them, too. I regularly tell my son that to have good friends, you must be one. If your circle is void of true friends, it might be time to ask yourself if you are a good friend.

Let's also be okay with letting some friends go. Let me caution you that not everybody can be your friend. Some you have to keep close but feed with a long-handled spoon. It is important to know that your friends represent you. When somebody causes you hurt or pain, or they decide to walk away, it's okay because everybody has a season in your life. Never regret that friend who walked away, or you had to ask to leave for whatever reason. Always appreciate what they brought into your life, whether a new understanding, laughter, wisdom, kindness, or support in that season that you needed it. Not all friends are meant to be your friends for life, so enjoy them while they're there and be the best friend you can be. I can assure you when you need to take a minute to be with your true friends, not only will they give you a minute, but they will also give you as many minutes as you need.

In the end, I just want to encourage you in these words "relax, relate, release." If you were a child in the 80s and 90s, you will know exactly where this comes from. For those of you who don't just look up the Whitley and Debbie Allen scene in *A different world*. You will learn what relax, relate, release means. Much of what we try to do as Black women and nonprofit leaders is control, contrive, and constrict. This only results in struggling and strangling the life out of our journey and our leadership. All you can do in this work is give your best. Black woman, your best is most certainly amazing. Your

80% is better than most people's 100%. It's not just enough to rest on that; you must still work at giving your 100% every day, you still have to work at doing your best in all things because we all know we are judged on a different spectrum, but we also know, without a doubt, that we are going to deliver on the expectation better than most. When you start to find yourself slipping, frustrated, down, head hurting, and chest pounding, just remember to take a minute.

You've got to know that better about yourself than anyone else, but in case you don't, empower someone else to take stock of you. Let them remind you to take a minute. Maybe that's your spouse, a child, a friend, or your assistant at work. I have three people responsible for telling me when it's time for me to take a minute. I have empowered every assistant in my last three jobs. I tell them, "Your job is to recognize when I am not giving my best, and say to me, 'I think you need to take a personal day' or 'why don't you get out of here this afternoon and go get your nails done' or 'you know what, Benaye, there's not a lot on your calendar tomorrow, so I'm going to clear everything else, and when you come in, I'm just gonna shut your office door so you can take care of whatever is on your desk that needs to be taken care of.'" I have empowered my friends, my girlfriends, to say, "Girl, I'm a need you to take a minute or several. Stay home today, go out for drinks with us but you are stressed to the hilt, and you need to take a minute." My third person is my son. I didn't empower him to do it, but he knows me so well; he's so like me that he'll say, "Mom, I think you need a nap. You need to go to bed early tonight." It's so funny whenever he says it because I look at him, and I think if my eleven-year-old is aware enough to know I need a nap or I need to take a break, then I need to take one.

Listen to yourself. Listen to the people around you. Then, when it's time, whether you know it or not, you feel it, or someone has told you that you need a minute … my friend, sister, Black woman in nonprofit leadership, I implore you to take a minute.

CHAPTER FOUR

Brenda J. Gomes

"Instead of letting your hardships and failures discourage or exhaust you, let them inspire you. Let them make you even hungrier to succeed."

- Michelle Obama

Dear Black women in the nonprofit sector, my message is to always remember to take care of yourself. I know this is easier said than done with all the tasks and responsibilities on your plates. As Black women, we place so much on ourselves and often feel we must prove ourselves to others. You are a beautiful Black queen, and your wellbeing is paramount for you to continue your amazing work. The pressures we place on ourselves cause us to forget how wonderful we are and how we need to protect our minds, bodies, and souls. So please, take care of yourself, love yourself, and believe in yourself during the challenging times. I aim to share some of the pitfalls I've encountered so you can avoid them and not have them negatively affect your wellbeing. Then, I will offer some suggestions on how to mitigate these pitfalls or prevent them from occurring. Before I begin, I want to tell you a little about my journey here.

My journey in the nonprofit sector began almost 20 years ago. Like many of you, I observed the disparities and injustices in my community. As I grew up, I knew I wanted to create change, so I decided being a lawyer was a way to 'save the world' and assist others.

My major changed several times in undergraduate school, but my goal to attend law school remained steadfast. However, unfortunately, my post-law school plan was not as clear-cut. My plans ranged from starting a nonprofit for teen moms to working for the Department of Labor or the CIA and even a public defender. As fate would have it, a funny thing happened in law school; I discovered the legal system was imperfect. I know, right? My experience in law school slightly deflated my notions of 'saving the world' once I realized I had been viewing the legal system through rose-colored glasses.

My naïve butt believed that the truth would set you free if you had your day in court and a lawyer by your side. The bottom line is all those legal cases I read in school were discouraging, and the cases reported in the news did not help. My eyes were opened to the fact that justice is not blind. In most circumstances, your socioeconomic status and/or color play a part in the outcome. Despite this realization, I continued my studies and graduated.

While obtaining my law degree, I worked full-time and attended law school in the evening. My job exposed me to some phenomenal nonprofits in the community and their impactful work. They were making a difference and changing people's lives. Thus, my interest in the nonprofit world sprouted. Yes, a light bulb moment occurred; I discovered my career path to helping others. As they say, the rest was history. Sorry for the corny cliché. Enough about me; I felt it was essential to give you some context into how I became involved in the nonprofit sector. Like many of you, it was the desire to help others.

Let's get back to my chapter's purpose. I'd like to begin with my experience with the Black Women in Nonprofit Leadership (BWNPL) cohort. When the fabulous founder, Errika Y. Flood-Moultrie, told the group we would each write a chapter for a book dedicated to Black women nonprofit leaders, I was beyond excited. However, it was more challenging than I imagined when I sat down to write. My mind was blank. What can I offer these beautiful, intelligent, compassionate, and savvy women? I grabbed a glass of wine and reflected on the last several months with the BWNPL cohort and my time in the nonprofit sector. My experience with the BWNPL cohort allowed me to strengthen my skills, learn new ones, recognize the importance of self-care, and bond with amazing Black women.

I will never forget the three simple words, "You are worthy." You will frequently see the word "worthy" in this chapter because our extraordinary leader ingrained it in our minds throughout the cohort. I wish to instill the same idea in your mind that **"you are** worthy." Always remember these three words and put them everywhere in your daily life; on the bathroom mirror and taped to the bottom of your computer monitor. Live by these words. You are probably wondering what this has to do with taking care of yourself. When we don't feel worthy, it can affect us mentally; if not addressed, it can affect us physically. Let's talk about taking care of ourselves.

My cohort experience and journey as a nonprofit leader have provided me with the insight and key takeaways that I can now pass along to others. I've distilled these insights into another powerful message, "Take Care of Yourself." I know you're thinking, "Really? That's your big revelation!?" It sounds so simple, but reflecting on my experience, taking care of yourself is not simple.

First, full disclosure; I was guilty of not caring for myself for decades. I would often metaphorically 'beat myself up.' Typically, when my voice was ignored, things weren't going as planned, or when I was simply overly critical of myself. It took me some time to recognize this harmful behavior and, second, to identify the triggers causing it. Only then could I eventually halt the negative thoughts and self-talk that left me emotionally and spiritually bruised and battered. I had to learn how to give myself some grace and not internalize everything when people were not hearing or supporting me. If you don't, it will adversely affect your work and personal life, including your health and mental wellness. To take care of yourself, you must get out of your head and remove the negativity from your life. I want to pass along some 'don't beat yourself up' (DBYU) moments (or pitfalls). This way, when they occur, you will recognize and stop them before they spiral out of control. I will also provide suggestions to create an arsenal of tools to assist you during DBYU moments.

As a leader in the nonprofit sector, you are in this position because of your leadership, skills, compassion, and desire to make positive changes in the communities you serve. It is frustrating when you cannot make the positive changes you desire, and your ideas or opinions are ignored or downplayed. DBYU when those scenarios occur, take a step back and breathe. It took me a long time to grasp this notion and believe me, it is still a work in progress. Thus, I offer you this advice: try to mitigate some of your frustrations when this happens.

I am by no means suggesting you allow others' behaviors that negatively affect you to continue without being addressed. There are personal agendas, lack of knowledge of those making the decisions, and maybe racism or sexism that all contribute to the stifling of your ideas and opinions. However, please do not allow your wellbeing to suffer because of it. I will talk more about focusing on your wellbeing later but let me elaborate on this point for now.

Several years ago, I was the director of a nonprofit's education and training department. Opportunities included GED and ESL classes and training programs such as welfare to work and youth development training. I was responsible for the youth development program, which became "my baby." This program provided many

53

training opportunities to prepare youth for the workforce and further their education plans. One program provided construction training. The organization built affordable housing, and the youth received hands-on training to build the houses. Finding a contractor that was effective at building homes and teaching young adults the craft of home construction was essential.

There was a nonprofit with previous experience training individuals before and during the construction process. I met with the leaders of the nonprofit construction program and visited their site. I was very impressed with their track record and their training plan. I knew they would provide the best training environment for our program. I spoke with the CEO about the organization and highly recommended we utilize them for the project. Unfortunately, the CEO hired another construction company. In my heart, I recognized this decision was not in the youth's or program's best interest. I knew the construction workers at this other company would not provide a suitable educational environment for the program. I expressed my concern several times by presenting an argument backed up with facts and my legitimate concerns. Nothing changed, and the CEO told me I could leave if I didn't like it. I took it very personally and allowed it to consume me for a long time. The house was built, but unfortunately, many program participants dropped out because of a lack of instruction and patience, favoritism, and unprofessional behavior. I beat myself up and questioned whether I had fought hard enough and was the right person for the program.

It took me a while to recognize I had given it my all, but it was not my final decision to make. It was a battle I did not win. Honestly, I felt it would have ended differently if I were a man. I would be lying if I said that was the last time I beat myself up. However, it has stuck with me the longest. As in any job, your idea, approach, or opinion may not be accepted, and that's okay. If you do the work, you should walk away knowing you did your best. It's them and not you. Keep your ideas and opinions flowing and remember DBYU. I know this is common sense, but as leaders in the nonprofit sector, our passion for the work and clients can make it very personal.

Another contributing factor in 'beating myself up' comes in the form of self-criticism. I am highly critical of myself, tend to put a lot of pressure on myself, and overanalyze and get in my head when my plans or ideas do not go as planned. We have all heard the saying, "Pick your battles." Sometimes, it really is that simple. However, if your supervisor or peers continually reject your ideas, alternative steps must be taken. Perhaps a one-on-one conversation with your supervisor is necessary. If nothing changes after the meeting, it may be time to move on to an organization that will appreciate your ideas and opinions. Whatever the reason, don't beat yourself up or question your skills and experience.

In the nonprofit sector, we wear many hats, which amounts to more work. Our capacity to work effectively for our organization and ourselves will be affected at some point. We can only juggle so many balls before one or more falls. You must address it if you determine too much is on your shoulders. Ask for more help or say "No" to new projects. Don't beat yourself up because you need to ask for help or feel overwhelmed. As Black women, we feel weighed down by the pressures of society and a constant battle to prove ourselves. Please, don't add additional weight with a self-beat down.

This brings me to impostor syndrome. As stated previously, beating ourselves up can conjure feelings of doubt in our abilities. It can lead to what is known as imposter syndrome. Don't allow imposter syndrome into your world. When we question our effectiveness, we feel inadequate and begin to question our abilities, which leads to self-doubt, ultimately affecting our self-confidence. I expressed earlier that the BWNPL cohort gave me a great experience, but I did not mention the arsenal of knowledge, tools, and resources it provided me to utilize in my life and enhance my journey. One resource is an excellent book, *The Empress Has No Clothes: Conquering Self-Doubt to Embrace Success,* by Alexander Kopelman and Joyce M. Roche. This book is Joyce M. Roche's autobiography about her struggles with self-doubt and feeling like a fraud, but most significantly, it is about how she triumphed over imposter syndrome. Looking at her bio, you would never think she had self-doubt. Joyce attended an Ivy League school, became the first Black woman vice president of Avon and president of a leading hair care company, and is currently the CEO of Girls Inc. How does this happen? Why does this happen? What is imposter syndrome?

Imposter syndrome, in a nutshell, occurs when you doubt your abilities and question your worthiness despite your competency. The syndrome can affect everyone. The term was introduced in 1978 by psychologists Pauline Rose Clance and Suzanne Imes. The original term was imposter phenomenon. Clance and Imes focused on high-achieving women. According to the Harvard Business Review, variables like racism, xenophobia, and classism were missing, and, most significantly, women of color were absent from the study.[1] As stated earlier, the syndrome affects everyone, but it impacts women of color more often. Those adverse feelings we place on ourselves are heightened when we don't see people like us in the workplace. As a result, we can feel we are letting down our gender and/or ethnicity. Yes, another ingredient to add to the self-beat down.

These dysfunctional feelings are exacerbated by a lack of support from peers and/or supervisors. As a leader, I feel detached from my peers because of the nature of my role. Unfortunately, the lack of support can be a part of the workplace's construct for Black women. These feelings hinder our greatness if we do not check them. If you do not tell yourself you are worthy, it affects your confidence level and it could become a self-fulfilling prophecy. It comes from the idea if you believe something about yourself, good or bad, it will manifest in your life. If you think you cannot do something for long enough, you psych yourself into believing it. You also start believing it if someone tells you that you cannot do something enough times. If you continue to allow self-doubt in your mind and think you are an imposter, this can manifest into depression and anxiety. Don't allow these negative self-doubting thoughts to stay in your head.

[1] *Stop Telling Women They Have Imposter Syndrome, by Ruchika Tulshyan and Jodi-Ann Burey, (February 11, 2021), Harvard Business Review.*

Earlier, I provided an example of when I felt my voice was not heard. I struggled with feelings of inadequacy and questioned my competency because someone dismissed my opinions and ideas. It took a minute to get out of my head before the negative thoughts led me to a dark place that would affect my work and personal life. Imposter syndrome can hinder your trajectory if you don't check it.

Thank you for indulging me with my DBYU rant and falling prey to impostor syndrome. The good news is I have some tools and tips to help halt the self-beat down and imposter syndrome before they affect your wellness, strengthen your conviction in yourself, reinforce your worthiness, and, ultimately, take care of yourself.

My first suggestion comes from my experience with the BWNPL cohort. The cohort completed a personality assessment to assist us in our leadership journey. It was an insightful tool and another resource added to my arsenal. You may have already taken a personality or behavior assessment. There are several good ones, like the DISC assessment, Myers-Briggs, HIGH5, etc. I have completed the DISC assessment, Myers-Briggs, and Strength Finders. I highly recommend taking an assessment if you have not already.

About ten years ago, I completed an assessment as part of an organization-wide initiative. It blew my mind how accurate the insight was regarding my strengths, areas of improvement, and communication style. Joyce M. Roche suggests taking an inventory of your skills, strengths, and achievements in her book *The Empress Has No Clothes* to reference when imposter fears start creeping into your head. This will help validate your worthiness; please include an assessment in your inventory.

It's also a great tool for understanding other people's strengths, communication styles, etc. I believe it is powerful to have this information at your disposal. In my line of work, it is an excellent resource to help teams work more effectively. As a supervisor, I can review my employees during one-on-one meetings and dive into their strengths and areas of improvement, thus, allowing me to engage that staff person's strengths and create a development plan. As for you, share your assessment report with your supervisor to delve into your strengths and areas of improvement. You will better understand the individuals around you and who you collaborate with within the organization.

Now, I realize not every organization has the resources to provide everyone with a complete personality assessment. However, I encourage you to reach out to your human resources department and your leadership to make a case. At the very least, see if your department and supervisor can take the assessment. It is a powerful development tool and excellent for tapping into your strengths and your teams' strengths and determining how people like to receive information or communicate in general. It's a great management tool and will help strengthen your team and your interaction with them.

The more you are aware of your strengths, the better armed you are to validate your worthiness when doubts start popping into your head.

Joyce M. Roche spoke to the cohort and mentioned believing your press. She suggested writing a press release about your achievements, strengths, and overall fabulousness. Use your inventory to assist in writing your press release and pull it out when you need a reminder. Don't forget to pull information from your personality assessment.

My second suggestion is to surround yourself with positive people and identify your support team. This may consist of family and friends, but I recommend also having a go-to support group of women to help lift you. I often mention what the BWNPL cohort provided me during my experience, and I said it offered many resources and tools to strengthen me as a Black woman and a Black woman leader. It also provided great speakers who educated, enlightened, and encouraged us. One such speaker was Cynt Marshall, CEO of The Mavericks. I cannot express how inspired I was by Cynt. There were several takeaways from her time with us, but I want to share a couple with you.

She discussed the importance of having a HASU network (hook

a sista up). If you do not have a group of women like this around you, you need to create one. They can hook you up with some positivity and joy. You will need them to remind you that you are amazing when you are not feeling so amazing.

Another nugget Cynt shared was the values she lives by, personally and professionally. We all have values that we stand by, but do we write them down, print them out, and have them at the forefront of our daily lives? It triggered me to think about my values. Most pertained to my personal life. I stepped back and considered, "Are my values reflected in how I live and work?" After thinking about it, I created my list, comprising family, integrity, joy, open-mindedness, consistency, reliability, growth, perseverance, and respect. So, my third suggestion is to encourage you to think about the values you live by each day or want to live by each day and write them down, print them out, frame them, and place them at work and home to help ground you and not allow others to pull you away from those values.

My fourth suggestion is to recognize when you are overwhelmed and take action to lessen your load. We are reluctant to ask for help or say no to additional projects or tasks in the workplace. There are often budget cuts or loss of grant funds at nonprofits; as a result, the extra work falls in our laps, and because we are awesome at achieving results, people place more on our desks. As I said, we can only juggle so many balls before we start to drop them. Our work suffers, and most significantly, we suffer. Too much work will lead to burnout and affect your mental and physical wellbeing. The cohort provided me with the much-needed permission to say, "Timeout! I am overwhelmed, and something needs to give." Telling my supervisor I was overwhelmed and needed help was a sign of weakness for me. If your leadership supports you and a culture of employee self-care, they will provide you with the time or resources to assist you. If they do not, find a work environment that will support the wellbeing and self-care of its employees. Yes, we need to make a living, but not at the expense of our health. If you are overwhelmed or on the verge of burnout, please take action to lessen your workload.

My fifth suggestion is to practice self-care if you are not already doing so. Self-care is the act of taking care of yourself. I shared ways to take care of yourself in the workplace, but self-care is very personal. Only you can practice self-care for yourself. As part of the cohort, we practiced various techniques to ground and center ourselves in the moment, and here is a list of those and more:

- Yoga session
- Breathing and stretching exercises
- Journaling
- Exercising
- Listening to music
- Mediating
- Getting the appropriate amount of sleep
- Removing as much negativity as possible from your life

- Improving your eating habits
- Setting time aside for you
- Doing something that brings you joy
- Doing daily affirmations
- Dancing like no one is watching
- Connecting with your support network
- Laughing, maybe by watching your favorite comedy movie or comedian

There are many other ways to practice self-care. I use a couple of apps with breathing and mediating instructions. They helped me remove the stress of the day before going to bed. Everyone is different; try a few and see what works best.

My sixth and final suggestion for taking care of yourself is to utilize daily affirmations. Here are some I created and some I discovered:

- I am worthy
- I got this
- Today is my day
- I believe in me
- I love me
- Unapologetically dope
- I am a beautiful Black queen
- I am a force to be reckoned with

- I believe in myself
- I am doing my best
- Do something today that makes me smile
- You are amazing
- Intention over reaction
- Stay positive
- You are an inspiration
- Never give up
- You are loved
- Be bold
- I deserve to be happy
- No one is perfect
- I am at peace with myself
- I am worthy of love and happiness
- I am beautiful
- I am successful
- I love the skin I'm in
- I overcome challenges
- I have the power to change my world
- I respect myself
- I am proud of myself
- My life is filled with joy and abundance
- Happiness flows with me

I encourage you to write all the affirmations down on separate pieces of paper and add your own, then pull one out each day. Take a moment to think, affirm, and believe it. Your arsenal is now complete.

As I leave you, remember to take care of yourself. Don't beat yourself up and build your arsenal or add to it. You have more impactful work to complete and more lives to change. You are a beautiful queen, and you are worthy.

CHAPTER FIVE

Caazena P. Hunter

"Invention, discovery, and empires are built of chances taken with high degrees of failure."

- Stacey Abrams

Keeping it 100: Black Women in Nonprofit Leadership

Identity "Will" Wheel

Who are you?

I'm not here to talk about what I heard; I'm here to talk about what I know. I'm not saying my experience will be your experience, but we can all learn from others' experiences. The first thing I want to discuss is showing up as you. Showing up as you is the most important thing you can do. We tend to worry about acceptance, be it with family, friends, or colleagues. I want to say no matter what, you must show up daily as your full self, which happens in many ways. I know you are thinking, well, I can't possibly show up as anyone else, but to that, I say I do, we do, and you probably have shown up as someone other than your authentic self. I feel like I'm stalling taking you through my identities right now because it's hard, and discussing some identities is more challenging than others.

I am African American. I lead with this identity because it is the most important to me, and although I experience oppression and -*isms* based on many of my identities, I believe this is the most important. I am a 41-year-old-woman. I identify as childfree, not childless, because I have no desire to have children.

I'm a non-smoker and eventually quit a job when a big tobacco company asked the market research firm to ensure we discarded any information about underage smoking or health issues caused by smoking. I do not believe in compromising my moral compass or data for dollars.

When a job asks you to do something out of line with your values, do not do it. I'm bilingual, with Spanish as my second language. I was born in the United States and am a U.S. citizen. I acknowledge I am on stolen land built by stolen people. The land I am on was stolen from Indigenous people, including the Jumanos, Kiikaapoi, Tawakoni, and Wichita. Stolen people built the land, my ancestors, Africans who were stolen from Africa and brought here only to be enslaved. We must always stand in truth, which is part of our authenticity.

I am currently able-bodied. I say currently because that identity can instantly change for any of us. I identify as middle class because of my income. I have a bachelor's degree in Spanish and sociology, an international studies certificate, and a master's in sociology from the University of North Texas.

My dad has always encouraged education and instilled the importance of education officially and unofficially in all his children. He never stated education would be the great equalizer but that, as a Black person, it's even more important. I experienced so many inequities and micro-aggressions in education that it was unfathomable. I have always charted my own educational course.

I worked on a Ph.D. for about ten years, including two on my dissertation, only to decide it was no longer in line with my goals. Education has always been of utmost importance to my parents, especially my father, and me too because I'm a daddy's girl. I have always been a fan of learning and consider myself a lifelong learner, but for me, it no longer has to be connected to academia.

I have worked in nonprofit for more than 15 years. I currently work for Young Leaders Strong City (YLSC) as the director of program design, where we work to educate, equip, and activate youth to realize their visions for racial justice and equity. The cohort affirmed my authenticity and my decision to join YLSC.

I also provide consulting and coaching services to organizations working toward racial equity and individuals working toward personal and professional growth. I was born and raised in the South, specifically in Texas, and even more specifically, I grew up in Pleasant Grove. As a kid, I considered Pleasant Grove a pleasant area where I went to school with all my friends. The neighborhood has since become more dangerous, and, like many neighborhoods with an abundance of Black and Brown people, it is neglected.

I'm heterosexual and acknowledge the associated privileges. I am a realist and recognize things as they are, but I also challenge things and work toward changing them. My father, Johnny Hunter, is a Vietnam veteran, and my grandfather was a World War II veteran. My father shared his experiences and the brutality of war and its atrocities, as well as the racism he faced when he returned from the war.

I am the youngest of three children. My sister Robin is eight years older, and my brother Curtis is ten years older, which means I'm legitimately the baby of the family. I was my maternal grandmother's youngest grandchild. I know what it means to be protected by and surrounded by family members who genuinely want you there. My mom always told me that my brother and sister begged her to have one more child, and in true sibling fashion, when I was born, they stated we should have gotten a dog instead.

"The voice of a Black woman should always be HERSELF ... No edits - no erasure - no pressure - no expectations - no additions - no intruders." - Malebo Sephodi.

I started with the most important identity, and I'm ending with the second most important, that I am not religious, which tends to be surprising in the Black community.

I have shared a brief overview of my identity as I bring all these

71

aspects of who I am to every nonprofit I work for, but most significantly, they all influence the 'why' of my role within nonprofits. Who you are is important because you must show up authentically. Authenticity is being real and being yourself 100% of the time. Sis, when you show up, please show up fully. I encourage you to create a wheel of identities, so you truly think through your identity and the stories that go with each piece.

No matter what, you must stay true to yourself, as countless people in your life will try to shift you to do what is expected, but if it's not who you are or for you, please, leave it where it is. *(Call to Action: Who are you? Create your identity wheel and list your most important identities. Which provide you with advantages? Disadvantages? Which do you find yourself losing sleep over? Which have you hidden?)*

Name

I would like to continue this discussion of identity using two pieces of mine I did not include in the wheel as I need to hold space for them separately. My name and my hair get individual sections of this work. My name is Caazena Paaha Hunter. I am the daughter of Helen and Johnny and the sister of Curtis and Robin Hunter. My parents and siblings have what most would consider common names. My name is everything but common; it is steeped in creativity, originality, and BLACKNESS. I show up as Caazena Paaha Hunter everywhere I go. One part of this is ensuring my name is pronounced fully and correctly. I have a unique name and can say that I have not met another Caazena. Have you?

Names are important; they are the foundation of who you are and have meaning. Think about how you got your name. Are you named after a parent or other loved one? Is your name from the bible or a proverb? Are you named after a historical figure or artist? Are you named after an amazing memory?

When I was old enough to ask my dad what my name means, without missing a beat, he said, "I had a meaning in mind, but I'm not telling you. I want you to define your name as you define yourself." As it stands, my name means warrior for RACIAL equity because my work, my passion, is not ensuring my people, Black people, have the same as everyone else but have exactly what they need now.

People often find my name challenging and handle it in many unacceptable ways. I always introduce myself and pronounce my name a couple of times to assist people. The first wrong turn is when someone does not attempt to pronounce my name at all and makes up a nickname. Wrong answer. You will not just decide to rename me. Another problematic response is to ask me for my nickname without even trying to pronounce my name. Finally, another technique is to simply call me by my last name. Now, calling me by my last name is lazy, but acceptable.

My ancestors were renamed, and you will not be so disrespectful as to just make an executive decision to give me another name. My friends, family members, and colleagues I'm comfortable with are more than welcome to call me by my nickname, but upon first meeting me, you need to pronounce my name.

I handle this by saying, "That is not my name. My name is Caazena." If someone tries and mispronounces it, I just correct them and continue offering grace. People who respect your humanity will ask you to pronounce your name again because they want to get it right and will make solid efforts. Often, when they truly listen, they will get it right.

My dad told me, "I want you to define and redefine your name as you grow and change." He gave me a name and a lesson. I think Uzoamaka Nwanneka Aduba said it best when she said, "If they can learn to say Tchaikovsky and Michelangelo and Dostoyevsky, they can learn to say Uzoamaka." Please do not dim your light or allow people to rename you because you deserve the full respect that everyone else gets, and it starts with being called by your name.

Hair

Now, sis, before people get to your name, they can see you coming. Again, you must show up authentically. Hair is of great importance as it can be a creative and cultural outlet. I've had 42 years of hairstyles. Of course, as a small child, I had a baby afro, ponytails with barrettes, press and curl, bangs, perms, finger waves, freezes, bobs, crimps, Shirley Temple curls, deep waves, straw sets, roller sets, comb coils, two strand twists, updos, French rolls, microbraids, box braids, bantu knots, knotless braids, kinky twists, feed in cornrows, and asymmetrical haircuts. This list is not exhaustive, but it is a start. I used to have a love-hate relationship with my hair, but now it is all love every day.

I remember sitting in the kitchen as a little girl with a towel wrapped around my shoulders, getting my hair pressed (straightened with a heated metal comb) by my mom with the infamous blue magic and a pressing comb. I would hold my ears super tight so that she could get all the hair around the edges of my hairline, but sometimes I moved, or her hand would slip due to all the grease. I would scream because, from time to time, my ear got burned. I got my hair pressed so it would be pretty for church or "easy" to manage. Pressing was my special occasion hair when something was super important, and mom wanted me to look my best. Who knew this lesson would carry deep into my adult years? The message was that my hair was not good enough in its natural state and needed to be changed. Also that my hair in its curly form was too much to deal with, so it had to be straightened to be more manageable. We must be conscious of the messages we send little girls when doing their hair and the racist messages we have internalized about our own hair. After a while, the press was not good enough to maintain my hair's straightness because if it gets wet or I sweat, it reverts to its naturally curly state.

The next stop on my hair journey was a perm. I was heading to middle school, and, like most middle schoolers, I got a perm. Now, every stylist in my teenage years was late and double-booked clients.

I would wait for her to show up, only for her to bounce from head to head. This taught me to be mindful of my and others' time. If people do not respect your time, they do not respect you. I had moved to the perm phase of my life. I was always about 10 minutes late because she was 30 minutes late, and I brought a snack and a book or something to entertain myself because it was an all-day experience. Perming was next level in hair torture for me because perms always burned, and I remember repeatedly getting chemical burns on my scalp because I had to have manageable straight hair that allowed me to look like all the other teenage girls.

My ears got burned when my mom pressed my hair. My scalp got burned when I got a perm. I sat under dryers for certain styles, and that burned. I endured nights of having to "sleep pretty" to ensure my styles stayed in place for workdays. Hairstyles and appointments tend to be time-consuming, expensive, and, at times, painful. I say this, sis, because, after all, you endure for someone at your job to say that you cannot wear a certain style is absolutely unacceptable.

While entrenched in a White marketing research firm in 2006, I decided not to perm my hair anymore and did the big chop. I was inundated with questions from friends and family because something had to be wrong to suddenly decide to rock a TWA or Teeny-Weeny Afro. The next space I worked in was a predominantly Black private school where all hairstyles were welcomed and embraced. I continued my loose natural journey for 14 years, and no one ever accosted me about my hair. When I typed that, I remembered I was accosted when I first decided to stop perming my hair and did the big chop.

I was accosted by none other than my brother. He entered my room and did a mocking impression of African dancers, concluding by saying, "I thought I had a sister, not an African brother." After that, I was ready for anything the world threw at my short afro. I stopped perming my hair in 2006 when it was not popular in my community. I wore my natural hair in countless ways, and 14 years into my natural hair journey, I decided to loc my hair. I consulted with friends and associates for about two years before that, and individuals with locs always said it was the best decision they ever made and to trust the process.

My family members immediately asked, "What about work? Are locs 'allowed?' Will it be professional? Oh no, you shouldn't do it; that's permanent." I began my sistaloc journey right before the pandemic in February 2020. Sis, all of this is to say that although India.Arie said, "I am not my hair," in my opinion, hair is a big deal. Hair is a political statement. Ebony magazine stated, "In the 1960s, Black folks finally said, 'To hell with that!' After decades of subjecting ourselves to European beauty standards, we decided to take back our hair. This newfound self-acceptance was widely known as the 'Black is Beautiful' movement, which sprang from the Black Power movement." I want to encourage you to say, "To hell with that," and take back your hair, and taking back your hair is defined for you by you. I wear head wraps and my locs, and I plan to color them when they are mature. Please, sis, do not dim your light or creativity when it comes to your hair to fit professionalism as defined by white supremacy norms. I spent two years going back and forth about getting sistalocs because of racism. I finally decided if an employer won't have me or if I can't advance because of my hair, the organization is not for me. When it comes to my hair, I should be able to have all the styles as well as all the opportunities. However, I believe there are instances in life when we cannot have it all, whether at the same time or not.

Having it all

Oprah once said, "You can have it all, just not all at once." I believe people who strive to have it all think perfectionism is achievable. I spent many years believing in perfectionism, but that is an illusion because we are human beings having a human experience, which means mistakes will be made. Again, mistakes will be made; it's just how you handle them. I believed in perfectionism because of Helen and Johnny. My dad is a Vietnam veteran, and my mom's a Black woman, and errors were not an option for them. My dad often talked about how mistakes could cost you your life, and my mom is the epitome of a problem solver. Well, the notion of making mistakes does not fit neatly within the strong Black woman stereotype.

I had a strong Black woman for a grandmother and have a strong Black woman for a mama. They have given their all to everyone. The problem with giving your all to others is that nothing is left for you. Now, here's how giving it your all can show up so that when you see it coming, you can adjust accordingly. I find myself being very mission-centered working in nonprofit. The people I have worked with are mostly Black and Brown women. These women could be my friends and family members, and the truths they experience are all too familiar.

I am not saying that you should not do your best work, but you should have realistic boundaries regarding work. My boundaries got extremely blurred, which is so easy in a nonprofit when you wear countless hats and have more tasks than you could possibly accomplish in the given time. Also, not to mention we were in a global pandemic, and many people were working from home.

How are you creating work-life boundaries? I noticed the work creep due to technology and boundary blurring. Work creep for me looked like responding to emails while I was at the movies or museum with my nieces. The emails could absolutely wait, but I thought I could just do a little more and go a bit further above and beyond. I committed to an organization for seven and a half years, and for five of those, I had no promotions but more work every year.

I worked nights and weekends, and although we could adjust our schedules at times, it did not make up for the family events I missed. I noticed I was working while eating my lunch, carrying over PTO days, not having complete days off, working while sick, asking for a code to lock up the building, and returning unused sick days. Black women, you, like every other human, cannot have it all at the same time. You cannot be fully present for the pertinent lives of friends and family members while also working, and that's it. Working really long hours and always on call for work interferes with and impacts your experiences with friends and family members. We carry tiny computers in our pockets that connect us to work 24/7. My role within my job is 100% remote, and I often find myself checking emails at awkward times of the day and, worse, responding (or at least saving it in my draft so that people don't think I'm strange or working at weird hours). Have you ever been out and thought, "I can multitask," and then sent one more email? Well, by saying "Yes" to that email, you missed your nephew's touchdown, part of the explanation of why your partner's day was so awesome, or why your niece is working your sister's last nerve.

I was assistant director of community engagement for a prominent national nonprofit organization, and because I worked remotely, I struggled with creating solid boundaries. I am also a racial equity consultant for several amazing nonprofits.

Creating racial equity is my absolute passion, and that is why the work does not stop. I am also passionate about being an aunt to several nieces and nephews. I want to be there for the football games, plays, and concerts. I love live music and want to attend the latest concerts offered by Sofar and Trap Karaoke. I have a pretty dope boyfriend, and we love traveling and eating out. I want and need to make time for ALL THE THINGS, but this means I must create boundaries and make sure my time is respected and used efficiently. Sis, you can have it all … just not at once.

The reality is for every "Yes" you give someone else, you are saying "No" to something for yourself because there's only so much time. Now, what I am saying, and more importantly what Auntie Oprah is saying, is yes, you can be an amazing employee, parent, and friend and take care of yourself, but you cannot have it all at once. This means to be really amazing at one thing is at the sacrifice of other things.

You may throw yourself into work projects, but what does that mean for your friends and family? As I write this, I just had an A-HA or Ha-Ha moment because it's ironic. I discuss white supremacy cultural norms, and as I'm thinking about and grappling with the strong Black woman stereotype, it is just as harmful, and it's killing Black women every day as it creates inhumane, unrealistic standards that impact health. *(Call to Action: How will you create boundaries for your work and personal life?)*

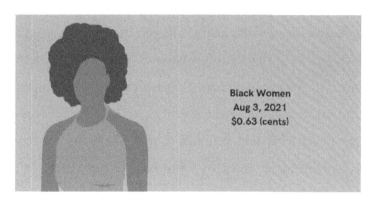

Black Women
Aug 3, 2021
$0.63 (cents)

"To face the realities of our lives is not a reason for despair—despair is a tool of your enemies. Facing the realities of our lives gives us motivation for action. For you are not

powerless ... You know why the hard questions must be asked. It is not altruism; it is self-preservation—survival."

- Audre Lorde.

Hey, sis in nonprofit, what's your number? I'm asking how much you make each year. We don't tend to talk about this in polite conversation or discuss it with family members and friends. I believe this works to our disadvantage, and we cannot afford to face any additional financial disadvantages. We already face racial inequities in all our lived experiences; therefore, we must advocate for ourselves. Our ancestors were Africans who were brought to this country and enslaved. Enslavement included an abundance of brutality and working for free. Please do not confuse this with the beginning or end of our story as a people, but it is definitely part of it. Our nation was built on racism and perpetuates this notion of white supremacy.

Generally, it takes women an additional three months to make the wage earned by a white man in the previous year. It takes Black women an extra eight months into the new year to earn what white men earned in the previous year. I once worked for a company for seven and a half years. I received an increase of about two percent each year. I only received a promotion after five years, and that was after training my supervisors. As a woman, but especially as a Black woman, you must always negotiate for more money and/or benefits pertinent to your happiness. Negotiation simply means obtaining or bringing about discussion. Specifically, in this scenario, discussion around compensation for a job, which may include options to be location independent, additional days off, and, most importantly, more money. Please remember that no one else will advocate for you. You must constantly and consistently hone your craft, learn new skills, and look for new opportunities. When was the last time you received a raise? What is the going rate of pay in your field? *(Call to Action: Where do you need to be financially for yourself/your family? When was the last time you explored other employment opportunities? Well, that's too long; please begin exploring.)*

Thus far, we have discussed things you can do as an individual to show up authentically, but now we must discuss your why and how for doing the work you do in the nonprofit space. First, you must understand your personal identity, which is where we started. Personal identity consists of who and whose you are. Next, you must understand why you are doing what you do within a nonprofit. I work for Young Leaders Strong City because working with youth for their visions of racial equity and justice will positively change the trajectory of our society.

We talked about identity because it is important to show up for this work authentically. Authenticity is being real and showing up fully as yourself. Racial equity simplified is ensuring everyone has what they need. A more complex definition by race forward states racial equity is a process of eliminating racial disparities and improving outcomes through the intentional and continual practice of changing policies, practices, systems, and structures by prioritizing measurable change in the lives of people of color. Below are a few reasons why equity is important to me. *(Call to Action: What is your why?)*

- I do racial equity work:
- because Black students made up 21.6% of the DISD school population but 51.6% of out-of-school suspensions during the 2019-2020 school year
- because I once worked for a company and saw old Halloween pictures posted on the internet with a picture of a white man pretending to be Gary Coleman, thus, in Black face
- because housing discrimination and segregation still exist
- because Black women earn 63 cents to every dollar earned by a non-Hispanic white man
- because the net wealth of a typical Black family in America is around one-tenth that of a white family
- because Black women are underrepresented in senior leadership
- because of the maternal mortality rates for Black women
- for all the Black women who are training their white supervisors who have less education and experience
- for all the Black women that have been told they cannot wear braids, locs, or an afro
- because I've been watching Black people be beaten and murdered by the police since 1991
- because my uncle and aunt were murdered for being an

interracial couple in Plano in the 60s

- because the system works just as it was designed, and the policies, practices, and systems in place were built to create racial inequity and need to be discarded

"African-American women have been victimized by race, gender, and class oppression. But portraying Black women solely as passive, unfortunate recipients of racial and sexual abuse stifles notions that Black women can actively work to change our circumstances and bring about changes in our lives. Similarly, presenting African-American women solely as heroic figures who easily engage in resisting oppression on all fronts minimizes the very real costs of oppression and can foster the perception that Black women need to help because we can 'take it."

- Patricia Hill Collins in Black Feminist Thought*, 1990.*

Next, you must be explicit about how you want to do your work. My life's work is racial equity on the path to equality. I have a full-time job that allows me to center the voices of students for racial justice and equity. I am also a racial equity coach and consultant. Below are a few of the ways I do this work. *(Call to Action: How will you continue to do your work?)*

- leading racial healing spaces for racially diverse and race-based affinity groups that provide a courageous space
- measuring where organizations are on the continuum to

becoming fully inclusive, multicultural, and anti-racist

- coaching organizations through the creation of a racial equity theory of change and racial equity policy statements

- conducting workshops and webinars to assist organizations in moving the needle of racial equity forward

- co-creating and implementing teen equity summits, community care cohorts, and councils for high school students

- coaching Black Women towards personal, professional, and financial growth.

"Caring for myself is not self-indulgence, it is self-preservation, and that is an act of political warfare."

- Audre Lorde in A Burst of Light*, 1988.*

"Self-care is a way of maintaining both wellness and balance in the energetic economy of social and economic intercourse. Activists and caretakers who do not attend to self-care are vulnerable to burnout, and burnout in turn can breed alienation from both issues and communities ... Self-care and care of others needs to be balanced."

- Layli Maparyan in **The Womanist Idea***, 2012.*

The only way for this work to be sustainable is by taking care of yourself as you are doing it. I have watched my grandmother, mother, and sister give so much to others that they do not have anything left for themselves. When I was a kid, my parents owned a grocery store and a nightclub, and they worked endlessly.

The saying goes that people work harder when they work for themselves, and my parents modeled that. I had a babysitter who cared for me all the time, and I saw her more than my parents. You must have a life outside of work and time to take care of yourself. You may have work, school, friendships, kids, a spouse, and/or hobbies that all need your attention, but you must have the energy to show up for all these people and things. Do not give so much that you end up breaking because it is definitely possible. What is your plan to care for YOU? *(Call to Action: Design a plan for taking care of yourself each day. What brings you happiness and peace?)*

I want to be remembered as someone who used herself and anything she could touch to work for justice and freedom…. I want to be remembered as one who tried.
~ Dorothy Height

Image: Getty Images / Hulton Archive
WomensHistory.About.com

Ten steps to surviving nonprofit life as a Black woman:

1. Keep looking.

2. Learn constantly.

3. Ask for a raise every year.

4. Apply for the more challenging position.

5. Root for other Black women.

6. Find a mentor.

7. Find a leadership cohort.

8. Take time to stop, breathe, and not worry about productivity.

Showing Up Black

When you show up Black, some will say:

Her use of AAVE (African American Vernacular English) is too Black

- o Her locs are too Black
- o Her name is too Black
- o Her interactions are too Black
- o Her style is too Black
- o Her desk decor is too Black
- o Her suggestions are too Black

Well, they didn't say it, but it was translated into:

- o She's not articulate
- o She's not connecting with our customers
- o She's confrontational
- o She is not dressed professionally
- o She does not fit into the company culture

And still:

o   BE(YOU)tiful

Acknowledgment:

I want to thank my Big Mama, Cream Lucille "Creamel" Cook, who laid the foundation for my mama and continues to pour into me. My paternal grandparents Daisy and Herbert "Tough Joker" Hunter. I want to acknowledge Helen and Johnny "Dogoon" Hunter, my most immediate givers of life and daily sources of light. They taught me to take pride in who I am and stand for what I believe in, no matter what. A dad who reminds me to live my life because you can get killed walking your doggie and to always read more. My mom who encourages me to find a solution to any problem. To my siblings, Robin and Curtis, thank you for encouraging me to leap no matter what and embrace a little flexibility and chaos. Lastly, to all my bonus siblings in all forms I LOVE Ya'll and you made this possible.

CHAPTER SIX

Candace Barnes

"Know that you can start late, look different, be uncertain and still succeed."

– Misty Copeland

Dear Black women in the social sector, you are Essential, Valuable, and Worthy!

I want to share a few things with you. Things I hope will help you, whether for affirmation or discovery, while on your journey. I want to offer a heads-up if you are new to this, and I want to high-five you, my sista, if you can relate.

I have worked in the nonprofit world for most of my career of over 25 years. When I joined my first organization, I was young and eager to soak up as much as I could, and I learned a few things along the way, including the main thing that no matter what, I have always been worthy, valuable, and essential. I've just had a hell of a time believing it consistently.

"Do they hire many Blacks where you work?" my maternal grandfather, John, asked when I told him I was about to reach my one-year anniversary. "How do they treat you?" he kept poking. At the time, I wondered why he was asking those questions, but over time, I realized they were exactly the questions that needed to be asked! By the time I really understood this, my dear grandfather had passed on.

Instead of asking me if I liked my job or if it paid well and had good benefits, he was more concerned about how I was experiencing "they," the power structures he was so familiar with. His questions and words still impact how I look at things moving forward. He worked as a sharecropper and eventually transitioned into working in a plant to support his family. By the time I came along, he was close to retiring, and when I entered the workforce, he had exited. But he said enough and asked enough to pass along his experiences, which were my foundational learning.

My paternal grandfather, Prince, told me to always tip my skycap when I travel. He worked for Braniff Airlines and explained the skycaps were usually the least appreciated, even with all the work they did to get passengers to their flights. He served as a skycap, and I noticed that almost everywhere I flew, the skycaps were often Black men or other men of color. Because of my grandfather, I always made it a point to overtly express my appreciation, and I still do.

Prince was a WWII Navy veteran who retired from Braniff during the pricing dispute with Southwest Airlines. It wasn't until well after he had passed on that I learned about and realized his color prevented him from taking advantage of the GI Bill, which helped returning veterans purchase homes for their families. Now it all makes sense. These two figures in my life were essential in helping form my beliefs about work, my work ethic, constant gratitude, and "won't complain" foundation. I survived off that for a long time, and I'm not mad because it is who I am and what I am made of, but there comes a time when you must give yourself the green light to do something different. By different, I mean to take up more space and be recognized as the leader and force that I am.

So, here I am, walking into my new nonprofit job in a city I know hardly anything about at 24 years old. I was hired as both their receptionist and HR assistant – the first face of the organization. Prior to arriving, I had worked in a corporate office environment in my home city for three years and moved up to become a supervisor before deciding to move away. Those three years are all I have to draw on when I think of corporate America.

The rest of my career has been in the nonprofit sector, outside of a couple of one-year gigs I did along the way. I could immediately see the difference when I entered the nonprofit scene. It was definitely a place I felt I belonged and wanted to stay. The mission, the purpose, and the people were all vibrant and relevant to me, and I still feel the same way today. Everything I learned about leadership was gained first through my family and community and then through the nonprofit sector.

I advise you to look back over your life and assess yourself. Don't allow others to define you. I had to look back and realize I was a leader from the time I took over the Peter Rabbit play in kindergarten. After weeks of rehearsing, when it came time to perform in front of our parents, a couple of my five-year-old classmates forgot their lines and positions and had stage fright. I politely pulled a couple of them into their spots on the stage and whispered their lines to them to keep things flowing. I was too excited about saying my lines, and I wasn't about to let things get out of order and miss what I had worked so hard to practice over and over for weeks. All the parents laughed, and we completed the play. My mom periodically reminds me of this shining moment, and I remember it like it was yesterday. I had to look back over my life and realize that, even in the smallest of moments, I have been essential, valuable, and worthy.

I didn't give moments like this much credit at first. As time has passed, there have been larger, more significant moments of leadership that deserve more credit. Look back and give yourself credit for EVERYTHING. It all counts, and it is all part of your story and why you are who you are and why you are worthy! This is especially helpful when you face that ugly impostor syndrome feeling we all get when we, as Black women, walk into a room and feel the need to fight back the urge to be silent, to just nod in agreement and to walk back to our safe spaces shaking our heads. I won't say this will stop completely because we all know everyone may feel this at some point in life, but we, as Black women in nonprofit leadership, are usually experts and leaders in this space, yet we feel compelled to concede when we should often be the main ones speaking.

Often Black women have done the work, lived on the other side of the mission, earned the credentials, and have the capacity to lead, yet every decision, idea, and notion has to be vetted, justified, and qualified. It often cannot simply be considered innovative and cutting-edge, like ideas presented by other colleagues. Practices like these, ignoring and undermining the leadership of Black women, continue to cause harm and deepen the trauma felt. The nonprofit sector also suffers. Angela Davis said it best, "When Black women win victories, it is a boost for virtually every segment of society."

We, as Black women, have repeatedly shown through the decades that we show up consistently as leaders in the fight for the common good, whether persevering through slavery, women's suffrage, civil rights, the Me Too movement, or fighting for racial justice in the Black Lives Matter movement. Our leadership capabilities, passion, and perseverance should deem more of us as thought leaders, champions, and best-in-class in the nonprofit world. Yet most Black women who lead in a nonprofit space share a similar story of being one of very few Black leaders who had to fight an uphill battle for the opportunity and respect earned long before it was received. Even with these practices in place, we must continue believing in our value and worth.

When I started to work in the nonprofit industry, I needed a mentor who was also a Black woman. I say this because, as a Black woman, I am at the intersection of gender and race, and it takes another Black woman to understand what this means and how challenging it is. When I think back to those early days, I realize that a mentor who looked like me would've helped provide the support and access I needed to advance in my career. I needed to actively seek a mentor, but I didn't think that way back then. I was excited to have a great new job, which provided purpose with a mission of helping people in the community. At the time, I felt full, like I had found a place to grow and learn, and that the leaders of the company would see me, my work, and my efforts, and that would be enough.

While I had some good managers, over time, I began to realize that, depending on who I reported to, my performance was measured differently than others. I was expected to go above and beyond more frequently than others, and it was not always measured as going above and beyond. A great mentor will counsel and advise in situations you may not be seasoned enough to navigate effectively. Having the support and backing from someone who you feel has your best interest at heart is encouraging and helps to build confidence. I recommend you actively seek out a mentor, especially in this nonprofit space - Someone who will pour into you and advise you, tell you when you are wrong, and push you to assert yourself when appropriate.

If you have someone you can trust supporting you, it will help strengthen your sense of self and help you build confidence in your abilities, no matter what the work climate looks like. As Michelle Obama stated, "Choose people who lift you up."

Sis, it is also important that you support and lift up other Black women. This is a two-way street, and there is room for all of us. We are not in competition, and we must take an active stance in helping to impact the trajectory of each other's careers. Mentoring and sponsoring other Black women is important. While mentoring involves advising and providing direct counsel to someone, sponsoring is using your social capital and influence to advocate on behalf of other Black women and endorsing and recommending them even when they are not in your presence.

Networking and connecting are great things but don't always do it just to further your personal gains. Reach out to other Black women leaders and get to know them to help connect them with other trusted mentors and allies. Intentionally fostering connections is also a way of advocating for someone. Even if you don't feel you have much influence or social capital, continue to speak the names of your fellow colleagues to help raise their voices and spread awareness about them. You don't have to be well-known or highly visible to make a positive impact. A thousand small voices can surpass the impact of one mighty one. In fact, make that an action item. Make it a point to amplify the voice of another Black woman in any capacity you can. You will build a connection and earn a loyal and trusted ally and be better for it.

If you are in a position to help professionally develop another Black woman by providing knowledge, sharpening skills, or even sharing information about opportunities that will provide training and development, make sure you are intentional about doing this. Black women are less likely to receive the professional development and support needed to advance in their careers. This is especially true in the nonprofit sector due to budget constraints. As a seasoned HR professional, this is an area that resonates with me. Providing equitable access to training and development throughout my organization is my way of ensuring opportunities to learn are available to all employees, which is also a positive for Black women where I work. Again, you do not have to have a highly visible role in making a positive impact.

It is a fact there is a large diversity, equity, and inclusion gap in nonprofit leadership. According to the *2018 State of Diversity in Nonprofits and Foundation Leadership* white paper, 87% of all executive directors or presidents are white. Nonprofit leadership continues to fail to mirror the community it serves. This is no surprise to me. I don't need these statistics to know the gap remains huge in terms of the number of leaders of color in the nonprofit sector. I work in a field where high-level recruiting firms will say there is a very limited number of diverse candidates when in fact, executive recruiters don't do enough to attract a diverse candidate pool.

Still, Black women in the social sector, you are needed, and there is room. You belong, and you are valuable. I advise you to make yourself available to the diverse talent pool by keeping your credentials updated so you can apply for leadership positions that interest you. The social sector needs you. You are qualified, and you are enough. I am sharing these words of affirmation the same way they were lovingly showered upon me by another valuable, incredible Black woman nonprofit leader. As she spoke these words, they rang very true to me. I just needed to hear them from someone else. Be that someone else for each other.

It is time we change the narrative around there being a limited number of Black women nonprofit leaders. A substantial talent pool is not being tapped due to the implicit bias of hiring executives and boards. This is why it is important to advocate for each other and also recognize that white allies will mentor, sponsor, and stand up for Black women and amplify their voices.

With all the focus on racial justice this past year, we are living in a time where companies have drafted racial equity statements and committed to making internal improvements to change the lack of diverse leadership in the nonprofit and corporate space.

The public murder of George Floyd in the middle of the Covid pandemic flipped the nation on its back and permeated globally to raise social awareness everywhere. I remember being so distressed while watching the news, where the video of George Floyd's death was shown several times each day. In a matter of weeks, organizations were posting commitments on their websites pledging to fight against racism, and several companies began hiring diversity, equity, and inclusion officers. People of color were reiterating that we were not okay at work during this time, even when work was remote.

Organizations are now seeking leaders of color to lead in this space to embed racial equity into internal work operations, work and culture, and externally. This is our time to make an impact. During the 2021 inaugural year of the Black Women in Nonprofit Leadership cohort, this message was conveyed to us several times by our amazing leader, Errika Y. Flood-Moultrie, and several of the phenomenal speakers and presenters who poured into us, from Cynt Marshall, CEO of the Dallas Mavericks to Dr. Froswa Booker-Drew, Leah Frazier, Noelle LeVeaux, and Jarie Bradley, to name just a few. And they are right; this is the time we, as Black women, have the world's attention.

We need to claim the space that belongs to us as innovative leaders, experts, and champions and make the difference we are naturally here to make. As I think back over my 25 years in the nonprofit sector, it was all worth it, and now is not the time to stop fighting the good fight. The social sector needs us, and we are the best thing for it.

And Finally, Practice Self-Care.

After all of this, we must ask ourselves and each other: Are you good, Sis? Check in on yourself and other Black women as often as you can. As Black women, we dismiss our mental and sometimes physical needs, all to maintain that dreadful Superwoman complex! Overcoming some of the obstacles involved in being a leader of color in the nonprofit sector is exhausting. Just showing up each day can be a lot, with all of the collective trauma of micro and macroaggressions, implicit bias, structural racism, code-switching, swirling Covid variants, racial injustice, and other debilitating situations that harm us daily; it is important to take care of ourselves.

Your mental health is vital and needs to be checked frequently. It is important to give yourself permission to check out. Don't listen to the news; unplug from work and allow yourself some quiet unconnected time. I think of unconnected time as not answering phone calls and texts and having no screen time. Figure out what drains you and what energizes you. Think about what your needs are and advocate for yourself. Deal with supportive people who won't make demands and who are understanding of your boundaries. Self-care time is all about you and what your needs are. Replenishing your soul and feeding your spirit is helpful and can be accomplished by simply breathing, meditating, and resting.

And as you exhale and think through all you've accomplished as an amazing Black woman leader in the social sector, know you have an army of other Black women behind you, and there is room for your awesomeness. You deserve to be heard, whether your voice is big or small, you are enough, and you are valuable, essential, and, most importantly, worthy!

CHAPTER SEVEN

Chris McSwain

"Perseverance is my motto."

- Madam CJ Walker

You're the secret; you're the sauce

The general concept of *career* was mischaracterized in young me. I knew what it meant to work and work hard; I saw my rearing squad do some version of that every day. They got up, punched clocks, built things, cleaned spaces, and reported to people in suits with directives and power. I thought that was how work worked; an exchange of a thing - your time, mostly, for another thing - a check, thankfully. I didn't know that in a more specialized and intentional way, work could look like charting a path into a space that allowed you to do something that fulfilled a call while also amplifying your gift, voice, and influence.

I couldn't foresee that real-life opportunities to advocate for people, causes, and missions that were an extension of your core self lay beyond the applications and interviews. I also couldn't have known that doing all this while Black, a woman, from the hood, and rising in the age of the worldwide water cooler (AKA the *innanet)* meant you'd become an anomaly. I couldn't see any of this, particularly for myself. And yet, here we are.

I didn't have my sights set on becoming a leader in a sector. I knew I wanted to do more than work a job for a check, but I also didn't have enough experience or examples to show me how that might look. So, getting to the story of how I've navigated to and through my current space is offered in two parts: deep gratitude in reflection and full acknowledgment of the wonder of ordained surprise with no perfect formula and certainly no well-laid guidebook. I'm still learning as I go. I'm even asking what a destination even looks like. But I'm leaning in deeply and appreciating how it's crystallizing and making more sense as I journey. While I know there is still a fashion-week-long runway ahead, I know I'm walking well. Where I serve, live, and do life is making a difference. It's making me.

Where I am, what I do, and how the heck I got here

Let's start with a caveat: titles don't do it for me. I know we're often trained to pursue them, and for the sake of hierarchy, structure, and professional context, they denote some things about your prowess. Sure. Fine. Let me be clear, though. I don't share my title apathy with disdain because I appreciate the entryway-ness of them for guiding a conversation about the work I do; however, I am not limited to some positioning nomenclature that is mostly convention and structure and less personal and gift-amplifying. That said, I'm a director-level marketing and communications professional in the nonprofit sector and have been in my current position for nearly five years.

I work for one of the region's most credentialed and respected community foundations. It's a pinnacle moment on many fronts. I work for an organization that is investing in the community and raising the bar of generosity. The foundation is well-known, respected, and, most importantly, doing work internally to ensure that our core values are not merely externally presented but internally owned. It's a great place, and for however long the season shall be, I know this opportunity has been a blessing.

Prior to this role, I'd hopped and tumbled around the sector, navigating roles with organizations diverse in size, mission, and structure. A mid-80s-born millennial, I graduated college in the year of the first recession with my sights set on powering music artists into their full potential as a publicist in the entertainment industry.

Two traumatizing internships, a bleak job market, and one out-of-my-price-range Manhattan apartment later, I took my first "real" job with a small organization smack in the middle of Harlem's famed 125th street. Our mission was to empower nontraditional entrepreneurs with access to capital by offering microloans based on a peer lending model. Despite the odds, it was beautiful work with a small staff and a deep and abiding appetite for helping people reach their highest and best selves. As the marketing coordinator, I was tasked with telling the organization and its people's story, those doing life and business with little. I loved the work and energy of the small organization grind.

With a staff of five, I sat within arm's reach of both my boss and her boss. I learned the tenets of how nonprofits are structured administratively, how fundraising works, and what it takes to appeal to the human experience to garner support for a mission. It lit a fire under me to hone my ability to make people care about causes using my voice and pen. It instilled a passion in me to connect mission with action. It allowed me to organically create a niche and make a mark.

Eventually, I left that organization and navigated several larger organizations in New York, staying true to my role as a communicator, learning to strategically write content for organizations and leaders, and telling the stories that would imprint donors and move them to give. I worked on and off in development teams, served as a spokesperson, and became a media-relating, message-carrying, social media nonprofit gal.

It's been a source of great joy, learning, challenge, doing, and undoing. However, charting my course in this space is where I've met the most brilliant minds, been challenged the most, and uncovered parts of my magic that I might not have done if I didn't do this work where I do it.

What I wish I knew as I traveled here

That was a lot, I know, but I wanted a contextual backdrop for the other sides of the still-developing story. I cannot say that I explicitly knew this professional niche was going to be mine. I knew what I'd studied (a public relations major and an English minor), and I knew what I had a general knack for (writing), yet I didn't know I was necessarily pursuing a specialized segment within the sector. I was just happy to have gotten a job.

I didn't know you could design a career path, choose an industry to navigate, and become expert enough to influence or lead thought. There was no crash course on how to design a career during my academic journey. I thought I'd go to school and pick a major and that between my studies and what was available, it'd all coalesce in a way that would allow me to do the things I was good at. I had no concept of navigating an industry or becoming adept and attuned to what existed outside the 9-5 window where I was expected to be each day. The concept of leading and empowering from the space of my mind hadn't cemented. It wasn't that I doubted my ability per se, but I hadn't seen examples of this kind of authority within proximity. Everyone expert enough was seemingly out of reach, from a pedigree and toward leadership and expertness that was beyond my ranks. Yes, I knew college would set a course for me, but I thought, at most, it'd get me a better-paying role than those I'd witnessed among the people around me growing up.

Now, 14 years later, deep in the thicket of solid, post-collegiate employment and adulthood, I can see it and, more significantly, see ME in it. By all accounts, I am still journeying, but as my experiences unfold, I am becoming less responsive to what is available and more proactive about letting my me-ness inform what should be. Instead

107

of merely form-fitting roles and opportunities as they have been presented, I compared what was being offered to what I knew I could offer, even if that wasn't explicitly asked for in a job description. In the space of pursuing roles and opportunities, women often feel we need to prove we can rather than show who we are. While one impacts the other, there is a difference.

I remember my second "adult" role, this time at a larger organization that focused on health advocacy serving people with a rare neurological disease. I joined as a communications manager with very specific functions that I performed dutifully. There was a growing sophistication in the era and the use of social media at this time. Not many touted themselves as experts, but some of us had trampled into social wizarding because we grew up with it in college. When there was an organization all-call to formalize the strategy for using Facebook as a platform to increase client engagement and help amplify the brand, I was excited about using my organically bred status-posting savvy in my work. I threw my hat in. I knew if I landed an opportunity to steer the social media strategy, I'd be able to leverage who I was (a natural storyteller) into what I did. I remember presenting to the committee uncertain if I was qualified in the skill, but I knew I could do it. I helped steer the organization's direction in the social space and innovated around the growing platform. None of this work was in my initial job description, nor was it a particularly polished or carved-out space. I just jumped at the chance to create in a space where I knew I had a knack. And, at 23, with minimal experience, I landed my first nationally visible opportunity within my already-existing role. It was my first experience bringing *me* into my work.

The takeaway: Organizations have roles and needs AND blind spots. Don't fear being proactive, suggestive, and self-advocating when sharing how you can meet those needs, but also bring new elements and untapped opportunities based on who you are and the unique gifts you bring. Your job is not only to check a list of what to do; it's also to illuminate what needs to be done.

The way you move as you get to where you're going

As much as course study and postgraduate resources help us chart a course for the careers and roles we want, I don't know if there is or could be a preparation study to help us navigate *who* we become as we work. As we establish ourselves by the output and execution of the work product, I believe it is vital to develop our personhood presence amid our position.

Talent and grind can get you where you want to go, we know that. However, I believe character is the real foundation of worthwhile success. How you express that character in the spaces you serve is a key and lasting element to navigating through your life in and at work. And let me say this too because I get it; we all have a version of us that shows up for work that hides or conjures character quirks, those we think we should /should not have to be successful. I could park there for a good minute to share thoughts on assimilation and posturing, but I'll say this: who you are is who you are, FULL STOP. *We discredit the divine uniqueness of our being if we are more concerned with acclimating to a space instead of requiring that the space widen to embrace ALL that we are.*

Read that again.

Separately, I should add that just because the nonprofit sector is generally positioned as a noble and 'for others' industry, there are still very real structures and bureaucracies that can make the interpersonal dynamics hard to navigate around and among. Anytime you deal with people whose identities are tied to their work, the money they make, and the status they hold, you will undoubtedly have to make choices for dealing with, knowing, and laboring among them well.

Who will you be in relation to others? How do you want to be known? Do you want to be known at all? Will you develop relationships with people outside of how you rely on each other in the shared space? How will you navigate the unspoken but sizeable power flexes created by org charts and tenure? In moments of key decisions, will you defy safety and convention to stand up for what is fair, right, and good? How will your workplace's culture reflect the fullness of your soul and presence? Will you welcome her there too?

These kinds of questions inform the behaviors that are just as crucial to the experience of career-building as the roles you own. Deciding who you want to be is one of the most proactive ways to own your space and establish your voice. No doubt, as you evolve, there will be new iterations of this expression.

I remember an incident in my early twenties when I experienced some relational turbulence at work. A young woman on another team was a peer in age but held a title a step lower than mine, and for reasons I never fully understood or investigated, she had never warmed to me. Despite attempting to engage in polite conversation and reading recipes from her spare-time cooking blog, she was curt and cold. During a hectic event season, when I worked on a shared project with her department, she told her direct supervisor I was frazzled and unreliable, citing three typos on a page of content that I'd written. Her concerns traveled from her boss to mine and into a meeting about pacing and my performance. It got real really fast.

The typos happened; I admit I was working on getting it done and wasn't giving myself enough checkpoints. Valid. However, while she was within her rights to follow up as she did, it wasn't the kind of energy my character deserved. I decided to approach her more with honesty than anger (although I was BIG pissed). While I was nervous about conflict, I felt a conviction about character, and I knew keeping quiet would only widen the chasm. I wrote an honest email, checked it against my spirit (and, well, for typos, too), and sent it to her. The next day, there were three lines in my Skype chat from her, "I hear you. I respect you. And wow, what a well written email."

No matter where I've been and will go, I know my commitment to being a good, honest, and relatable human anchors me. My goal

111

isn't to be a fan favorite but to be the kind of intergroup leader and peer who measures success by the way people feel in my presence and what they are inspired to do after working with me. Achieving this does not look like every day pep rallies, pizza parties, and emoji-filled emails either. For me, the road to this has meant self-regulation, boundaries, having difficult conversations, and establishing a rhythm of checking my actions against my core values and ensuring I'm showing up authentically.

No accomplishment, accolade, or amount of money will let me compromise that. At all.

The takeaway: Your 'you-ness' matters. Nobody else can bring that element to the workspace. No matter what the role or assignment, it is 100% your decision to bring yourself into the space with an intentional approach that far exceeds the work product.

Making a plan to move it forward

At the time of this writing, I am still relatively young. In my thirties, bougie-auntie single, and very much in the designing-the-life-I-want space. I'm assessing all things, including how I want to work and how I want my career and profession to be a part of the beautiful mosaic that is and will be my life. As I know my purpose in this world is attached to how I serve and express my gifts professionally, my career and the places I choose to serve will be a big part of the story my life writes.

I was not reared with the concept of pursuing and designing a career path. Mostly, I've listened to my instincts about when it was time for me to shift from one place to another, and I've been fortunate to see how connecting dots and edifying relationships have opened doors in other cases. Now, my goal is to be more intentional with the way I am pursuing by making choices around what matters most. What kinds of opportunities will get me to my optimal space of fulfillment, joy, freedom, and creativity? What cause or mission is reflective of what my life is most aligned with? What environment and leadership energy will activate my untapped potential and help me achieve new things? Some might say a utopian mix reflective of the answers won't happen under the halo of traditional employment. I don't necessarily agree. While infrastructure and process compliance doesn't scream liberation, I think we can create an ecosystem that sets a precedent and honors our life desires and choices.

Getting to this place, at least for me currently, means conducting an audit and designing a plan for my career. I am giving words, vision, and image to how I want to work, live, and be. In real-time, that looks like listing the kinds of organizations and causes I'd like to support with my skills and how I'd like to do that. I'm auditing where my time is best spent and what work projects give me energy and produce magic. I'm listing the kinds of team dynamics I work best with and making notes about the level of flexibility I'd like to work on other creative projects. I am writing down the compensation number that will allow me to live and bless others the way I know I'm called to do. I'm even drilling down to what I want my environment to look like, the cultural norms I desire, and how I'd like to be managed (should I decide I want to be managed at all). This list isn't a guarantee by any stretch, but it gives me guardrails that I can use as I assess my next and best moves.

I can develop an action plan by whittling down what I want and don't and identifying what I'm willing to wait on. I am determining what I'd like to pursue with intention by creating something - a list of sorts - that I can sit with, see, and adjust as necessary. Knowing where I'm headed makes for a more focused, deliberate, and fulfilled woman of service.

The takeaway: You get to fly your plane, sis. Yes, life will do what life does, and we don't have control, but we can partner with the Divine to do our part. As a co-conspirator of your unique destiny, you can and should be proactive by writing out the vision for your professional life and creating an action plan that will help you get there. You have the tools and know-how to develop the system that will nurture and produce the next, most successful version of you. Will you take the reins and own it?

What matters most

The jobs of our dreams, the mile-long resumes, and highlight reels of awards and recognition are all wonderful. We are within our birthright to aspire to the accomplishments that our ancestors fought for and dreamed of. I want that for you. I want that for me. I want it for the generations of Black women and girls who will follow me to uproot systems, advocate for true justice, and implement new ways for us to live, work, and dream. For many of us, the path to that will be through the work we do in this sector. We will raise funds, design programs, and lead movements to those ends. Our names will be called when a need arises for the expert and the influencer to provide wisdom and insight. And yet, with all those things and the responsibility of that assignment, my sight remains set on allowing the fullness of ourselves to be the deepest and most prevalent element that we bring to what we do every day.

If you are more practical than philosophical, stick with me for a second; I'm going somewhere. While the steps for navigating this sector and the roles of our dreams come with real-life processes and intentions, none of it matters if we are not true to the deepest and most earnest parts of us. That means every document we write, process we create, event we produce, or program we direct should be on-brand for the version of ourselves we feel most accurately reflects the real us. It doesn't mean we will be perfect or that every new initiative will result in a win; it means we can stand behind our efforts, knowing we didn't compromise our character, work ethic, or beliefs. This, for me, is true success and a version I will forever strive toward.

The learning journey to achieve such confidence develops as we learn our lessons, do the work of focused reflection and redirection, stay tethered to our higher power, and go to therapy. Once we are aligned and certain of the goodness we hold and the power we own, we can get to work from that place of abundance, doing what we do like only we can.

CHAPTER EIGHT

Cynthia Thompson

"Defeat should not be the source of discouragement, but a stimulus to keep plotting."

- Shirley Chisolm

We all need a travel agent.

You can't get too far on your journey without a travel agent. Well, I suppose you can, but I wouldn't advise it. A travel agent is supposed to be your guide to help you reach your chosen destination or one crafted by a higher power. Either way, you should want a tour guide to help you create your plan, avoid pitfalls, prepare for the unexpected, get up after failure, craft your comeback, and keep you grounded. I wish I had this travel agent. I never got one, but I have learned so much along the way that I want to share. Here are a few things you might need: a journal to take notes, a mental compass for emotional and spiritual balance (I call it a Bible), a map (your plan), and a passport (collect stamps from each destination stop).

Dear Sis,

No one told me about getting a mentor. I wish I had known how valuable a mentor would be. I kept hearing about how I should get one early in my career, but I'm naturally a loner, so I just kept it moving. I had no idea how badly I needed one until years later.

Merriam-Webster defines a mentor as *"someone who teaches or gives help and advice to a less experienced and often younger person."*

No one explained what a mentor was. I'm not dumb. I knew it was someone who would advise me, but I didn't know who this person would be to me. Where was I supposed to find them? In my professional field, probably. Would I find them at my church? Hmmm maybe. Were they supposed to be a college alum, look like me, be the same sex, or what? Since I didn't have a profile of a mentor, I wandered through each job, intending to chart my path without someone telling me how I might achieve my goal.

Sherry Sims: "The most common impediment [for women of color to] finding mentors is not knowing how to ask for support or where to look."

Here I was, on a journey without a travel agent, not necessarily because I didn't want one but because I didn't understand what I needed or how to ask or look for help. Sis, do you have a mentor? Am I describing you? If I am, it's okay.

Dear Sis,

So, I've been traveling for a minute in this nonprofit business. I think I know where I'm going, although I sometimes question my journey and path. Yet, I am still without a mentor – a travel agent to help me get to my final destination. Have you figured out what you're looking for in a mentor? I mean, you want to get one who can at least help you elevate your profession, right? I've learned a couple of things in my search. Be a damn good listener, as in listening to understand, not to respond. Attend as many workshops, seminars, and conferences, in person, as possible. These are where I gather tons of information about where people are today and how they got there, all while learning about my professional craft. And let me drop this nugget in case you weren't aware: Networking is a necessary skill we must intentionally master. Networking takes discipline to get you to your next leg in the journey. Sometimes, Black people treat networking like a member-only club. Except in some settings, we're one of a few bits of pepper sprinkled in a sea of salt. We may not even want others to discover the group, yet we get excited when another one of us walks into the room. Sis, it's okay to share.

Rahel Tekola: "Networking gives you an edge because you never know when [someone else] can help you. And it [builds] your network, knowledge, and credibility."

One day, I had this epiphany. I decided to stop looking for this elusive mentor. I mean, all this time had passed, and I was still doing okay. Don't get me wrong; I still needed a mentor. I just discovered the act of mentoring doesn't have to come from one static environment or one source. People had been mentoring me, especially those from whom I took mental notes. Remember what I said earlier about being a good listener? After taking all those notes, you can set your final destination and map your route. The rest of your journey is determined by all the advice you've been receiving.

Dear Sis,

Do you know what you want to do? What's important to you? Those were the two most significant questions I heard repeatedly playing through random ear-hustling sessions during networking breaks at conferences. Or, at least, that's what I understood. Even knowing how to answer these questions requires help from someone other than yourself. *I learned to seek out unsuspecting mentors.*

One of the best things about working in nonprofit is that the circle is small and mighty, which is the same for Black females in nonprofit. I assure you someone has experienced something like the path you're traveling.

Deena Drewis: "Look at the people right around you to start, rather than seeking out the big shots right out the gate."

Ask questions and listen to how what is being said connects with your path. What you hear doesn't have to be an exact match. Nothing's perfect. Your route will change and may even have some detours, so pack light. Put it on paper – map it out.

Dear Sis,

I love to hear hustle because I pick up these little nuggets of golden advice. Someone once said, "Always act like you're going somewhere, and stay ready." As you get more comfortable with your traveling map, you'll refine your path to suit your personal and work ethics, and hopefully, your passion will blossom. An old boss told me that as I personally and professionally age, my personal and work ethics will align and meld into one. Neither will interfere with the other because they are one. If you're not passionate about where you want to go or who you want to be, someone may come along and set your compass for you.

Rahel Tekola: "Seize opportunities to better yourself and your career."

Dear Sis,

Now it's time to put in a little work. Grab your passport because it's time to start collecting stamps for every destination where you land. Start signing up for those lunch-and-learn seminars specific to your field of expertise. In-person is best. The more you attend seminars, the more you'll notice some of the same faces. You may see a person who draws attention from several people at varying levels of experience. That person could be a great mentor, but you have to consider whether they have enough time. Sometimes, their popularity might be indicative of being stretched for time. It doesn't mean they won't be good mentors, but you should be mutually beneficial. If you can, exchange contact information, follow up with an email, and schedule a time to speak by phone or in person.

Deena Drewis: "A mentorship is a professional relationship which can make for some vulnerable, personal moments. Find someone you trust and get along with."

121

Finding a mentor can be intimidating, but you're up for the challenge. Make the process suit you. If the above isn't your style, and it definitely wasn't mine, try sitting at a table with people who appear calm and reserved. I've been surprised by how easy it is to start a conversation table-side. In either scenario, pick their brain about their professional journey. What it took to reach their destination; hopefully, they have achieved it or soon will. Ask for advice on how to get to your destination. Ask for tips to refine your path. Sometimes, this question can be the most challenging part because you're asking someone to critique what you're doing. Constructive criticism can be challenging to hear but is necessary. The objective is progression. Your journal should be filling up with notes about your journey in real-time.

Dear Sis,

Don't forget your passport. You'll need it as your traveling becomes more strategically focused. Each destination will be stamped to mark the occasion. Your resume will start looking like your personal business plan. Each stop will tell its own story by title and length of stay. Your luggage becomes lighter as you travel because your expertise isn't caught up in paper. Your expertise has become your personal brand. No matter where you land or your layover, your strategy will precede you. All that is left to do is bring someone else along. Bring someone into your circle and show them how to travel.

Christiana: "I'm so thankful that I've been able to spend time with you.

122

You are a miracle."

Here are some things to consider when looking for a mentor:

- make the relationship easy
- everyone is busy; make the relationship mutually beneficial and be a damn good listener
- don't let someone's title intimidate you or make you fawn over them - the person you're seeking will be flattered, but don't make it weird; you can always aspire to be in a similar position, but you can't be them
- I said I didn't know what characteristics a mentor should have; your mentor could be on your level right now but has enough discernment to guide you
- look for people with similar interests as you, including your field of work
- be specific about what you want

CHAPTER NINE

Daneshe Williams-Bethune

"Knowing that it has never been done before makes me want to fight even harder."

- Misty Copeland

Dear Black woman in the social sector, I want you to know my story. I didn't choose nonprofit as a career, but I believe I was destined for this work. An opportunity landed in my lap, and I learned long ago to take advantage of opportunities. I was familiar with nonprofits because I grew up in a family that worked closely with social service organizations. My mother was a director of a large youth development organization. Her district consisted of mostly African American neighborhoods riddled with drugs and crime. She would take me with her when she presented to families, encouraging them to enroll their children in the afterschool and summer programs. I participated in all the activities with the kids. I was in talent shows, pageants, Black history programs, plays, speaker introductions, and church announcements. If there was an opportunity for me to be a part of it, you'd best believe my family had me in it. I was the poster child for IT. Nothing happened in local schools or communities I wasn't involved in at some point.

My grandfather was city council, mayor pro tem for our city, and a financial advisor, so he was always helping people. I noticed how he interacted with people with this smooth but distinctive behavior that made him a community-wide star. My childhood was steeped in being raised by a single mother while also being engulfed in a life of exposure.

When I started studying my major, journalism, with a concentration in public relations and a minor in marketing, we had to choose local nonprofits and help them build their brand awareness. I remember helping a children's home with a fall festival fundraiser. It felt great seeing those children enjoying themselves while the community got a chance to see how their donations made a difference. It gave me a sense of fulfillment and joy, but I left it at that.

As soon as I graduated from college, I thought I would work for a medium-large-sized marketing agency. Instead, I started working for my godfather and his cousin doing public relations for their country western and talk radio stations. Not the agency life I had imagined, but I had to be creative and use my college learnings. So, when a friend called me and said I have the perfect job for you, I was thoroughly interested. She told me the position was a minority youth outreach worker for an HIV/AIDS organization. I didn't know what that entailed, but I was ready for something different. I interviewed for the job and was hired on the spot and realized I would be teaching sex education.

I would go to schools, community centers, boys and girls clubs, juvenile delinquency centers, adolescent psychiatric facilities, and youth groups to explain HIV/AIDS. Because of the nature of the disease, I talked about sex a lot, and, as you can imagine, the kids would ask off-putting and strange questions. However, the organization hosted a one-week evening camp each summer for kids infected and/or impacted by HIV/AIDS. I'd make requests to companies, organizations, and individuals about ways they could support the summer camp. Though I didn't work for the development department, I enjoyed this type of work and, during my presentations, started providing donated door prizes I had acquired. It felt good to request items to support children in the program. I never felt like I was begging for anything.

After two years of working there, I applied for a development associate position at another nonprofit organization. Though I had never officially worked in a development department, I understood the work required to succeed.

My first official fundraising position was for another HIV/AIDS organization. When I interviewed for the position, the executive director asked me if I knew how to write grants. I politely informed him that I didn't, and he said, "It's okay, I'll teach you; it's not hard." I was excited to see someone who didn't look like me take an interest in my professional growth and was willing to teach me a skill I was interested in learning.

I realized that writing grants wasn't only about the words used but also establishing relationships. I built a friendship with my coworker, an older, beautiful African American woman who treated me with respect and like her daughter. She took an interest in me and was my first professional mentor. When I had issues with the development director and, ultimately, the executive director, she helped me navigate those waters, along with my mother. They had started to request things from me that didn't seem ethical or logical. I eventually wrote a letter to the board of directors, which proved to be a waste of time, but I learned a valuable lesson that I hadn't needed in my previous position – CYA, affectionately known as 'Cover Your Ass.'

After my daughter was born, I wanted to work part-time, but still in development. I interviewed for a part-time position at a large nonprofit. Two months after interviewing, the associate director of development informed me that their manager had quit and suggested hiring me for her position. WHAT??? Flabbergasted and honored to be asked, though I thought I was unqualified, someone else saw potential in me. This role required me to become strategic, build philanthropic relationships with some of the wealthiest individuals and families in the metroplex, and navigate multiple personalities and work styles, all while staying on top of my work, even when dependent upon others. I was responsible for identifying, applying for, and securing funding for various programs and services for over ten locations.

The associate director of development took a special interest in me and began giving me additional responsibilities outside my regular work duties. I was simultaneously working on my graduate degree, and she saw my tenacity and determination to do an amazing job. I would oftentimes serve as interim development director or lead on certain projects. I was the only person in the development department who met their annual fundraising goals. During my tenure, my team raised over $25 million for the organization from private and public funding. I built a relationship with the CEO and felt I could potentially take on a higher-level role. I was almost done with my graduate degree and thought that would allow me to gain a better position, but I realized the organization wasn't prepared to have African Americans in higher development roles or in any outward-facing capacity.

The organization was built under a "good ole boy" system, and that meant Blacks couldn't rise to the top. I learned that oftentimes you doubt yourself, not because you're incapable, but because you've been beat up enough to feel like you're incapable of more.

But I wanted more, and after I finished my graduate degree, I quickly started looking for another role. I found a job that appealed to me and would allow me to grow into a larger role and serve children. I interviewed five times with the leaders and board members. It was a gruesome process, but it allowed me to hone my interviewing skills, so all good. In my Charlie Murphy voice,

129

"WRONG! WRONG!"

When I started my new position as market director, I was responsible for Dallas County proper, then, six months later, for all of Dallas County, and six months after that, I was responsible for Collin County. My territory coverage had doubled, I had more dollars to raise, and I was not offered any assistance with my personal growth, mentorship, or leads. It felt disrespectful to have a larger territory but no one to assist me. The pressure became overwhelming; I was abandoning my family, missing school activities, gaining weight, and being overly stressed.

Staff expected more from me than I could manage, and my supervisor had no problem layering it on thicker. But I still managed to gain more corporate contacts and awards from coworkers and expanded three boards in two years. Some coworkers watched my work and became jealous that I didn't share my contacts. No one else had picked up one finger to make a phone call, take notes, assist with research, etc., so when my supervisor left, and a new one arrived, I was excited. He was an accomplished Black man with several years in nonprofit and a proven leader. A Black male coworker told me before he started that he would get rid of all the Black people. And you know what? He did. He didn't talk to me and was always surrounded by the "other" girls in the office. And six months after he started, he laid me off and hired a white girl in my position who was given access to my hard-earned contacts. It was a kick in the gut, but I should have listened to wise counsel when it was given.

I learned that no matter how hard you work when someone wants your spot, you'd best believe they'll do anything to take your place. I also learned that you can be collateral damage when someone wants to be perceived as 'more than.' Two years after I was laid off, the same trick he used on me was used on him, but he wanted to sue the organization. Karma is a bitch, and I was sipping my tea.

God also revealed a message to me after being laid off. I wondered why I had been laid off after working so hard for that organization. Weeks after leaving, slowly, more and more people started quitting the agency. At least five people I knew quit, and God revealed that I was being used to help encourage others to leave.

Being laid off was a blessing. It allowed me time to rest, relax, and release all the stress and time I had spent working for them. I sat on my couch watching soap operas for six weeks before I started looking for another job. My family did not suffer financially, and God continuously provided for us in unimaginable ways. When I finally started looking for a job, I found one that would allow me to work from 8:30 am to 5:00 pm, no evenings or weekends, and they offered me $20k more than my previous job. I was one happy camper, and though the title wasn't as grand, the stress was less, and the pay was more. I had a white female supervisor who understood I was valuable to the organization and to her. We made a good team, too. She would call all her rich friends and get them to do a site visit with us. Once on site, I would present our programs and give them a tour, and then they'd ask us to submit a proposal or would write a check. It was a good gig.

I attended probably every nonprofit luncheon in town and met great people. I've always worked to build my network, and this job allowed me to do that. After two years of working for the organization, the president was released and replaced with an older white man from the financial industry. After meeting me, he appreciated my work but didn't feel I should interact with donors. He felt I should stay in the office and write grant proposals. I immediately started looking for other jobs but didn't know what I wanted to do. As luck would have it, a person I worked with at a previous job contacted me with an opportunity.

I was elated when I received the phone call from a former coworker regarding the chief development officer position at a homeless shelter. It would allow me to move on and embark on a new opportunity. The new CEO at the homeless shelter had been a board member and volunteer for a long time, but this would be his first time serving as an executive director/CEO.

Without me knowing, promises were made to staff that made the working environment hostile for me. One employee had been working at the mission for over 20 years. She had served in many roles, so, of course, when they decided to create the chief development officer position, she wanted the role. I don't think she had anything against me personally, but she was upset that I was in "her" role. I tried my best to work and consult with her because I knew she knew the answers to all my questions. She had special relationships with the donors and knew when they would give and what they supported. So, it was always "strange" that when I asked her questions, she never knew the answers or was "confused" by my requests.

I've encountered many individuals who have worked for organizations for long periods. Oftentimes, they have a sincere love for the organization they work for but feel they deserve to be promoted even though they've had no professional development in the field. Employees can also become very stuck in their ways and not be open to new ideas, concepts, or suggestions, and that can hinder a nonprofit and the work to improve others' lives. Progress can be difficult for them to comprehend and understand.

I want you to understand that individuals will try their best to dim your light. For me, men in the nonprofit sector were intimidated by my presence or my ability. Either way, it caused me undue stress, trauma and to often made me question my abilities as a fundraiser in this field.

Next, I was excited about my new opportunity to serve as an executive director of a small youth development nonprofit. When I interviewed, I was asked to help groom an employee who had been at the agency for more than ten years to where she could ultimately become an executive director. At first, I was taken aback because I knew they hadn't asked the other executive directors to groom her because she hadn't been given any professional development and had only recently started taking a nonprofit management certification class. However, they wanted me to train her so she could take my position.

When I started, the organization wasn't meeting its student recruitment numbers, had lost two major fundraisers, had no individual donors, had no cultivation and/or stewardship program, and was dependent upon grants and special events to raise most of its funds.

I worked with the staff, who were not fans of me. They had made the organization about them and not the students. I was considered an enemy of the state because I wouldn't conform to their ways of operating the nonprofit. But that wasn't my assignment; my assignment was to help turn the organization around.

For the first four months, it was a living nightmare. Every day, there was drama with the staff. If I had an idea or a question, it would be turned down, or I was told, "We tried it before, and it didn't work." Those answers are the most frustrating because they indicate no one wants things to be better; they are comfortable with the way things are. It also has an air of my way or the highway. That was frustrating. I never thought they had a color issue with me, it was more that one person wanted to be the executive director, but she had been stiffed several times for the role, so she was upset and unwilling to help the organization succeed. She had so much love for the organization but was willing to watch its demise based on her theory that she knew what was best for it.

I wasn't surprised when she and another staff member quit in February. And two weeks later, the PANDEMIC happened, and it changed everything. The sad part about them leaving was that we also lost students in the program. This program serves kids who'd be the first in their families to graduate from college, who come from low-income households, single-parents, or multi-generational households, so these young people can fall into two categories, reach their full potential or fall behind. It was sad to see kids leave because of the staff. I don't know if the kids understood why; they were chosen for the program, and it's supposed to help them get to college. I pray for all the kids, but especially for those who are no longer part of the program.

As soon as the pandemic started, I lost program staff, didn't have funds coming in, and depended upon available staff and board members to help carry the program with our remaining participants. Also, I didn't know much about the program, but we tried our best to ensure the kids continued to have an experience, even though it was virtual. The students weren't fans of the virtual program, even though we tried hard to keep them engaged and interested. But the pandemic did help us in some ways; the PPP funds helped keep us stable, and we reduced our expenses by 60 percent. Moving all the programming to virtual also allowed us to be creative in how we worked with the youth.

And this is where connections mean so much for nonprofits and why people don't like us often serve as CEOs. They have built-in connections, help that comes without asking, and ways to garner large gifts in the blink of an eye. Several nonprofits struggled during the pandemic, and many had to close their doors because they lacked one thing: funding, while others thrived, especially those providing basic services like food, rental, and utility assistance, along with housing help. Some had board members who weren't impacted by the pandemic and could still write large checks, and, lastly, some nonprofits had cash reserves and may have laid off staff but redirected the remaining staff to still assist clients, albeit on a smaller scale. Here lies the difference between Black-led nonprofits and white-led nonprofits; the connectivity.

I won't say my success over the years isn't from my own doing. The opportunities to be in front of the right people allowed me to present good philanthropic programming to those who had the means to give. And those opportunities came about because I often had a white connection to the right people. I'd also say my passion for the people helped convey the importance of our work to others.

I have prided myself on bringing opportunities to the table for nonprofits. I've closed several deals, from creating a hospital sexual assault counseling wing to securing national partnerships with large, franchised companies and using familial philanthropy to raise millions of dollars. But I never realized the trouble I would have when I moved to this new nonprofit that had none of these connections to dollars. It's been an uphill battle, and I've felt unqualified to handle it, despite my success over the years.

To have worked in nonprofit for years and to have made a difference in thousands of people's lives is a blessing and one I'm proud of. But being the executive director for this nonprofit feels like a life's mission. The work the nonprofit does is unmatched. Its impact on changing attitudes and behavior through exposure and experiences isn't like your typical youth development organization. I strongly believe in its work, and the youth who are being served are amazing. They are specifically chosen because someone has seen a spark in them, one that needs a little fire to help it grow. And I'm proud to be a part of the flames of their future success.

In April 2021, I decided not to discuss the issues I encountered when I started with the organization in October 2019. I was tired of holding onto that trauma and reliving it every time I talked about the organization and why we were in the current condition. Once I made that decision, I started to move forward and went from survival to thriving mode. I changed my thought patterns and started to put actions into place to set us on a better course. Imagine having to resurrect the Titanic with little help and plenty of parts floating out at sea. Well, I decided to leave those parts at sea and build a new ship. A new ship gave me the autonomy to build new rooms, gain new passengers, add new vendors, and reach out to those who helped build the first ship while helping them understand and be a part of the new vision.

It's going to take time, but I'm willing to put that into this organization.

I want you to know that working in nonprofit can be frustrating. It can be pleasing. It can be heartbreaking. The one thing it's going to do is test your ability to move forward. I can hold on to all the trauma, disappointment, drama, troubles, and betrayal, but that doesn't help me be my best.

I wish you the best in your career path. I pray for your prosperity and that you continue to make waves and continuously help those who need it the most.

CHAPTER TEN
Dominique S. McCain

"If you want to fly, you have to give up things that weigh you down."

- Toni Morrison

Principles to live by as a BWNPL

1. **Lean into how YOU lead**

Today, I watched a clip of Adele being asked about someone who inspired her, and she referenced Ms. McDonald, a teacher she had in 8th grade at 12 years old. When she described what was so special about Ms. McDonald, it had everything to do with how Ms. McDonald made her feel as a student. She referenced helping to spark her love for literature and "getting her." As it became clear the question was a trick to surprise Adele by having Ms. McDonald in the audience, the audience began to erupt in applause, and Adele was moved to tears. The first thing Ms. McDonald said to her was, "I am so proud of you." I was struck by how emotional this multifaceted success became by hearing those words from this woman, A BLACK WOMAN! I'd be lying if I didn't

139

say that I've often said, "The whole world crawls into the lap of a Black woman for love and acceptance."

I picture the sprawling lap of mammies and nursemaids bringing the earliest concepts of comfort, care, and servant leadership to the world – the ability to influence and touch lives through love and nurturing. I bring this up because, as Black women in nonprofit leadership, there are often erroneous messages about what it takes to lead and be at the "top" or c-suite/executive level.

That this book and this cohort exist is evidence of the anomaly that is Black women in nonprofit leadership. That said, many characteristics and criteria are presented as antithetical to who we are. I have taken so many personality, strengths, weaknesses etc. assessments, and each has identified relationship building as a key/core strength; however, I've found myself feeling very isolated as messages of "strategy over relationship" are touted across the nonprofit sector. I encourage you to lean into your most authentic self in this work, as it is the most powerful and purposed part of you. If nonprofit work has service to others at its core, then the sector should be fertile ground for the natural skills and leadership styles of Black women.

As a Black woman who has helped, empowered, and directed others to their purpose, it goes without saying that I have only been able to do so because I have been helped, empowered, and directed to my purpose by other Black women. From my grandmother Erma's loving guidance to my mother Charlet's stern resourcefulness, I am the product of a long line of Black women who have poured into me. Their pouring has fueled my existence. As early as I can remember, I've been goaded and led to greatness through the affirming words of Myrtis and Debra; through the real love and real-life talk of LeDora and Priscilla. Ladine gave me the sister I needed, and Audrey's consistency kept me kind. I went from a girl looking for guidance from women with lives and experiences I wanted myself to a young woman seeking out her tribe. And for this, I am grateful to God, Jehovah.

After several failed attempts, I finally met my first sister-friend, Nickie Landry. This friendship would change my life forever. This was the first friend who accepted me fully and the first peer I also respected as a role model. I can vividly recall when my sister circle went from mentors and mothers to sister-friends. It would be easy for me to rant about why we need each other and how each of us is our sister's keeper, but instead, I'd prefer to just tell you of the magnificent benefits I have reaped. If I didn't know any better, Jesus himself would be a Black woman, 'cause Lord knows, they have saved me.

Recently, I suffered a loss greater than any other in my life. My grandmothers Erma and Hattie died in the same year, and I literally felt like a cannon had blown through my body. A huge piece of me was instantly missing. In the following weeks and days, I spent hours on end crying, sobbing, and wailing, and only the comfort of other Black women kept me afloat and alive.

Shortly after suffering this loss, after just enough time had passed for me to be functional again, I joined a cohort of women who led nonprofits, and I didn't know what to expect. Like any other professional development, I signed up expecting to learn some, share some, and, most importantly, take a break from the hustle and bustle of work. I saw it as a way to rest my mind and my code-switching muscles. Not in a million years would I have imagined it would become the most treasured and transformational engagement of my life. "Why?" you ask. Because this cohort represents the space where I have been the most seen, heard, and cared for in my entire career.

This cohort started me on a journey to being healed. Healed from shrinking myself (imposter syndrome), healed from overworking myself, healed from being undervalued, and healed from my perfectionism and inner critic.

How did this healing come about? Through the authentic interactions and relationships that I formed in this group. I have received just a small token of their greatness from every single woman; these tokens have added up to a treasure trove of love and support that have filled me in ways that years of "going it alone" never could.

When asked, "What did I expect from the cohort?" I was super clear that I wanted to show up and not be expected to "carry the load," which had become my pattern in every aspect of my life. I didn't realize at the time that I was asking for the ability to depend on others, lean on others, and rest myself trusting that whatever was needed and/or required would be taken care of. I didn't expect to not do my part, I only expected to not do it all. This was the best expectation I could have set, and I have been more than pleasantly surprised with the power, strength, and tenacity of this sister circle. Every woman has given some part of herself and, in turn, has also allowed me to give some part of myself.

2. They will not chase you down, *so if you want freedom, you must take it*

I have seen a white male CEO and other white colleagues literally "chase down" an employee who has expressed being at their wit's end with the whole operation on several occasions during my five-year tenure at a large educational nonprofit. I initially had compassion and pity for the white women who did and/or said something I know for certain my ass would have been put on the streets for doing or saying. But here's the thing. If, as a Black woman, you are working longer hours, meeting more goals, growing more team members, and fucking spreading your Magic (Black Girl Magic, that is) all over the joint (and I'm certain you are), and yet, you don't make as much money nor receive as much recognition and affirmation, then stop that shit! They will not chase you down to pay you more; they will not chase you down to recognize and affirm you.

I'm sure that, like me, you don't even realize how much you matter and how much you do for the benefit of the company. However, let's be clear; they won't chase you down. By chase down,

I mean beg you to stay, demonstrate their appreciation of you, or give you everything you want and/or need to continue sustainably. If your love language is "words of affirmation," then seek that in your personal life or from those who love you. We are rarely given flowers on the job or by white superiors because we are so often gifted in ways that are not in keeping with the whitewashed cultures and narratives that pervade the nonprofit sector. We are often underestimated and overlooked. It is crucial that you know your strengths and what you bring to the table because often, you will need to be so intrinsically sure and motivated that what seems to be a dismissal or ignoring of your value will not harm you.

This "chasing down" can take multiple forms, but you should not expect any to apply to you. It might look like a CEO-adjacent white woman being offered time off to "take care of" herself after months of asking not to be given too many more projects as she is facing overload.

For another, it looks like not being held accountable or having a consequence for the blatant disrespect of her supervisor's lateral colleague. The disrespect was allowed because the lateral colleague in question is a Black woman. This white woman was believed over the Black woman, and she was provided all sorts of support for mental health and growth, only later to be found stealing by falsely documenting her worked hours. Only then was she let go, and even then, it was a slow and compassionate process of termination. If only the same compassion had been shown for the number of Black women who were forced to resign, including me, because of a lack of compassion and understanding from their white and/or bi-racial supervisors.

Meanwhile, we Black women in nonprofit leadership are asked to bend over backward and deal with constant microaggressions and retaliatory threats. Like being asked to "not talk so much" or said differently, allowing room for others' voices, when others who are consistently asked to speak up don't. We are also asked to take on additional projects on top of our work for no additional compensation, and we are asked to solve the most audacious, long-standing problems faced by the organization with no value assigned to our suggestions and ideas.

We need to offer a dissertation to justify our strategy, but white people can make it up and pull it out of the air. The privilege of having your word and perspective valued and trusted with no real evidence is one we will not be handed but instead must take. And yet, after you go on your way, meaning you take your freedom and build your own org., or you find an org to support that supports you, they somehow find the money and motivation to create a position strikingly similar to what you wanted to do inside their org. Those who choose not to speak will speak up when we remember we have nothing to prove. Stop killing yourself, sis … they don't value you like you think, and they never will, so Sis, do what is best for you and yours.

The moral of the story is that if we as a people must chase

ourselves down … when our "selves" tell us we are fed up, we need to act. As the grand dame of Black literature so eloquently plants in her work *Beloved*, when Paul D tells Sethe, "You are your best thing." We are absolutely our best thing. Ourselves and our other sisters/Black women.

I am sure you've also heard, "All kinfolk ain't skin folk." Tap into God's given discernment and pray that He reveals who He has assigned to you and who He has not, and you will be able to determine who is part of the best thing and who is not. This leads me to the next principle I'd like to share.

3. Don't commit Black-on-Black Crime

I know, I know, they say we should not allow the figurative Black-on-Black Crime (BOBC) narrative to persist in professional spaces, but I'd say this is one of the most important principles to live by. In my opinion, we do the whites' work when we succumb to the systemic ill that leads to BOBC. It is rooted in the philosophy of scarcity. Why would it ever be necessary for me to hurt, harm, or undermine the authority or social capital of another Black woman?

In my opinion, there is never a justification for this. There is never a GOOD reason, so it should never happen. Now, let's be clear; that does not mean we won't have to "check" each other, coach each other, or even fire each other, but it does mean our intention, like the Hippocratic oath, should be to "do no harm." I do not believe in doing harm to anyone unless they are trying to harm me, but I absolutely recommend that we are intentional to NOT harm other Black women. And before you ask, yes, I have been professionally and personally harmed more than once by other Black women. But, if I'm honest, the help outweighed the hurt even when the hurt was bad, like the trauma I suffered at the hands of my mother's poor decision-making and desperation in her younger life. None of that outweighs the strength, tenacity, and standards she set for me as the foundations of my successes and legacy. Black women have shown up for me, even when I didn't know I needed them to. Loving each other as a community takes on many forms, and one is supporting and having empathy for each other in the workplace. This can be easier said than done, so I'd like to offer you a perspective that might just make you think, even if it doesn't compel you to live by this code.

I have a sister who is, by all stretches of the imagination, a *"whole lotta extra," a big ball of fun and love and, most importantly, she is hilarious.* She's the kinda sista that makes you laugh and smile until your belly and face hurt; a self-professed "clown." She taught me one of the greatest lessons of my life and she's my cohort sister. The other thing I should tell you about her is that she is a DOCTOR. I share this to basically show the versatility that she, like many other Black women, brings. She was perfect as a session facilitator on Black Women's mental health because she brought levity to an extremely heavy topic.

Initially, I was skeptical about whether I'd be able to take her seriously, but the lesson she taught me is that to judge another Black woman is to judge myself as a Black woman, and to accept another Black woman is also to accept myself. I'd be willing to bet that most BOBC in the workplace comes from feelings anchored and rooted in judgment and a lack of acceptance of either self or others. For weeks after her session, I couldn't shake this feeling that I had totally misjudged her. Below is an excerpt from my journal entry post that session:

"The topic of Black women's mental health is so many things like a Black woman ... the complexity, depth, and general lack of knowledge of Black women about Black women is always jolting for me. But the greatest lesson I am taking away today is the NECESSITY to fine-tune my vision and heart to be able to see and embrace (love) the value that every Black woman brings into the world. If I could love on all of them, I would. Maybe loving on them more will teach me to love on me ... How is it that Summer's sense of humor brings deep belly laughter out of me, even though she is one of the most brilliant women with knowledge of a topic that is so deep and important? Who did I assume she was? Who do I now know and value her as? Is her value only about what she has done for me in this moment of time? What is it that makes me predetermine someone's abilities or value?"

I realized that day that I was inadvertently holding Black women to a standard above other groups. I was expecting perfection from them, including myself, when, many times and in many ways, I have tolerated and dealt with mediocrity from others.

Why had I only applied Howard Gardner's theory of multiple intelligences to my students in the past, and hadn't taken the perspective of multiple intelligences with Black women? I discovered that it is a white supremacist mindset to think and hold Black women to a standard above and beyond who they show up as and are. Instead, I should have committed to accepting them and me as enough! I believe the path forward is to lean into identifying each other's strengths and values with the clear understanding that we are all interconnected, and what I need, you have, and vice versa. Since we are all imperfectly perfect, our communal value strengthens us and makes us a WHOLE UNIT. Each of us is enough and has value.

Ode to Black Women and Me:

Hey Girl … you are full GROWN and ENOUGH … even when you are incomplete or not quite sure, you are ENOUGH …

ENOUGH to be the center of attention

ENOUGH to be the head and not the tail, remembering that tails have a real function too!

What is it to be the Alpha (head) or the Underdog (tail)? It is a PRIVILEGE because both are necessary for the structure and stability of the pack.

You, my sister, are …

Challenging, like a Rubik's cube

Complicated like calculus

Fun and easy going like CandyLand, yet

Peaceful and serene like still water.

And you are all of this wrapped up into one!

You have the rage of an uncontrolled wildfire and the spontaneity of a wildflower that springs up unannounced.

You ... work the work ... the process must be processed to get a clear sense of how it all fits in that container called YOU.

When not needed ... you are still enough even when that container is empty.

You are enough of whatever you want to be, and whatever IT (all that is assigned to you) takes.

I love you.

4. **Be wise about your time**

"In a country that prioritizes commerce above all, a nation where money has always talked louder than rhetoric, the proof of a perception shift will be evidenced in the payment rendered, enough to put us on par, I hope, with less talented whites who've been earning more for decades. It's easy to say Black Lives Matter; the question is, do they matter enough for this nation to treat and compensate them fairly?"

How much do you value your time? From my perspective, time is the most valuable and equalizing entity there is. We are all given

150

the same amount of it daily, weekly, monthly, and annually. But often, time and the sense of urgency associated with it can be manipulated in ways that are not helpful, like when it is in the hands of a racist system and/or when it is being handed out as a sentence or suspension. Then, it, too, is manipulated and used against those of us with brown bodies. Beware of this tactic in the workplace. Do not let the concept of TIME be used against you.

When you feel overwhelmed, stressed beyond your capacity, and pressed or pressured to be quick to make decisions, set goals, or meet the expectations of those who have a very different perspective or perception of "the work" that you are doing in nonprofit leadership, know that "time" is more on your side than you know. I am reminded of a sermon I heard once titled "Surviving Jezebel."

As you may or may not recall, Queen Jezebel threatened the prophet Elijah by declaring he would be dead in 24 hours. She was determined to kill him; however, the end of Elijah's earthly life was much later and not even to death; it was by God taking him up into heaven. So, not only was the queen unable to kill him in 24 hours, but she couldn't kill him. His life was not taken by human hands but by God's. I share this thought to encourage you to take the time you need to make the decisions that are most significant to you and for you.

I also reference time as a commodity of great value. Often, as Black women, we are asked to participate, contribute, and collaborate in ways that take time but do not pay or provide us with any benefit outside of the experience. We are also often underpaid or paid less than our less melanated, more male colleagues. As a woman in nonprofit leadership, get clear about the value of your time, and allocate your time appropriately to the things that will provide you the greatest return on your investment. If you don't already have strategic thinking time, rest time, and personal breaks on your calendar, add them. Your ability to schedule the time you need to execute your duties will support you in using the "time" you are paid to actually do the work you are paid to do. When I am asked what I get paid to do, my most accurate answer is, "I get paid to think."

When you become responsible for the strategic level of work, it is critical that you set aside the right amount of time to think through and build the strategy. This is important because it wards off burnout and the infamously bad habit of "putting out fires" all day and doing the thinking work after hours. Bad deal, sis! Remember one of the key principles to success and use your time wisely!

CHAPTER ELEVEN

Dr. Garica Sanford

"Do what works for you, because there will always be someone who thinks differently."

-Michelle Obama

Dear Black women in the social sector, when I started my journey, I needed to "**R**elax, **R**elate, **R**elease!"

Be honest. Were you able to say those three words in that order without hearing the high-pitched voice of Whitely Gilbert? For those of us who watched *Different World* religiously on Thursday nights in the early 90s, the phrase "Relax, Relate Release" instantly takes us to the scene when Whitley Gilbert (played by actress Jasmine Guy) is seeking therapy to process emotions connected to her ex-partner who, in her words, is "marrying the perfect woman and going off to live a perfectly lovely life (in Paris) while I'm hopelessly in love with a boy who can't even tell the difference between a salad fork and a pitchfork."

The wise therapist, played by the incomparable Debbie Allen, gives Whitley the infamous 3R mantra to help her move forward instead of being stuck in what could or should have been true for her. As Whitley leaves the office, she repeats the mantra several times in her iconic voice while arching her back and chest as she says each word. It's definitely Google-worthy if you've never seen the scene.

However, with full transparency, when I watched the show as an adolescent, the connection to the mantra was the dramatic persona of Guy's character, which made it a humorous scene that was fun to recreate with friends. The meaning of Allen's words didn't fully resonate until I watched reruns of the television show as an adult. And while Allen's wisdom was about a personal aspect of Whitley's life, it's not hard to understand how the phrase made it into a book for Black women leaders.

Most of us did not obtain our leadership role(s) by relaxing or releasing anything. Ask many Black women in leadership, and they will tell you they "had" to do exactly the opposite. Given that Black women are often underrepresented AND **misrepresented** by society, many who obtain what the world defines as success via leadership roles and titles do so by adopting very different mantras.

Many of us were fueled by Black cultural aphorisms that served as motivation and encouragement as we navigated a world not traditionally welcoming of women, let alone Black women, given historical inequities deeply steeped in the fabric of this country. Aphorisms like, *"You have to work twice as hard to get half as far,"* and *"Never let them see you sweat"* were likely first heard long before there was a dream or plan to achieve any professional title. Sadly, most of us heard these sayings as children because our caregivers knew that whether our future included being a successful C-suite leader or becoming an entrepreneur, we would face challenges connected to our racial and gender identity.

Growing up, I was definitely aware that, even with multiple degrees, various credentials, and tons of professional and real-life experience, I would not be buffered from repeated experiences of being overlooked for someone less qualified, occasionally being assumed to be "the help," being complimented on how well I spoke, and frequently being held to different and unfair expectations compared to my white colleagues.

That to be seen as a competent leader, I had to **always** have everything together … more often than not, be the first one in the office and/or one of the last ones to leave … balance speaking up with not talking too much or being too quiet … and more significantly, accept mistakes are not permissible because not only would they jeopardize being seen as competent in comparison to my White colleagues but they could also negatively impact the next Black woman's ability to move into a leadership role. To say the least, the mental and emotional double-dutch of being a Black female leader is exhausting.

Black women are naturally oriented to care for others, and many choose leadership roles that create greater opportunities to do so. However, in doing so, we often sacrifice ourselves and fall into patterns of self-abandonment, whereas we suppress our needs, fail to honor our values, silence our voices, hide parts of ourselves, and ignore our emotions. When you repeatedly face experiences that create a feeling of having to prove yourself, you often feel like you can't fully be yourself and, instead, must be more than yourself to make it. Consequently, in the end, you lose more and more of yourself because experiences like impostor syndrome are real and impact even the most seasoned leaders. So, while I was undoubtedly aware of the terrain I would have to navigate as I pursued my educational and professional endeavors, I was not aware that the increased effort to do more and be better would create a belief that only my strengths and what I achieved made me worthy of leadership.

Many Black women walk away from their passion and purpose because the pursuit of it is too great of a sacrifice for their overall wellbeing. Sacrifices along any journey are to be expected, yet they must be time limited. Continuously operating in spaces that require the ongoing sacrifice of self is neither sustainable nor healthy. Furthermore, it is impossible to be an impactful and effective leader when continuously operating from a place of scarcity, feeling unsafe, and not being fully seen and valued beyond what we produce. Consequently, what I and many Black women in nonprofit leadership need is our own Debbie Allen reminding us to "relax, relate, and release." Without readily accessible mantras and aphorisms that offer validation and compassion for our experiences, we often fall into the trap of thinking that the way up and out is to do more, which only leaves us more depleted and unfulfilled. Instead, it is imperative that an integral part of the leadership journey for Black women centers and prioritizes caring for self. More importantly, that it is understood as a right instead of something that must be earned or deserved after we check enough boxes on our to-do list or climb a certain number of rungs on the leadership ladder. What I needed most when I started my leadership journey was guidance about how to **relax**, who to **relate** to, and what to **release** as I stepped into leadership roles in the social and nonprofit sector.

Relax

Relax via Reflection and Rest

As you enter or continue the leadership path, it's not surprising that your workload changes. While for many, the quantity of the work will shift and may decrease, the mental workload and way you have to engage with the work is different. Oddly, in some ways, it feels lighter and yet also heavier at the same time. You may not have as many direct tasks and projects to hold but are now responsible for overseeing and supporting the work of others while holding a firmer understanding of the organization's mission, values, and strategic plan.

When you speak, you now must consider alignments and gaps between your individual perspective and that of staff who report to you, the vision of the team, and the larger mission of the organization. You must also increasingly consider the impact of the inherent authority your new role holds, and that when you speak, it is from a position of power, despite the internal cognitive dissonance you may be battling.

When I first transitioned to a leadership role, I was confused as to why I felt more fatigued at the end of the day, despite having a bit less to do regarding day-to-day tasks. Over time, I realized I was in a new round of mental double-dutch while still navigating the round tied to my identity of being a Black female leader. I faced people questioning my promotion, not feeling my voice was honored the same as my colleagues and being held to stricter expectations about the structure of my work schedule.

I quickly found myself wondering if I had made the right decision. To silence the imposter syndrome and my inner critic, I fell into the trap of trying to prove myself by saying "Yes" more and being one of the last, if not the last, to leave the building most nights. As time progressed, I didn't recognize myself at work anymore. While I was "successfully" navigating the role and being what my directors deemed productive, I became a shell and found myself going through the motions without real connection or presence.

I wish I could say it only took a few months for me to realize that this way of working was not sustainable, but it took years for me to make a sizable shift that made a sustainable difference. At first, I attempted to combat things with more time off and jumping on planes to places that offered peace, connection, and joy. However, I came to realize that as soon as I returned to the office, the endless

158

rounds of mental jump rope were still waiting to embrace me as soon as I walked in. It's also true that 98.9% of the time (probably closer to 99.5%), my work laptop was packed in my carry-on bag.

The pivotal moment that forced me to pause and have a long and radically honest sit down with myself occurred when I dropped my work laptop on my foot WHILE ON VACATION. At that time, laptops were not as light and thin as they are now, and mine was the equivalent of a stack of bricks. Looking back, the laptop had started to function like a security blanket. I had recently received feedback that I wasn't in the office as much as some of the other directors and that there was a narrative that I worked less than my colleagues. Now, I'm an overachiever and often settle feelings of inadequacy by doing more. At the time I received the feedback, I was sitting on different committees and supporting several tasks and projects not directly tied to my role. I was also the only director in my immediate circle with young children, which meant there were definitely days when I left earlier and ended up finishing some tasks at home after my children were in bed.

However, prior to having my child, I was typically the last one to go home two to three days out of the week. So, while internally I knew the narrative was inaccurate, I once again tried to overcompensate by being more available, even when I was on paid leave. The laptop drop occurred as I was getting my bags out of the car and preparing to catch a flight. And despite excruciating pain that left me limping, I STILL TOOK IT WITH ME ON THE TRIP.

Talk about working twice as hard and never letting people see you sweat (even when no one is watching).

As I sat on that plane, I kept hearing a voice asking, "What are you doing?" And it wouldn't go away. Even as I sat on the beach and sipped my favorite cocktails, it was there, relentlessly nagging me. It even followed me back onto the plane. Every time I tried to ignore it, it grew louder and didn't subside until I created time to relax through rest and reflection rather than take more vacations.

I came to understand that my use of vacations was allowing me to hide versus rest because, without addressing the larger context, the restorative benefit of time off was not accessible.

The Rest

- **Prioritization of white space**. Once I returned to the office, I completely overhauled how I managed my schedule. I intentionally blocked and reserved unscheduled time on my calendar instead of continuing to go through the day from one meeting to another without a break. where nothing was to be scheduled and where I didn't immediately fill gaps by checking off tasks on my to-do list. When a meeting ended early or was canceled, I didn't rush to fill my schedule. Instead, I took time to listen to a little music, take a walk outside, connect with someone in my support circle, and sometimes, just sit for a bit and enjoy a quiet moment. This was a major shift given most days, I only left my office to transition from one meeting or appointment to the next and rarely left the building even if I was there for 12 hours. I was the queen of *self-abandonment* and regularly ignored or delayed responding to cues like hunger or fatigue until I completed a task. Everything and everyone were prioritized except me, and it took a huge toll. Transparently, it took a while before I could consistently make these shifts without worrying about how it would contribute to the narrative about my competence or commitment as a leader. However, the more I did it, the more anchored I felt. Shame and guilt were dethroned and I could more consistently pass on playing rounds of mental double-dutch. More significantly, my self-awareness and attunement were strengthened, which resulted in my ability to better validate my narrative about my leadership abilities.

The Reflection

- **Consistent time to reflect.** As I prepared to step into a new leadership opportunity, I completed a phenomenal leadership program that focused on developing the leader's person. The timing of the program was kismet. It reiterated that my approach to leadership was missing a major component: attunement to the leader's humanity. Attunement to me. A major tool I received from this program was establishing a weekly practice of reflection. While I frequently engaged in planning and organizing to ensure I navigated my responsibilities efficiently, I rarely carved out consistent time to reflect on what was going on internally as it related to my identity as a leader and its intersection

161

with my whole self. I began using my white space to more comprehensively and regularly assess my wellness. In addition to assessing and addressing my **professional wellness** by clarifying my career goals and sense of purpose, I checked in with myself across other dimensions of wellness: **physical** (assessing what was going on within my body), **emotional** (tracking how I felt and the reason), **psychological** (monitoring my thoughts), **spiritual** (checking in with my soul), **social** (understanding how I was connecting with others), and **personal** (reflecting on how I was connecting with myself). By doing so, I could more **intentionally engage in truly restorative care** by aligning my acts of care to the area that was in need.

When I first started my leadership journey, it would be impressive if I gave myself 10 minutes a week. So, as part of my reflection practices, I began to ask myself each night whether I had taken my 10. There were and continue to be days when this doesn't happen, and that's okay. It leads me to be curious about what got in the way and set intentions for the next day. I no longer look at dropped balls or not getting something down with a critical eye, and instead get curious and offer compassion about the reason.

Relate

*Prioritize how you **Relate** to yourself and assess the impact of how you **Relate** to others*

Leadership is relational. Even if you don't directly ascribe to this model of leadership, it's hard to deny that a large portion of what we do as leaders is cultivate and nurture relationships as we drive productivity, measure outcomes, and move an organization's strategic plan forward. We must be aware of relationships with various stakeholders, including direct staff reports, consumers, community partners, and our board. And while some leadership programs provide tools and frameworks to help us better navigate these interpersonal relationships, there is often less emphasis on the intrapersonal functioning of the leader.

I have come to learn that, like my belief that as a psychologist, I am the biggest tool in the room with my therapy clients, the same is true for leaders. Who and what I bring into my work environment greatly impacts how I function with others. Consequently, when you are constantly in your head attending ongoing rounds of mental double Dutch, it's hard to be fully present and show up how you want to.

As I previously mentioned, early in my leadership journey, I often felt like only the shell of myself could be present. Consequently, the staff I worked with experienced me as distant, and that's probably putting it nicely. My boundaries became rigid to buffer the impact of my experiences.

However, over time, this had become overly rigid and inauthentic to the core of who I am. I really had to take some time to reassess my boundaries.

Nedra Glover Tawwab has a fabulous book and workbook that provide tons of wisdom about assessing and understanding our boundaries. In her words, **"Boundaries will set you free."** And this is what happened as I gained more clarity about my function and became more aware of the boundaries of others in my professional space.

Over time, I became more aware of meetings and interactions that left me drained or energized. I noticed that when I felt energized, seen, and valued in interactions, my boundaries relaxed a bit, and the fullness of me came online. In spaces and interactions that left me depleted because I experienced the energy of others as overwhelming, critical, or invalidating, I withdrew and became very rigid with my boundaries. As I became increasingly aware of these patterns within my day or week, I became more intentional and strategic as I went into meetings.

For spaces I knew would leave me drained, I was intentional about what came before or after those meetings so I could enter the space grounded and care for myself afterward. And for the spaces and interactions that resulted in me feeling more energized, I tried to be more aware of how my energy impacted others. By doing both these things, my boundaries moved to a healthier and more authentic place because I better trusted my ability to navigate both ends of the spectrum. I also had more intentional and fulfilling connections with colleagues because I was no longer simply going through the motions.

164

Perhaps one of the biggest boundaries that developed and offered liberation was awareness of my "Yes" and "No." I gave myself permission to say "No" more purposefully and became very intentional with my "Yes." I took time to pause before I volunteered to take on projects and tasks that were not directly connected to my role. I assessed the impact they would have on my wellness across all dimensions and questioned why I wanted to say yes. If a "Yes" was connected to a desire to prove myself or to my work ethic, I gave myself permission to say "No."

Conversely, if it was connected to my passion and goals or to support my team and colleague, I *considered* a "Yes." I also increased my ability to say "No" without tons of explanation about the reason (which had become another pitfall). I embraced the notion that it was not my responsibility to help others feel comfortable with or accept my "No" as long as it was anchored, purposeful, and nourishing. Toni Jones's song of affirmation *No is Bae* was heavy on the playlist rotation and reminded me that my "No" offered care and "would take care to me" by providing "clarity to my priorities," which meant I had to "be solid in my 'No.'" I also ensured I prioritized saying "Yes" outside of work and in the personal relationships that meant the most to me.

Release

Release the desire for balance and seek rhythms

I'm sure we have all heard and been encouraged to establish a work-life balance where there is harmony and equal time and effort between our professional and personal lives. While achieving this desired balance is typically thought to primarily be the responsibility of the individual, employers have also learned that supporting staff in this area has a plethora of benefits, including increased productivity and employee retention. However, as I obtained leadership roles, it felt like there was an unspoken expectation that my new title and pay meant I was supposed to give most of myself to my professional responsibilities and arrange my personal life around them. I quickly learned the increased flexibility with my work schedule translated into being expected to be available more and working later. I tried to emulate patterns of more senior and seasoned leaders who answered and sent emails after the office closed, on weekends, and, yes, even when out of the office on paid leave. Given this was the organization's leadership culture and my high-achieving and overcompensating disposition, making changes that allowed me to navigate my leadership role from a more integrated perspective was not easy, nor has it been a linear journey. It is an ongoing process to challenge mental patterns and beliefs about the ways we have been socialized to define productivity by quantity and busyness over quality and efficiency.

My journey led me to quickly realize that balance had to go out the window. The reality is that there are times in my personal and professional life when one will require more time than the other. Instead of operating in a space of tension to make sure they were equally attended to, I learned the patterns and waves so I could establish rhythms. In my role, there were predictable times of the year when things at work would be crazy busy; this didn't change and wouldn't change given the nature of my job and external deadlines for the programs I led. Instead of trying to fight this, I leaned into it. I prepared my family for these times of the year so we could adjust schedules and commitments when I had to work instead of it being a reactive adjustment.

Similarly, during times of the year when the demands were less, and there were fewer external deadlines for my professional tasks, I leaned into my personal rhythms a bit more. I left work earlier to nurture my personal connections and values. I also regularly made time to reflect on whether my rhythms were in sync or needed to be adjusted. When they were out of sync, I became curious to reason and looked for opportunities the following week to readjust. I also looked at my daily rhythms and adjusted boundaries around when I responded and sent emails. I turned off notifications for work most weekends and ensured that when I was out on paid leave, I was truly out. By operating within rhythms, life flowed better, and I undoubtedly showed up better as a leader. Transparently, this was, and still is an adjustment for others. I received an email at 8 pm and woke up to another one before 9 am asking if I had received it. Amid navigating feelings of guilt or worry, I've learned to politely say "No," and let them know when they can expect to receive a response.

I was also more intentional about sharing the shifts I was making with some of my colleagues and director, not only to inform them of the changes but also to hopefully begin to shift the culture. If nothing else, I wanted staff who reported directly to me to know caring for themselves was equally important as whether they met professional expectations and benchmarks.

Release (and burn) the cape

As I finish up this chapter, I can't help but wonder what my 95-year-old grandmother would think if she were alive to read it. It was rare to see women in my family truly rest. Not sleep, but rest with the intention of restoring and renewing.

I know I'm literally preaching to the choir at the mention of the narrative that Black women are seen as superwomen who have the innate ability to overcome atrocities and make the impossible possible. However, like the unintended impact of the aforementioned mantras and aphorisms, this narrative of Black women being superhuman has also had a detrimental impact on our wellness.

While the truth of the narrative that accurately highlights Black women's ability to overcome and achieve despite a world not designed for us to do so and, at times, directly attempting to stop us from doing so, the idea also reinforces messages that have been detrimental to all dimensions of our wellbeing. To be perceived as superhuman sends a message that vulnerabilities are weaknesses, that mistakes are not permitted or to be hidden, and that asking for help is out of the question. I definitely struggled with this growing up and

168

continued to do so over the course of my career.

Over the past few years, it has been so refreshing to see the narrative about what defines strength being challenged more and more in the media. When a social media post recirculated a while ago about someone's desire to never be called resilient again, being exhausted by strength, and for a desire for support and softness, my soul felt seen. I gave permission to release even well-intended messages and beliefs that were no longer in service to me. I made room for my imperfections and flaws without believing they diminished my light and contributions. I stopped subconsciously expecting perfection from myself and recognized that doing so was rooted in fear of not being accepted and valued.

For Black women in leadership, the question has never been whether you can do the job; rather, the point to ponder is what you are (myself included) sacrificing to do it and what is the impact on your overall wellbeing.

Black women in the social sector, be kind to yourselves. Make self-compassion and rest a daily practice and distinguish it from hiding. Create rhythms that honor your professional and personal values. Use "No" as a complete sentence. Expand your support circle and ensure it includes other Black women. Create and honor your boundaries. Reflect. Prioritize white space. Rest. Honor you as much as you care for and honor others. **R**elax, **R**elate, **R**elease (and make sure you arch your back like Whitely Gilbert when you do it!).

CHAPTER TWELVE

Dr. Summer Rose

"Self-esteem comes from being able to define the world in your own terms and refusing to abide by the judgments of others."

- Oprah Winfrey

Lessons and Blessings

There are no rules.

This world will make you believe that there are certain rules you need to follow. To be accepted. To be hired. To be promoted. To be successful. I am no exception. My earliest lessons came from my family. Both of my parents are hard workers. They have worked hard all my life to make a better life for me than the one they had. They were born in the time of segregation and were among the first few classes to be integrated. For them, education was the ticket to the American Dream: work hard, play the game, and get ahead. I cannot remember what age I got the talk about having to "work twice as hard, to get half as much" but it was somewhere between elementary and middle school. This is where I was further socialized to follow the rules. Stay in line. Don't talk in the hallways.

Make the honor roll. I must be honest; I swallowed that lesson whole. I was the best. There was not an honor roll that my name was not on. I read voraciously. This might be telling my age, but I was part of The Babysitter's Club. Ya'll remember those books? Well, they used to have a club. You could pay a monthly subscription fee and they would send you up to three books, a newsletter, and some kind of silly "prize" that I just had to have every month. At the end of the year, I went to the mailbox looking for my package, but it was not there. There was a letter addressed to my mother and the top, left-hand corner had The Babysitter's Club logo. I took it to my mother; she opened it and found her check returned to her and a note saying I had read all the books they had. See, even the club couldn't keep up with me! Just kidding, lol. But you get my point.

I take education seriously and I work hard. It was the "play the game" that took a little getting used to. It really wasn't until I was in my late high school/ college years that I got some on-the-job training in playing the game. I have learned A LOT about how to fit in, be accepted, and succeed in a white world. I have often felt uneasy ... conflicted ... hell, angry when I have achieved goals because I "spoke so well," "comport so well," "make everyone feel so at ease." I have a lot to UN-LEARN. I want to share some lessons and blessings I have encountered on my journey of un-learning.

Lesson 1: You matter. In a world that works hard to tell you you don't, YOU DO.

I have been very blessed to have parents that poured a sense of self into me that is so grounded, you couldn't shake me even if you wanted to. My father is 6ft 6in, 300 pounds and has been my whole life. My mother is 6ft tall and has never been bigger than a size eight. I took after my father. When I was a toddler and did not know I was bigger and stronger than the other kids in my daycare class, my parents did. They began to tell me how big and beautiful I was. My mother would praise me for my posture. I liked wrestling as a kid. I used to tell other kids that my dad was the size of Andre the Giant. In that way, it made sense to me that I was taller than everybody else. I've been 6ft tall and wearing a size 12 shoe since 7th grade. My parents made sure I knew that because I was their child, I would (genetically) take after them, and that was something to be proud of.

On top of knowing who I was, they made sure I knew whose I was – a child of the King. I was raised in a Christian household. In other places I have referenced that I thought my mother had keys to the church because of how much we were there. But I know that was on purpose. She bathed me in The Word and covered me in prayer so I would be prepared for whoever dared to call me anything other than a child of God. It was in church that I learned that someone loved me so much that they died for my sins, even before I was even born. And in return, I just needed to align my life with His walk.

Now would you believe that someone who had been that fortified, would still fall victim to second-guessing my value in this world??? I had a sixth-grade English teacher that probably should not have been teaching anything. She was the principal's younger sister and the cheerleading coach. I am unsure what qualifications she had to be an English teacher, but she had a Ph.D. in hating! She always seemed surprised when I had the highest scores on all the work she assigned. She would ask me how I studied for the last test as if she couldn't fathom how I continued to outscore my peers. She made it her mission to keep me off the honor roll and I made it my mission to prove her wrong. I never understood her problem with me, but as a kid I thought surely it was something I had done. I thought if I was nicer to her, she would be nicer to me. It only seemed to annoy her more. She seemed insistent on making me feel I was not as smart as I knew I was. I learned that nothing I did or didn't do would change her opinion of me, so I stopped trying. I just did me and MY village cheered me on. To this day, they think I'm an outstanding writer and orator. Thanks family ☺.

I wanted her to like me, see my unique gifts, and help me better myself. Arguably, that is not her job. I believe that is the exact job of a teacher, but that's not the point. I had to see in me what the world tried to deny, most times for no other reason than I have black skin. I can list a number of other times when folks have been surprised by the talent that came out of my black body, like college professors who couldn't believe I was attending school free of charge, graduate admissions personnel who couldn't believe "Summer Rose" was this tall, full-figured, Black girl standing in front of them, and clients who look past me when they arrive for a session with DOCTOR Summer Rose. I have been underestimated in every setting. It's almost fun now.

Being in this cohort with Black women from various cultural upbringings, full of talent that has also been slept on, has been so redeeming in this season. I remember sitting in the very first cohort meeting. Even though it was virtual, the energy was electric. We were all teeming with excitement for what was to come. To have a place to rest, laugh, and learn. I very quickly learned that I was not alone. There were others who were brilliant, who had built organizations or were carrying organizations on their back with their special gifts, who had Googled "unprofessional [insert anything]" and found images resembling them staring back from the screen, and who have agonized over how to be uniquely them in a world full of media portrayals that are ill-informed, ignorant, or just plain incorrect. I recall a conversation with one of my cohort-mates where the question was posed, "What would happen if all the Black women just stopped? Stopped working, stopped fixing, and stopped cleaning up?" The world would come to a screeching halt. You matter.

Blessing 1: There is so much beauty and power in being able to gather with others who affirm your existence and your experiences. It is the refill I didn't even know I was thirsting for.

Lesson 2: Do you. No one else can.

As I mentioned above, I have always been a hard worker and an overachiever, but for a long time, I was not doing it for me, I was doing it for the people around me who I did not want to disappoint. Even knowing that, as a Christian, I was to work like I was working for the Lord and not for man, I can admit that I was not. I liked the feeling of being successful and the acceptance I gained when I was successful. Honor roll. Sports. Scholarships. Bonuses. I became a master shapeshifter. I could read a room and become whatever the situation called for. I jokingly say I have a Ph.D. in code switching, I'm a "white walker" of sorts. White people really like(d) me. I am not proud to say this now, though I once was.

Remember when I told you my parents told me to "play the game?" I was impressed with my ability to play the game like no other. I would wake up, pray, and then get dressed in all my white cultural values and be ready to slay the day. I was never too loud, opinionated, sassy, or smart for the situations I found myself in. I was so good at being the type of Black woman who white women want to be friends with and who white bosses want to promote. I fit perfectly in the box they built for me. What was less apparent at the time, but became glaringly clear, was the toll the box-fitting was taking on my soul. It was exhausting doing impression management all day, every day. My home became my sanctuary because it was the place I felt I could be truly me. I began to dread going to work and attending team meetings. I even dreaded opening my inbox because I knew there would be some request, some need for me to be something for "them." They were fans of my contortionism. Meanwhile, I was dying on the inside.

Someone once asked me, "When all the people you are doing these things for are dead and gone, who will you be doing it for then?" That question led me to do some serious introspection about what I actually like, what brings me joy, and what has God gifted me with so that I bring HIM glory. This ultimately led me to pursue my current occupation as a psychologist walking with people who are hoping to heal from some sort of brokenness or detour in life.

This role has really allowed me to hone in on what God uniquely placed in me. Relationships are my superpower. Period. When you are in a healthy relationship with someone, you feel light and understood, and you feel felt. I have been doing this my whole life but did not understand it like I do now. I think before, I was doing it for me, when God intended for me to do it for others. I hope this does not come across cocky, but I love how I love people. It has been transformational for me and the people on the receiving end.

Once I got clear with myself (and God) on my passion and purpose, it was almost like an awakening. I stopped trying to shrink and contort to make others more comfortable. I am loud, opiniated, sassy, AND smart. When I began to own that and exist more authentically, I felt light and understood, and I felt felt. Living authentically brings you the people and opportunities that were meant for you. You are not bogged down by the expectations of others. You are less self-critical and more self-accepting. It becomes easy to say NO to people and opportunities that are not in alignment with who you are and where you are going. Girl, it is so easy to be me. It was so much work trying to be someone else … I quit!

My experience in the cohort has served to confirm that I do not need to be anyone else but me. Loud, laughing, listening Summer. I think the essential ingredient that has made this so easy to do during my time in the cohort is safety. I think for many of us Black women, we shrink and dim our lights because it is unsafe for us to live authentically. I looked forward to every third Thursday of the month because when I showed up as a professional Black woman in nonprofit leadership, I also brought everything else that I am and was fully embraced.

As I reflect, I realize the pandemic brought me emotional and physical distance because I could move away from the white corporate world while working from home. The cohort then gave me emotional and physical safety to evaluate myself, my goals, and my trajectory with people who give me all the feels (I really love them!).

Blessing 2: When you are planted in the right place and passions, your light shines brighter than ever. That light then attracts all the good things your weary soul needs. Figure out if you are planted in the correct environment, people, and passions to do you, Boo.

Lesson 3: Take care of yourself because that is no one else's job.

THE Dr. Froswa Booker-Drew graced us with her time and talents twice during the cohort. During one of the sessions she facilitated, she shared different narratives of Black women that have evolved over time. One that particularly stood out to me was Black women as the always happy, caretaker of others. She cited a quote from Carolyn West (2017) that said,

> "The expectation that Black women constantly provide service and emotional labor, always with a smile, persists in modern times. In fact, Black women from all walks of life, from corporate professionals to service workers, complain that coworkers and supervisors ask them to assume multipurpose caretaker roles as guidance counselors, nannies, and therapists."

Whew! When I tell you I felt that in my spirit ... truer words have never been spoken! As enslaved people, we were expected to work and serve in the most extreme negative conditions, and we had to be grateful each day that our lives were spared. The society we live in has continued to condition us to believe we are always to be in service to others and we must always be pleasant while doing it, and it does not matter if you have the bandwidth.

Wait a minute, ya'll ... I AM A PSYCHOLOGIST! I know better! But yet, here we are.

Aren't we the worst at taking our own advice?! I cannot tell you how many times I have said any of the following phrases:

- You cannot pour from an empty cup.
- You have to care for you so you can continue to take care of others/your responsibilities.

- Put you on your to-do list!

- On airplanes they tell you if the plane experiences a change in cabin pressure, three oxygen masks will fall from the ceiling. Please secure your mask first, before attempting to secure the masks of those around you.

That last one is a personal favorite! I can say that so effortlessly, you would think I work for an actual airline. As a Black woman and a psychologist, I often find myself putting the needs of others before my own. Sometimes it is an active choice, like when I'm getting into bed for the night and a friend or family member calls me for advice or to vent. For me, that is different than when a supervisor continues to pile things onto my figuratively full plate, even after I have expressed that I am at capacity.

The former fills my cup, the latter drains it! I find fulfillment in being there for the ones that matter most to me, but even that has to be done strategically because it can quite literally become a full-time job. The key word is boundaries. To maintain my sanity, I have had to learn how to have healthy boundaries. Being able to say no, not immediately responding to calls or text when I know that I do not have the time to engage meaningfully and being honest about what I can and cannot do are all examples of healthy boundaries I have used in my personal life. Sometimes this is easier to do than other times, but for the most part, the people who love me understand and respect my boundaries. I have even received feedback from friends about how they have been encouraged to do the same through my modeling.

But for some reason, I really struggled to have healthy boundaries in my work life. While in the cohort, not only did I discover that I am not the only one who has this particular struggle, I also learned that this is a bad habit that I have allowed and reinforced by stretching myself too thin.

Fun fact: I facilitated the cohort session on Black women's mental health. During my own presentation, I referenced an Instagram post I saw that said, "I don't know who needs to hear this, but take your lunch break, your evenings, your weekends, your holidays, and your PTO. You agreed to a job in exchange for pay and benefits. You did not sign up to sell your soul and every moment of your personal time."

I felt so seen (and exposed) when I sat with that post. I had come to believe that I owed my job all of me. I'm sure some of that comes from my natural tendency toward being a high achiever, but I also realized that I had allowed my work positions to be all-consuming and I needed some better boundaries. The cohort helped me better integrate that I am more than just my job and encouraged me to be my own advocate in the workplace.

For example, during the pandemic, I have lost several loved ones. I had just gotten the news that a close family friend passed suddenly minutes before I had a meeting with my supervisor. I joined the Zoom call looking like a snotty mess-eyes bloodshot, nose red, and actual snot flowing. After I explained the news I had just received and discussed the significance of the relationship with the person who had died, my supervisor asked if there was anything she could do. I was still in shock, and I think I said something to the effect of, "I don't even know what I need right now." She then proceeded with the meeting, discussing recent happenings and deliverables. I could not believe it, nor could I understand it … who goes on with business-as-usual minutes after a huge loss?!?! To make things even worse, we were supposed to have another meeting with some additional team members right after our meeting. I was finally able to choke out a tiny "no." I told the supervisor I would not be able to make the next meeting and that I was probably going to cancel my clients for the rest of the day so I could grieve. I added that I would follow up on the deliverables by the end of the week and I got off the virtual meeting. After I digested my grief and did the things I needed to do to take care of myself, I began thinking about how I would address the lack of empathy and support I felt during the meeting (from another therapist!!!). After I prayed about it and consulted a trusted friend, I summoned the collective strength of the cohort to have a conversation with my supervisor. In the conversation, I spoke to how I was made to feel and the response I would have wanted in that moment of mourning. The craziest part came next. I was told that supervisor had been able to respond to others in the way I described, and the reason it did not happen for me was because I always seemed so strong and capable that it was assumed I would be ok and didn't need empathy, space, and grace. I think I might have actually grabbed my pearls! What Dr. Froswa had shared was true, and the stereotype of the Strong Black Woman was alive and well!

My supervisor and I were able to engage in a dialogue about the narrative that Black women don't bleed and how our workplace culture is complicit in maintaining this stereotype. It was freeing and corrective! I learned that just as I have model boundaries and taught people how to treat me in my personal life, I needed to do the same in my professional life. Maybe I knew that before the cohort, but the cohort definitely helped me to understand this on a more intimate level and gave me the voice to make it happen. Not only am I taking care of me, but hopefully, I am creating sustainable narrative change for others that come behind me.

Blessing 3: My voice has power. Once I found it and used it, liberation happened.

The last lesson and blessing, all-in-one, I have received through the cohort is that of **Black sisterhood**. Although I joined the cohort under the pretense of professional development, it has been so much more- it was like coming home. I mean, where else do you go and learn about a Black woman attorney/ author/ entrepreneur (with a powerful story) dedicated to transforming the criminal legal system, get poured into about how to navigate the workplace by going deeper into yourself, and do the electric slide in the same place, on the same day?! Black women loving on each other, breaking bread together, and encouraging each other are so powerful. In one of my journal entries, I remember writing that "they" know how valuable we are "they" just hope that we don't. Now that we know, watch out world!

Every third Thursday of the month, in the year 2021, was a refill for me. I did not have to "play the game," put on my white cultural values, shrink, or compromise my wellbeing in the space we created. Together we created a space of safety, authenticity, and truth-telling, and in return, I gained confidence and renewal. Also, they are hilarious. I mean, like, they seriously keep me in stitches! Each one of them has offered me so much in different ways. So, while the topics covered every month grew my knowledge and skills, they grew my heart and my village. There was softness and strength, learning and loving, reflection and growth. All of this occurred with people who looked just like me and who understood the nuances of existing as a Black woman in a white corporate world without me having to explain. I have felt so affirmed, and that has given me the courage to take personal and professional risks toward being the best version of myself. (Shout out to my executive coach- a phenomenal Black woman who pushes me to be a professional troublemaker and holds me accountable!)

I told the ladies during our first session that I "collect people," meaning as I journey through life, I encounter people that add such value to my life, and I don't let them go. They can all officially consider themselves "collected," and that is the biggest blessing of them all.

CHAPTER THIRTEEN

Hillary Evans

"Let nothing dim the light that shines from within."

- Maya Angelou

Dear Black women in nonprofit leadership

YOU ARE ENOUGH.

Ten lessons for finding liberation and leading with your whole self

Lesson #1: Turn a moment into a movement

I am proud and grateful to be part of the inaugural Black Women in Nonprofit Leadership (BWNPL) cohort. The timing of this 2021 BWNPL cohort began at a profoundly challenging and unique time for humanity.

At the start of the cohort, the nation's bedrock of democracy was under attack as we witnessed the United States Capitol under siege. The January 6th insurrection came after a historic election where Kamala Harris became the first woman, the first Black American, and first South Asian American to be elected vice president of the United States. During the inauguration of President Joe Biden and Vice

President Harris just a few short weeks after this siege, the words from National Youth Poet Laureate Amanda Gorman renewed a sense of hope. Her poem, *The Hill We Climb,* ends with saying:

When day comes, we step out of the shade of flame and unafraid.

*The **new dawn** balloons as **we free it.***

*For there is always light, if only we're **brave enough** to see it.*

*If only we're **brave enough to be it.***

We needed a **new dawn** and time **to heal** after a year of enormous loss from the global pandemic to the murders of George Floyd, Ahmaud Arbery, Breonna Taylor and far too many other Black lives. As anxious as we have all been to resume some sense of normalcy, author and poet Sonya Renee Taylor's quote resonated with me when she said in 2020:

*We will not go back to normal. Normal never was. Our pre-corona existence was never normal other than we normalized greed, inequity, exhaustion, depletion, extraction, disconnection, confusion, rage, hoarding, hate and lack. We should not long to return, my friends. We are being given the opportunity to stitch a new garment. One that **fits all of humanity and nature**.*

Later, this quote was attributed to author and research professor Brené Brown, and she credited Sonya Renee Taylor and asked others to share Sonya's powerful words. I listened to Brené Brown's *Unlocking Us* podcast from September 2020 where she interviewed Sonya and discussed this quote attribution mix-up.

There are several takeaways from this podcast episode relevant to BWNPL. First, Sonya (a Black woman) mentioned that the attribution mix-up was emblematic of what happens to Black women's voices during movements. We often see Black women's voices attacked, hidden, silenced, or stolen. We must reclaim our voices.

A second takeaway is the power of allyship. Brené (a white woman) took the opportunity not to upstage but elevate another female voice. We need more allyship and others to elevate voices, particularly Black women and other women of color's voices.

The third takeaway is around what Sonya Renee Taylor calls our inherent divinity, meaning we all come into this world already uniquely made. Taylor posits that it is incumbent upon us to dismantle this ladder of social hierarchy that creates a false sense of inadequacy, inequity, and not being enough.

In my chapter, I will delve deeper into these ideas around allyship, enough-ness, reclaiming our voices, and other lessons I have learned as a Black woman nonprofit leader and throughout my life's journey. However, I wanted to circle back to **this moment**. It is our time and **will always be our time to lead**. It is not a moment but a movement for others to see our worth and be liberated by it. For anyone not ready, kindly step aside and make way.

Lesson #2: Live your life story

We all have a story to tell. My life story began in Austin, Texas, where I was born and raised in a strong, middle-class family. My parents always provided unconditional love for my older sister and me. Family is the rock of my existence and has given me the foundation to grow and become in life. I realize, through life's struggles and celebrations, how important family is and to never take them for granted. Family comes FIRST. I must remind myself of that when I bring work home, especially when work disrupts this harmony.

My passion is social justice and working on behalf of marginalized communities. A big part of my life's journey took me to the nation's capital, where I spent nearly two decades, which led to earning a law degree, marrying my law school sweetheart, and becoming a mother, birthing two daughters who are my pride and joy.

My path to the nonprofit sector was not something I had imagined initially. However, there was a civil rights law and policy course in my third year of law school that allowed me to see the broader systemic impact that good and bad policies can have on communities. This perspective planted a seed that grew my career in nonprofit and policy advocacy work. Additionally, through a legal internship on Capitol Hill in the late Senator Ted Kennedy's office and working directly with staffers on his Senate Judiciary Committee, I began to see how the sausage was made and how legislation becomes law.

Immediately following law school, I did voter protection

advocacy work in Michigan for the November 2004 presidential election. I then clerked at the U.S. Equal Employment Opportunity Commission, adjudicating employment discrimination claims on an appeal brought by federal workers.

My first real stint at a nonprofit was with a national trade association. I shadowed two senior lobbyists, one who had worked for President Jimmy Carter and whose husband was a former U.S. Senator, and the other who had run a legal aid office in North Carolina and had engaged in state-level advocacy work. This role allowed me to delve more deeply into the legislative process and lobbying. It also took me to different parts of the country, where we organized conferences for legal aid practitioners and equal justice advocates working on behalf of clients who could not afford a lawyer.

My fondest memories were engaging with the client community. One client leader had been arrested and charged with murder at 16 years old and sentenced to 22 years. He served 15 years in prison, the remaining years on parole, and came home to start his own nonprofit helping formerly incarcerated people re-enter their communities. This client leader and I had met with senior-level officials at the Federal Communications Commission; we advocated for reducing the exorbitant rates for prisoner phone calls that many families could not afford to pay. This rate reduction was necessary so that incarcerated people could remain connected with their loved ones while serving time.

Another client leader who had a profound impact on me was

189

Darryl Hunt. He was wrongfully convicted of rape and murder at the age of 19, served 19½ years, and was then exonerated through DNA evidence. There was an HBO special, *The Trials of Darryl Hunt,* that was life-changing for me to watch and learn more about Darryl's story and his innocence. It allowed me to see the overwhelming disparity of Black people in prison.

Both these client leaders were teenagers when sentenced to prison, which revealed an unjust system that would later lead to my work in juvenile justice reform. Very sadly, Darryl, who was a gentle and kind soul, took his own life in 2016. His suicide shows the deeper impact of incarceration on mental health that can persist and manifest even after prison.

My tenure with this national nonprofit ended with me experiencing a reduction in force. While it was incredibly disappointing and humbling to be laid off, given my hard work within the organization, it was time for me to leave. This experience allowed me to see that when one door closes, another opportunity awaits.

In my next role, I worked with a local nonprofit in the District of Columbia focused on access to courts and administration of justice issues. Many people forget that DC is a city within a city. There are those who are focused at the national level on federal policy impacting the entire country, but it is also a city/state where families and people have lived for generations and have built communities.

My work focused on child welfare and juvenile justice, and I authored a first-ever report on equity in school discipline policies and practices for traditional and charter public schools in DC—an effort to divert young people from entering the school-to-prison pipeline. The data and recommendations in this report resulted in local legislative change, eliminating out-of-school suspension in early elementary grades. This work prepared me for continued advocacy on this issue in Dallas, Texas.

In the fall of 2015, my family closed the moving-van door and began a cross-country drive from DC to Dallas. My husband's job and a desire to be closer to family allowed me to return home to my Texas roots. While I had to look for work, my passion remained serving marginalized populations with a specific interest in reducing poverty and closing opportunity gaps in education.

While uncomfortable with the temporary reality of not being employed, I had a six-month-old and a four-year-old and was able to spend more time with them during these critical years of their development and transition. In nonprofit leadership, it can be hard to juggle work and family, and there may be pressure to rush back into work. However, if you can reduce your workload or take time to be fully present with your family, I highly recommend doing so or working with an employer that allows this flexibility.

Following a stint of contract work with several Dallas-based nonprofits, I finally got an opportunity to stretch my wings as a nonprofit leader, leading a start-up organization. A Dallas businessman and philanthropist needed a project manager to run an initiative supporting the school district's homeless high school students. His vision was to take a former school sitting vacant, renovate it, and create a center that housed both "drop-in" and residential services, all under one roof, for youth experiencing housing instability and homelessness.

After a unanimous vote from the Dallas school board and the city council, along with raising hundreds of thousands of dollars, we transformed a former elementary school into a center for homeless high school students. We also partnered with existing nonprofit organizations to bring support services to these youths. Collaboration is never easy; the success of collaboration is having the right leaders at the table and sharing the same end goal. My role was to raise the funds to support the building renovation and some of the program services and manage the collaboration.

Before the building renovation began, I met a man whose "home" was at the entrance doors of the building. In talking with him, I found out that we were the exact same age. He became homeless after being disconnected from his family and facing mental health challenges. I thought about the youth that would enter and exit these doors. The broader goal of the initiative was to help circumvent chronic adult homelessness and to lead these youths on a path toward self-sufficiency to thrive in life and never face homelessness again. We needed partners to see and support this vision and North star goal.

Lesson #3: Tackle imposter syndrome

At the same time as we launched this initiative, the founder had bigger plans to establish this start-up as its own nonprofit. I will never forget being in a meeting where the founder began to refer to me as the executive director before we had the conversation about it. I thought, "Who is he talking about? Oh, wait, he is talking about me!"

This brings me to lesson #3, tackle imposter syndrome. In *The Empress Has No Clothes* by Joyce M. Roché, imposter syndrome is defined as "the inability to recognize and celebrate our own strengths and accomplishments ... that feeling of being a fraud and not deserving of our success."

Initially, I had a hard time accepting this executive director title because I had self-doubt about living up to the role. The founder often told leaders to ask themselves, "Why not me?" We all have unique skills and talents, and sometimes we get in the way of our own success and in believing what we can do is possible.

Not only was I ready for this executive director role, but I also thrived as a leader, raising more than three million dollars in less than three years for this initiative. I established meaningful relationships with high-net-worth donors and foundations, reached consensus among diverse partners with many complicated dynamics, navigated human resource issues, and built the infrastructure of a new nonprofit to operationalize the vision of supporting these youths in crisis.

We named the center after the original school's name, Fannie C.

Harris, which had incredible significance. We spent months researching and asking community members who Fannie C. Harris was. After digging through the school district's archives, we finally uncovered that she was an African American former slave from Georgia and an educator at one of Dallas' first all-Black high schools during segregation. Also notably, her daughter Frederica Chase Dodd was one of the 22 national founders of the historic Black sorority Delta Sigma Theta. Fannie C. Harris was someone who overcame the unconscionable adversity of slavery and epitomized the importance of education as a pathway to freedom. Through her lived experience and life story, we can find hope and fortitude.

Lesson #4: Reclaim your voice

I am continuing to find and elevate the power of my voice as a Black woman nonprofit leader. Additionally, I either do public speaking well or struggle with it due to nerves and lack of confidence. Even though I have been speaking to large audiences since my younger days in student government, I sometimes get nervous and fumble words or worse – I go completely blank.

Now, for a moment of levity. Once, during my tenure as an executive director, I was giving a big pitch to a room of funders. I came to the word "operationalize," and that day, it sounded like something entirely different. For the life of me, I could not get the word out. After three attempts, and while absorbing the awkward silence and feeling like I was standing there in my birthday suit, I moved on. The truth is, so did the audience, and chances are they forgot about me fumbling the word

194

within minutes, hopefully. Even the best speakers get tongue twisted or may not be as eloquent at times.

Why, then, is there this pressure, particularly as Black women nonprofit leaders, to always speak perfectly or with authority? And alternatively, why are folks surprised when we do speak with eloquence? We often hear, "She's so articulate," which begs the question, are we not articulate normally? We, unfortunately, live in a world where Black women's voices are undervalued. Some feel that they must speak for us or speak over us. This brings me to lesson #4: reclaim your voice.

During the 2020 vice presidential debates, then-candidate Vice President Kamala Harris famously said the words to then Vice President Mike Pence, "Mr. Vice President, I'm speaking." These words had so much power and resonated with so many women, particularly women of color who get interrupted and talked over in many settings. In leadership and when speaking with others, assert your voice with confidence, and be unapologetic about it.

One last word about tone. As a Black woman nonprofit leader, I have often heard that my speaking tone can be aggressive. However, what about my tone makes you feel uncomfortable? Can we instead get real about the inherent power dynamics that women of color face who have been shut out of conversations or shut down altogether? Why should we muffle our voices to make others feel more comfortable and empowered? While I promote civil discourse and respect, I implore others to have empathy when a Black woman

195

speaks, please listen and give her the stage she deserves.

Lesson #5: Elevate other Black women's voices

I came to the August BWNPL cohort session feeling depleted and with a migraine. However, the cohort sessions and being in the company of other Black women fed my soul. As I sat, ready to embrace the next speaker, we were introduced to Brittany K. Barnett. I had first heard Brittany's transformational journey when she was interviewed on the local NPR affiliate KERA radio program in the fall of 2020. Brittany grew up in a small East Texas town. Her mother struggled with drug addiction and ultimately served time in prison.

Before becoming an attorney, Brittany began taking pro bono cases during law school of clients who were given life sentences for nonviolent drug offenses. She represented and freed these individuals who were buried alive with draconian drug sentencing and left to die in prison.

I remember getting up during this BWNPL session and saying what a rockstar Brittany is, and all I could do was hug her to show my gratitude for her awesomeness and humility. During this session, we each received a copy of her best-selling book, *A Knock at Midnight,* an extraordinary memoir about hope and freedom.

I could not put her book down once I started reading it. Brittany's book elevates not only her personal journey, but she also humanizes her clients' life stories that have been upended by an unjust system that devalues humanity and precludes freedom.

Following this session, I reached out to Brittany about speaking at my organization's conference. She agreed to participate on a mainstage criminal justice panel, addressing an audience of hundreds of funders across the U.S. Southwest. We also had a book signing for her book that sold-out at the conference. It was significant for Brittany to be there and to elevate her voice, as she lifts the voices of others who are unseen and unheard.

Lesson #6: Find trusted allyship

In leadership and in life, you need trusted allies along the way for support and to foster movements for social change. My experience as a nonprofit leader has often felt like *The Hunger Games*, especially when it comes to raising money for organizations or advancing in your career. To be honest, I am still building my circle of trust and determining who I will let into that circle. When trust is breached, it can be hard to rebuild and heal from it.

Part of building trusted allies is connecting with others who can be authentic and vulnerable. It is also important to have allies who may not share the same background or race but who are willing to grow and expand their perspectives. A couple of years ago pre-pandemic, I met and connected with philanthropist and activist Serena Simmons Connelly.

Our paths initially crossed at the initiative to support homeless youth. Serena was a highly respected philanthropist and an incredible human being. While we did not know each other long, she had an indelible impact on my life. Shortly before her passing, Serena organized small gatherings at her home to connect with others, particularly white women and women of color, primarily around issues of race.

She was vulnerable, which allowed others to feel comfortable in being transparent and vulnerable. We need more Serenas to build allyship and stronger communities. I am confident that her spirit and the spirit of allyship live on.

One final note. Finding allies will not just happen; you must be intentional about it. Priya Parker, author of *The Art of Gathering*, says, "[I]t's hard to build a movement if you don't know who's in it." The beauty of the BWNPL cohort is that you have a network of Black women with shared lived experiences who can help validate each other and establish meaningful connections. The BWNPL network will only make our movement stronger to be visible and supported as Black women nonprofit leaders who are affecting positive change in our communities.

Lesson #7: Take time out for self-care and wellness

At the beginning of the year, I made a pledge to myself to have self-care Sundays. This was an attempt to dedicate time during the week when I could do something for myself and not feel guilty. So, lesson #7 is taking time out for self-care and wellness. We, as Black women, carry A LOT, from familial responsibilities to showing up at work, where we often feel undervalued and overworked. No one else is going to prioritize your self-care but YOU. If you do not prioritize self-care and wellness, then your own physical and mental health will suffer, and others will absorb the effects.

The BWNPL cohort has given me a greater awareness of the importance of self-care and dedicating time to it. Opening our sessions with mindfulness exercises, from yoga to receiving strategies to deal with physical stress, have only expanded my practice of self-care and wellness. Also, the curated self-care boxes have been a phenomenal way to feel loved and receive personal notes and gifts that just make you feel good (e.g., the delicious cookies from Cookie Culture and Ego Tequila), and it is supporting Black-owned business entrepreneurs!

When the highly-decorated Olympic gymnast Simone Biles pulled out of the 2020 Summer Olympics due to the pressures of mental health, some criticized her decision and said she was being selfish because she could have given her spot to another gymnast. While everyone is entitled to their opinions, this criticism is egregiously unfair and represents other pushback I have seen Black women receive when they choose to put themselves and their mental health first.

I saw something posted on social media by @BlackLiturgies that really captured a powerful response to this backlash by sharing "Grateful for Black women who refuse to kill themselves for someone else's definition of 'greatness.' **INHALE:** I can honor my limit. **EXHALE:** This breath is enough. **INHALE:** I am free to walk away. **EXHALE:** I won't apologize for healing."

We must know when to say when, and before even reaching that point, live balanced lives that honor self-care and wellness so we do not succumb to exhaustion, depletion, and burnout. We owe it to ourselves and to others who love us.

Lesson #8: Know your worth & when to leave

A toxic work culture can create emotional distress that can break down your confidence and emotional well-being. Lesson #8 is knowing your worth and knowing when to leave a position or work environment that has toxic people, is misaligned with your beliefs and values, does not value your worth or allow you to grow, and, above all, does not bring you JOY.

I have had the great pleasure and fortune of getting to know and work with my executive coach Reggie Carney through the cohort. His listening ear and strategic guidance have given me enormous perspective in navigating my career and overall work-life direction. He cautioned me about staying in toxic work environments and equated it to spoiled milk in the refrigerator. Once you remove the cap, things begin to stink. So, get out before you are overcome with the STINK. He also encouraged that instead of us running away from something we make sure that we are running toward something.

Sacha Thompson, Founder & CEO of the Equity Equation, LLC describes how toxic workplaces can influence your mental health, sleep pattern, concentration, mood, and overall emotional wellbeing. She invites us to repeat, "I am an asset to my organization. I am proud of the work I am doing and will not allow a toxic workplace to diminish my self-worth because I know how valuable I am. Never prioritize work over yourself."

Additionally, equal pay and negotiating the salary you deserve is a conversation we should all welcome. During our BWNPL cohort session with brand strategy expert Noelle LaVeaux, she provided excellent insight on how to negotiate, particularly around salaries.

Throughout my career in nonprofit, I have had salaries that do not reflect my talent and value I bring to the organization. Part of going into nonprofit and servant leadership, I knew that I was not going to be making the competitive, high-paying salaries that my peers in the private sector make. However, being paid at a fair level that reflects the contributions and worth that you bring to an organization is essential. Noelle discussed how women typically are less likely to negotiate their salary when compared to men. We must be willing to have the conversation and offer other options if a salary increase is not achieved.

Lesson #9: Embrace your enough-ness

Struggling with my enough-ness in life has been a constant challenge for me. We live in a world with a lot of excess stuff; however, some of us are always wanting more. Nothing ever seems good enough. Wanting a better car, wanting to live in a bigger house, wanting to be thinner, prettier, smarter, and continuing down that spiral of never being enough.

My executive coach encouraged me to read Brené Brown's book the *Gift of Imperfections: Let Go of Who You Think You're Supposed to Be and Embrace Who You Are*. There are so many incredible nuggets in this book, and would highly recommend it to anyone who is struggling with their inadequacies or imperfections. Brené offers, "[o]vercoming self-doubt is all about believing we're enough and letting go of what the world says we're supposed to be and supposed to call ourselves."

I have struggled with these definitions and labels that society wants to put on us, particularly around my career identity.

What do I call myself? How can I live fully in my life's purpose and passion with happiness? But what if we instead accept who we are already made to be, embracing our imperfections and inadequacies as gifts? Sonya Renee Taylor invites us to understand our own inherent divinity and enough-ness. We come into the world already ENOUGH. Like the Japanese art form Kintsugi, which is broken pottery that has been mended with gold, may we begin to honor our brokenness and be liberated by the abundance and enough-ness that fills our lives.

Lesson #10: Be audacious & visionary

A few months ago, after being overwhelmed with the pandemic, unrest with yet another tragedy involving racial injustice, dealing with toxic people, and feeling frustrated, I found peace and solitude in going out for a jog. Dark clouds hung above me, and then a rumble of thunder rattled my soul. Instead of turning back, I kept running. Gentle raindrops fell, and then a steady hard rain washed over me. It was a baptism and precious moment of renewal, reminding me of the interconnectedness of life and the rich tapestry of humanity Under lesson #2, if you read this far, you will see that I did not end my life story because the rest of my story on this magnificent planet Earth is unwritten on paper but already written in the stars. Our stories are coalesced together through our glorious triumphs, defeats, grief, and joys of life. Let us be audacious and visionary to **LIVE LIFE FULLY**. Always remember that **YOU ARE ENOUGH**.

CHAPTER FOURTEEN

Jessica Armstead

"Don't sit down and wait for the opportunities to come. Get up and make them."

- Madam CJ Walker

The cast iron intern

Hey girl, my name is Jessica Armstead, and here is my chapter. I am going to start off like those old classic movies. You may be wondering how we got to this chapter, how it started, and where we go from here. Allow me to take you on this journey of my chapter. I intend to activate your heart and mind and a few of your senses. So, sit back, relax, and enjoy my chapter as you have enjoyed the others.

I am part of the Black Women in Nonprofit Leadership, but I haven't entered leadership in the nonprofit role; rather, I am the intern. I guess you can think of me as the cast iron skillet sitting on the stove in the kitchen.

Let me explain what that means. The cast iron skillet is a

tradition in Black households. It is not used or needed for every meal. In some households, it is put away until it's needed, but we're going to say in this household, or cohort, it stays on the stove. As the skillet stays on the stove, it soaks all the seasoning and spices from other meals being cooked on the stove, and when it is time to use the skillet, it has some of the spices and seasoning soaked in while not in use to help contribute to the meal. As well as the additional seasonings and spices the skillet has been created in a manner that it cooks differently.

Cast iron skillets can be used for sautéing, pan-frying, searing, baking, braising, broiling, roasting, and more cooking techniques; it is versatile. Another great thing about a cast iron skillet is once it's hot, it remains hot and stays hot for an extended period. This allows for even cooking in a way that regular pans cannot produce. Okay, now that we have the back story, let me make it make sense and start from the beginning.

In the first session, we had to introduce ourselves. When it was my turn, I simply stated, "Hello, my name is Jessica Armstead. I attend the University of North Texas at Dallas, where I am majoring in child development and family studies, and I am your intern for the cohort." That was it, that was my entire intro, or so I thought.

The amazing Errika Y. Flood-Moultrie was like, "No, ma'am. She is not just a student intern," then she began introducing me based on my resume and our interview for the position. To be perfectly honest, as excited as I was to be in the room with these women who are where I aspire to be, I began to get a little intimidated. After hearing their introductions, I was overwhelmed with mixed emotions "Wow, I am in the room with ALL of this greatness," while at the same thinking, "Why am I in the room with ALL this greatness?"

I would not consider it impostor syndrome, per se; I think it was more like the realization of my being in "THE ROOM." A room that looked like me, a room that had similar backgrounds as me, a room that had the same struggles as me, a room that had features like me, a room that had hair like mine, a room that smelled like essential oils, cocoa butter, and delicious food, a room full of smiles and laughter without someone in the corner giving side eyes, a room with rhythm, a room that understood references, quotes, and music lyrics, and a room in which I did not have to scale any piece of me back to be palatable. In other words, I was in THE ROOM that I hoped existed but did not know existed, and I WAS THERE; I was in THAT ROOM. Now I am in this room; what do I do? What do I bring? How do I contribute? What can I learn?

Sitting on the back burner

Some kitchens put their cast iron skillet away when it is not in use because they do not want to see the clutter, while others keep theirs on the back burner, the left one, to be exact. For my analogy, I represent the cast iron skillet that is kept on the stove on the left back burner. A portion of my intern duties included keeping the communication lines flowing, setting the atmosphere, conducting the icebreakers, recording the sessions, and ensuring everyone was having a good time. I mainly sat toward the back or on the side of the room. This helped me take good notes while being able to scan the room and anticipate the needs of any of the cohort members, welcome any guest speakers, grab lunch without disrupting the flow, and allow members to express themselves to me without distracting the session. Despite the multiple duties I had going on, I was able to listen and digest the topics being discussed and listen to the ladies' stories.

Soaking up the seasoning

While sitting to the side, listening to the discussions and topics and the personal stories being shared, I noticed something deeper about this room. There were moments when they forgot they were being watched or did not realize an intern was in the room and gave things I could not believe. I am talking about moments when they shared imposter-like syndromes, what they thought were downfalls, and when they felt they did not measure up. At these moments, I would look up from the screen in confusion, like, "Sis, do you not see what I see? What are you talking about? What do you see when you look in the mirror, like HOW do you feel less than ..."

As much as it pained me to hear these stories, it brought a sense of familiarity. Those eight hours a month became my favorite eight hours. I looked forward to every third Thursday, to the point that I shortened two vacations to ensure I made our sessions. On one vacation, my flight was scheduled for a Wednesday night but was canceled. I immediately started looking at other airlines and bus routes, willing to be on a bus for eighteen hours to ensure I would make it in time.

I called Errika and said, "My flight was canceled, but I will be there tomorrow. I might be thirty minutes late, but I am not missing it." She told me not to worry and to enjoy my vacation. Thursday morning came, and I was twenty-eight minutes late. I ran into the building luggage and all because I took a shared ride. I left my luggage in the hallway, pulled out my computer, and got to work like I hadn't missed a beat. They were like, "You went through all that just to get here?" I had to explain what this group and this Thursday session meant to me. I could show up in a room as me. I did not have to "fix my face," "fix my attitude," "flatten my hair," "tone it down," or "watch my mannerisms." I mean, do I need to go on? Not only could I be me, but I got to see others who were excited about being able to do the same.

I reminded them many times, and they reminded each other how amazing they were there as individuals and as a unit. It amazed me that they couldn't see it sometimes, but it showed me that feelings do not go away when you get to where you want to be. Even when they felt they were less, I was still inspired and only saw their greatness. As the intern, I only saw how far they had gone in their lives, careers, and journeys. I did not see mistakes; I did not see a lack of confidence; I did not see the negative things they saw in themselves. As a college student, I sometimes question whether I study enough, did I present myself correctly in a meeting, did I do this right, or could I have done that more.

As a first-generation college student, I sometimes feel lost navigating this academic journey. I wonder if I am doing it right and have moments of doubt when suddenly, I'll receive a social media message from an old schoolmate telling me they enrolled back in school because of me or a current classmate tells me they are glad I am here, or an advisor points out the difference I am making on campus. In my mind, I am a struggling college student wandering blindly through my course, just trying to make it work and get these letters behind my name, attempting to keep my edges.

In someone else's eyes, I am an inspiration when I'm just trying to keep from drowning. That realization came after hearing from my session-mates. Some thought of themselves in this dim light, but when I see them, I see bright, shining lights guiding me along my journey. I gathered all their seasoning, you see; while I was in the back observing, I was getting bits and pieces of the lessons, the confidence, the understanding, the perspective, their success stories, and their "I am enough" mantra.

You know when you are cooking, and you imagine how great it will taste, and while you season the food, you may get some seasoning on the counter or the stovetop? Well, that happened to me. I was on the back burner; I was gaining seasoning from the over thirty meals being cooked. Getting all the flavor and knowledge and the cast iron skillet was being seasoned for a great meal. I acquired seasoning, including salt, free love, confidence, the art of negotiation, self-respect, permission to be unapologetically me, permission to climb up the ladder and create my path, and friendship.

Meal prepping

The seasoning and spices have been manifesting in the skillet for months, waiting to see what meal will be prepared in the skillet and how. I have been provided with these new skills and life contributions to improve my quality of life. Will the meal be braised beef; will I walk into this corporate meeting and not have to give myself a pep talk before entering the room? Will the meal be baked chicken; will I be able to express my worth and let people know I am not settling for less than I deserve? Will the meal be sautéed vegetables, fried tofu, or seared salmon; what skills and love have I been collecting?

I was ready for the opportunity to pour out and see how much of the seasoning stuck with me. I was presented with another situation where I had to introduce myself in a room that made me super uncomfortable in Austin, Texas. They called on me first, and I stood up and literally forgot my name, what school I attended, and my major. I began to shake in fear and allowed my nerves to take over. I quickly said my name is Jessica Armstead, and I am from Dallas, and then quickly sat down. They moved around the room, and everyone began introducing themselves.

As the introductions took place, I began to hear these voices in my head. "Know your worth," "You are worthy," "Know your value and then add tax," and, finally, "No, ma'am, you are more than that." As the last person introduced themselves and sat down, the speaker started to talk. I stood up, interrupted them, and said, "Hello, my name is Jessica Armstead, and I am a junior at the University of North Texas at Dallas majoring in child development and family studies with a minor in business management. I began to express what I wanted to accomplish with my degrees and some fun facts about myself, then ended with, "Thank you for the time to allow me to reintroduce myself (even though I did not ask permission to do so)," then I sat down with the biggest grin on my face. As soon as we went on a break, I messaged the ladies and told them what happened. I let them know I heard them and their encouragement; I felt their confidence and produced a result of everything I have gathered.

The meal has been made

Here is the final meal; remember the introduction at the beginning of my chapter? Allow me to reintroduce myself.

My name is Jessica Armstead. I am a first-generation, non-traditional transfer senior attending the University of North Texas at Dallas, majoring in child development and family studies with a minor in general business. I will obtain my Ph.D. and use my degrees to open group homes and after-school programs with an emphasis on children in the foster care system. I am a leader on campus as the president of multiple organizations. I am a McNair scholar. I have a job and an internship. I accomplish that while maintaining a 3.94 grade point average. I am one of the most organized people you will meet. I enjoy smiling, helping others find their worth, and traveling. My dogs mean the world to me.

In my free time, I enjoy working out, dancing (even if the rhythm is not there sometimes), and spending time with family, as family is a precious thing. I have an adventure list, as I am too young to call it a bucket list, with some items crossed off, like scuba diving, skydiving, and solo travel to another continent. I am a daughter, sister, aunt, and friend. I wear my hair in its natural state as a form of being proud and as a silent statement of how I am in every aspect of my life. I love watching sports and helping people discover the voice they have within.

Dear Black women in the social sector, when I started my journey, I needed to see representation of where I aspire to be in life. I was fully aware that women are in the nonprofit world, but I did not know what they looked like. I saw what they looked like when they were provided an opportunity to be themselves and to heal. I needed to see what it looked like when women came together not as competition but to celebrate each other's win and be there when someone experienced a loss. I needed to see what it looked like when women in power came together and celebrated everything that it means to be a Black woman.

Dear Black women in the social sector, what I want you to know is that you are worthy, and you might not belong. The worthy part is you are worthy enough to allow yourself to take a break. You are worthy enough to say "No." You are worthy enough to celebrate yourself. You are worthy enough to get help when it is needed. You are worthy enough to receive healing from the past. You are worthy enough to think the world of yourself. YOU ARE WORTHY ENOUGH. That only needed a period, not a comma; just know that is a full sentence in itself; you are worthy enough.

The other thing I want you to know is you might not always belong, and that is okay. We have not always had a seat at the table, but we know how to create our own table. Who cares if you are not invited? You have two options: try to burst through the door and sit at that table or create your own, just know you do not have to settle.

Dear Black women in the social sector, I have learned to have confidence in who I am and not just what I bring into a space. I learned that I am more than just what I produce, I am the person behind the production. Reminds me of one of my favorite songs, "I am not my hair" by India.Arie.

Dear Black women in the social sector, what I want you to know is you have been equipped with everything you need to change the world. Make sure you know that you do not have to do it alone. Get you a group of women that can make you laugh, cry with you, celebrate for and with you, correct you in private, and adjust your crown when needed. You can and will change the world; you just do not need to do it alone.

Dear Black women in the social sector, my personal action item is to continue to be glitter in this world. I personally love glitter; there are people in this world who cannot stand glitter. Regardless of whether you like glitter, once you have been in contact with glitter, it is hard to get rid of it. No matter how hard you attempt to pick at it or try to clean it, it does not go away. Just when you think you have gotten rid of it and walk away, you turn around and see that glimpse of sparkly glitter reflecting light off it. It is just hard to get rid of. It affects everything it comes in contact with.

My action item is to continue to do the same with my encouraging, whimsical, high-energy personality. Some may love my personality, and for others, I might be too much. Regardless of where you stand on that spectrum, you will notice me, and something I say or do will resonate with you. It is typically the way I made you feel that you remember about me. I am often told when people are in a dark place, that all they have to do is text me, call me, or remember a moment with me, and it makes them feel better. I am about to continue to do that even when I am in dark places myself. I want to always continue to have that superpower.

Dear Black women in the social sector, I want you to know that my story is not over yet. I do not know if I am at the beginning or in the middle, but either way, I know it is not over. If you have not heard of me yet, it is okay, you might not ever know who I am, but you will know someone who has been affected by my work. My story may go unheard, but the glitter I leave will always be seen in the distance.

Dear Black women in the social sector, what I want you to do is enjoy this thing called life. You will be a success, you will walk through these doors, you will create new tables, you will find your group of sisters, and you will do so much.

Make sure you allow yourself grace and time to be great and enjoy life. Take your personal time off, lock yourself in the restroom and let the kids feed themselves, take the scenic ride home, treat yourself according to your budget, take that trip, call in sick and lay in bed, and do the things that we feel are a luxury. Self-care is not a luxury IT IS A NECESSITY. Take care of yourself, give yourself time, and find time to do the things you enjoy doing. Self-care is self-love, so find out what that looks like for you.

Thank you for reading my chapter. I hope this book as a whole blesses your spirit the way this past year has blessed me. I want to thank Errika for creating this amazing opportunity. I want to thank my parents, siblings, my favorite cousin, and grandmother for being my biggest supporters and for listening to me talk about this program. To the amazing Black Women in Nonprofit Leadership 2021 cohort, thank you for being there and showing up. You all inspired me more than you will ever realize. To all my mentors, counselors, and advisors, thank you for encouraging me to continue on this journey. Giving respect to all religions, I would also like to thank the God that I serve for answering the prayers my mother prayed on my first day of college. She prayed that God guide me to the people who can help me navigate through this journey as she has never been down this road. That prayer has been answered 100-fold.

CHAPTER FIFTEEN

Marjorie Murat

"Know that you can start late, look different, be uncertain and still succeed."

- Misty Copeland

A sassy Black woman's tidbits

PRELUDE

I worked for this nonprofit for several years. I started part-time and moved my way up to full-time management. An amazing internal job opportunity came up that would start my senior leadership, c-suite path if I was promoted to it. Without a doubt, I knew I was the right one for this job. Not only had I worked hard and built a great team, but I also had great working relationships with all stakeholders and raving performance reviews, but it annoyed me to no end that I had to go through an interview process.

In my interview with my then-supervisor, a white woman, and her supervisor, a white male, I was asked a very traditional question, and I had not planned to give a traditional answer. I was asked, "What do you think you would bring to this team that we don't already have?" I could have answered in the most generic way by saying things like my ability to work in a team, great communication and attention to detail, blah blah, but NO, without skipping a beat, my response was, "You don't have a SBW." Of course, they were puzzled and thought I had mixed up the acronyms for BSW (Bachelor of Social Work). They asked, "What is a SBW?" I said, "Well, a **Sassy Black Woman!**" It was not meant to be funny, as I was quite serious because they did not have one person of color at the senior leadership level. They laughed and said they had never heard that answer before; of course not! And yes, I did get the job! This experience and many others throughout the years have led me to not only keep a journal of lessons, which I call tidbits, but also the "S" in my SBW changed with different environments.

I have been a Safe Black Woman, a Strategic Black Woman, a Searing Black Woman, a Smooth Black Woman, and a Strong Black Woman. I hope you can find some humor but also some meaningful tidbits.

SBW (Sassy Black Women) tidbits for Black women in the nonprofit social sector

A tidbit is defined as "a small and particularly interesting item of gossip or information."

Dear Black women in the social sector, here are tidbits I have learned:

- You've heard the saying, "Laughter is the best medicine?" Well, sometimes, it's okay to use humor to get your point across. Humor can be an icebreaker if done properly.

- Whiteness is often, if not most of the time, synonymous with truth. I have experienced contributing to meetings without acknowledgment, but when my white colleague says the same, heads nod in agreement. Make sure your achievements are recognized!

- Always negotiate. Never settle. Once again, always negotiate. Remember it may not always be monetary but know that you can negotiate things such as extra PTO (Paid Time Off), working "x" number of days a week/month remotely, tuition, or professional development allowance. Know your worth, and if the company really wants you, they will negotiate with you.

- Be aware of people being too nice. People may weaponize that but stay true to who you are. Would you rather be kind than nice or respected?

- Have a personal circle, friends or family, people who will hold YOU accountable. If you feel like you don't have them currently, FIND them.

- Know that there is a dominant culture, and playing the game is okay. Just don't be a pawn- don't be one that others can manipulate and use. Be the player, be the SBW that is respected first, not liked. Being a Sassy Black Woman, I have learned that followers are liked, leaders are respected, you don't have to be liked to be respected, and that leadership does not equate to friendship.

Dear Black women in the social sector, when I started my journey, I needed:

- A mentor, a sponsor, someone who could have helped me navigate the rugged professional waters and help cultivate the leader that was in me. In one position I had, I was close friends with some of my peers, and we shared stories of successes, challenges, workplace gossip, and sometimes very negative conversations about our director. A promotion opportunity came up, and I became that friend and boss of that coworker/peer. Well, she threw me under the bus big time to my new boss, the director, and shared all the negative things I had ever said about anyone and everyone, including her.

Fortunately, this director saw my potential and realized that this was one of the toughest lessons I would have to endure in starting my management track. She was kind and understanding, and we were able to talk it through, though I felt so humiliated. My director admitted to having experienced the same thing and that her boss at the time was sympathetic to her as well, and in that moment, I vowed never to engage in that manner and to have a confidant outside of the workplace who I could vent to. Do the same, and don't get caught up in the workplace bullcrap; you never know when you may one day lead.

Dear Black women in the social sector, what I want you to

know:

- Make yourself number one because no one else will. If you don't take care of you, nobody else will.

- Prejudices exist – don't think they do not, but how you maneuver around them is the most important thing. As hard as it is, instead of internalizing all the racist remarks or microaggressions I had experienced throughout my career and letting them fester and eat at me, my experiences became my motivator. Let those words become your motivator!

- Be your authentic self but also know that your behaviors can work for or against you. Lack of self-awareness of how your behavior may affect others will be a deterrent. In wanting to get your message across, keep the message the same, and make the delivery different. This does not mean you are not being true to who you are. Put yourself in the place of the one receiving your message.

- Step into your power as a strong Black woman (strong, <u>beautiful</u> Black woman).

- The nonprofit network is small. Don't burn your bridges. You never know who knows who.

Dear Black women in the social sector, my personal action items are:

- Know that I must believe that I deserve it! Positive thinking goes a long way, and if you surround yourself with positivity, there is always hope.

- I will always root for the underdog, in any position I have, I will not only mentor but sponsor an employee with potential. At one organization I worked for, I had a person on my team who was a hard worker; she was one of the hardest working employees there and had already been with the agency for 7+ years. It really baffled me that she had never been promoted in that time, not for the lack of applying for opportunities. One of my coordinators resigned, and I encouraged her to apply for the position.

She did, went through the interview process, and my boss and I felt she was the right one for the job. Well, my boss's boss said no. The reason, she was too eclectic; she had colorful hair, tattoos, and piercings, and how would anyone take her seriously? I was devasted; I couldn't understand because, to me, those were minor physical things. We had a leader in her! In a conversation with my boss, expressing my disbelief and disappointment, she said three words that stuck with me to this day. She said, "Fight for her." And so, I emailed the naysayer with facts and data about her performance and how she would contribute to the team. I told her she needed to look beyond her physical appearance and listed all the other reasons why she should say yes. Her response was short and curt, "Fine, you can hire her, don't make me regret saying yes." I am happy to say after my departure from that organization, she was promoted to my job!

- To leave an impact, an imprint on those I come across and for them to remember me as an ally.

Dear Black women in the social sector, I want you to know that my story is:

- My story is not yours, but we all have a story, and the ending has not been written. Being a Sassy Black Woman has helped me navigate spaces where I am the only one.

Dear Black women in the social sector, what I want you to do:

- Remind yourself <u>daily</u> that some leaders are born women, SASSY BLACK WOMEN.

CHAPTER SIXTEEN

Melanie Calhoun

"I embrace mistakes. They make you who you are."

- Beyoncé Knowles

Dear Black women in the social sector

I want you to know YOU are powerful. Oftentimes, we only think of power in concrete terms. Those who make decisions. Those who have authority, who set the agenda. Merriam-Webster defines power as the ability to act or produce an effect, possession of control, authority, or influence over others. Traditionally, in our society, power is primarily associated with white men. Rarely do we see ourselves represented among those with traditional power.

In 2021, two Black women were CEOs of Fortune 500 companies for the first time in history. Let that sink in. TWO ... for the first time in history! While we celebrate their accomplishment, it is a glaring example of the dearth of opportunities for Black women to be associated with power. Everywhere we look, images of power seldom reflect us. Over a lifetime, we are inundated with examples of power and authority that do not align with who we see staring back at us in the mirror. It is no wonder many of us struggle with viewing ourselves as powerful. The lack of representation does not equate to Black women being powerless.

I want you to understand that your power is not defined by labels or titles. It is not achieved. I want you to know that your power is inherent. You arrived with it intact. I want to challenge the narrative of power we have been sold. There is nothing you need to do to attain it. No one can grant it to you. This goes against so much of what we have been conditioned to think. We have been told we need to earn power. Get the right education. Work your way to the top. Check all the boxes. Put in the blood, sweat, and tears. Then, one day we will finally gain power if we are lucky enough. This is a myth that prevents us from recognizing our worth and what we have to offer. Your power is activated just by you being your beautiful, bold, brilliant, Black self. Nothing more. Embrace it and never let it go. My hope is that you recognize this power you hold, own it, and use it to make a greater impact on the causes and constituents you have chosen to serve.

There is power in your position.

Whatever your title, your job description, your role, whatever it is, you bring the power! It is true that organizational structures have a hierarchy, and typically power is defined by where you land on the diagram. Those at the top usually have more authority than those at the bottom. In this situation, power typically follows a similar pattern that is established at the top and then flows downward. This is not the power I am referring to, though. I want to remind you that your power is not determined by an org chart. It's not confined. Your power lies within. You are powerful whether your title is receptionist or chief executive officer. Your power stems from what you, and only you, bring to the position.

When I was the volunteer coordinator for a local nonprofit serving older adults, I worked with a volunteer corps of primarily older Black women. When I joined the program staff, I was immediately welcomed by the volunteers with an unspoken warmth, trust, and understanding. I was able to bring shared deep cultural beliefs that made me approachable and respected. There was an automatic connection that granted me access and relevance. I was promoted to program director a couple of years into my role. When the promotion was announced, the volunteers gave multiple standing ovations and expressed their pride and excitement publicly and privately.

For over 20 years, the program had only been led by white women. I imagined what that moment meant for them, to see a Black woman finally given the opportunity and authority to lead. It was not the promotion that bestowed power on me, though. I owned that before the title. The power lay in my ability to connect with the volunteers authentically, regardless of my position. The ability to see them as more than what they brought to the organization allowed me to build deep relationships and equipped me to better serve and advocate for them.

In the social sector, the work is often focused on neglected communities of Black and Brown people who have constantly navigated power dynamics that leave them at a disadvantage. While many nonprofit organizations are staffed with Black people, leadership tends to maintain the status quo. When Black and Brown clients show up to the organizations where we work seeking assistance, there is an opportunity to relate with credibility and compassion in each encounter.

Everyone within the organization holds the power to connect in this way, but there is an additional power boost for those who look like the clients being served. There is a specific capability that comes from the cultural knowledge and insight you have. This is part of your superpower, and it is possible to leverage it regardless of your title or role within your organization. This power is accessible whether you are the janitor or the board chairperson. It lends credibility and validity to your organization. I've learned the importance of leaning into this power in our work. When we show up authentically and connect genuinely, it strengthens the impact we can make. It also deepens the engagement we have with the people we serve. This should be our goal as professionals in the social sector. We must be willing to use our power in whatever position we hold. We have a duty to show up and use our skills in service to the people and communities we serve each day.

There is power in your experience.

The life experience that you bring to your work is relevant: from your educational background to your family dynamics. It makes you who you are in all your exceptional glory. Your journey is unparalleled, which is why it is so important that you show up as your authentic self in every way. So often, we are told we need to fit a certain aesthetic to be accepted in professional spaces.

Most interviews include questions about degrees, years of relevant work experience, and cultural fit to determine whether an applicant will be successful. An applicant's life experiences are hardly ever given the same emphasis. This is a missed opportunity for institutions but especially those looking to make a direct impact in communities. Everything you have experienced in your life, good or bad, can be used to benefit others.

The challenges you have overcome, the failures you have endured, the successes you have earned, and the joys you have felt all have meaning and contribute to your personal power. They are your superpower that only you possess. You can and should harness this power in your work. To do so requires you to be vulnerable and open. Don't allow your fear to hold you back!

It took me a while to recognize this power. It was easy to let my education, knowledge, and accomplishments speak for me. It wasn't until recently that I came to understand how leveraging my background could push me to become better in my role. In my current position, I work with mostly older Black women. They remind me of my aunties and grandmothers and all the lessons I have learned from them. Drawing on the experiences and relationships I share with my relatives has allowed me to build deeper connections with the individuals I serve. It shows up in small, nuanced ways that only come from intimate cultural knowledge and appreciation.

Creating impact and developing community clout require trust. The foundation of this trust is mutual respect and understanding. For those of us working for organizations serving marginalized populations, we should not shy away from the experiences that connect us to those we are working for. Quite the opposite. We should use that experience to increase our access and strengthen our ability to effect change. Your ability to relate is powerful and should not be underestimated.

There is power in your voice.

Your voice is needed, and it is valid. There is power in your voice. You are unique. Your story is original. Your voice is unlike any other. We were each created with a purpose to fulfill; your assignment is different from everyone else's. Somewhere along the way, though, we forget this and begin to conform to others' expectations of us. We are taught to shrink to fit in and make others comfortable. We seek acceptance over authenticity. I get it! It is scary standing in the spotlight by yourself. So, we look for validation from others to assure us that we are on the right path. I am sure we can all think of times when our opinion did not align with everyone else's. So, instead of looking like an oddball, we go along. When we hold back and silence ourselves, we rob the world of our wisdom, our perspective, and our brilliance.

There is a message that can only be conveyed by you. Sometimes the messenger is just as important as the message. As Black women in spaces that frequently feel unsafe, we often choose to be silent. We are hyperconscious of the angry Black woman stereotype and take great lengths to code-switch in hopes of not offending. We spend a lot of time navigating the benefits or harm that come with speaking up because the title of challenger or troublemaker is not the honorific for Black women that it can be for others. Additionally, the lack of a shared voice in decision-making within most organizations is commonplace. I understand the various things we must consider when deciding to use our voice.

I also recognize that over time these mental gymnastics can make us feel like our voices do not matter. That is far from true! Sharing your perspective and challenging common ideas about the communities served by your organization can lead to better outcomes for your stakeholders.

I have learned the significance of using my voice to contribute a different viewpoint. It took me a while to move beyond my uneasiness about being vocal. I was unsure if I would be heard and doubted my contributions would be taken seriously. My lack of confidence caused me to shy away from sharing my outlook. Eventually, I realized I was doing a disservice by not including my voice in the conversation. I had to accept that my holding back was me willingly choosing to disengage. Deciding to speak up was me deciding to show up. In many instances, the insight I shared contributed directly to improving processes for greater impact. You can use your voice to speak on behalf of the unheard and ensure their needs and interests are included in the conversation. There is a need that can only be met when you speak up. To truly be impactful, we must become intimate with discomfort and be willing to stand in & speak our truth. Your voice is powerful!

There is power in your network.

We are stronger together. Combining our gifts, experiences, and voices creates greater influence. I want to encourage you to be deliberate about building your network. We all know the saying that it is not what you know but who you know. Find women who will encourage, equip and empower you to be your best. They will be your biggest supporters and speak your name in rooms you are not in. They are invested in your success. Seek out opportunities to create bonds with women at various levels with different strengths than your own. This only enhances your power.

In my experience, there has always been a sister who was willing to guide and mentor me. It was not always a formal relationship, but it was clear that I could look to them for support and instruction. Sometimes it came in the form of new opportunities or exposure to alternative perspectives. I used to find networking difficult because I did not like the transactional nature of the encounter. I was firmly planted in the "I hate networking" camp. This inhibited me from thoughtfully developing mutually beneficial relationships. Ultimately,

I had to accept that my discomfort stemmed from my false belief that I did not have much to offer or exchange in the transaction.

This was because I was discounting my own expertise and experience. However, by doing so, I was preventing others from learning from me and experiencing my gifts. I was limiting my own potential. You can only go so far alone. Your power is reinforced by your network. Your network also bolsters your ability to realize your outcomes. Collectively, we accomplish more. Merging our powers has the greater potential to provide better outcomes for our clients.

Think of the powerful examples of Black women leading in your own life and use them as inspiration. They may not have made the Forbes list or have fancy titles or advanced degrees, but each day they use their wisdom, talent, experience, and voice to make a difference in the lives of their families and communities. It is no less powerful because it happens outside of an office or board room. *This* is the legacy of Black women.

We take the resources available to us and combine them with our unique gifts and talents to improve the situation for ourselves and everyone around us. This same power resides within you. Bring it with you each day, and let it fuel your agenda. It is okay that your power doesn't fit the narrative or looks different than what is customary. Undoubtedly, when you recognize the power you hold within, and you choose to use it, the world will be better because of it. The impact of your influence will be greater and undeniable.

One of my favorite quotes is by Marianne Williamson, where she states, "Our deepest fear is not that we are inadequate. Our deepest fear is that we are powerful beyond measure."

YOU are powerful beyond measure. Let this be your reminder of the greatness and the possibility that resides in you. It has always been there waiting for you to realize and access it. I hope these words give you the confidence to stand in your power unapologetically. I want you to use them to assert your expertise and authority. I want you to know without a shadow of a doubt that you are worthy. You are deserving. You are enough! Go forth and wield your power to change this sector and this world.

CHAPTER SEVENTEEN

Nichelle Bennett

"We should seek out all the doors which still remain ajar, however slight the opening might be."

- Angela Davis

Fractured identities to wholeness

This section of the book contains brief autobiographical essays about the author's search for a healthy sense of identity as an African American woman who was born in the United States of America. The author is a twin, wife, mother, student, leader, employee, and more. Each season of life has taught her to understand her unique design and not be afraid to grow into the whole woman God has called her to be.

The unique you!

Same DNA, different fingerprints

I grew up in a home with my parents and four other siblings. I had one older brother, two older sisters (one was my twin, who is ONLY a minute older than me), and one younger brother. I would say we had a good upbringing and good life. As with any family, we had our struggles, but growing up in this Christian home, we managed to get through the trials and tribulations that came with life.

One of my biggest struggles growing up was finding my identity as an identical twin. Now, I have grown to appreciate my womb-mate and DNA-sharer but growing up as an identical twin, people think you are the same or, even worse, they categorize you in different ways to tell you apart. One twin is often labeled the sassy twin or the smart twin. To be honest, we both have sass and smarts, but the labeling almost caused a self-fulfilling prophecy because we often clung to those labels given to us by others to help inform us about our identity.

I did not realize how unique we were until one day, a D.A.R.E. officer came to our elementary school and told us about fingerprints. Prior to that time, I just had to pray that if my DNA was found somewhere connected to a crime, then I would have to somehow prove my innocence. I learned in that moment that even though I shared the same DNA with my twin, I was designed with a unique fingerprint that no one else shared in the entire world. I immediately went from thinking I was a mere copy of my sister to believing I was uniquely designed for a reason and that being a twin made me even more special.

Roxane Mann wrote a reflection titled, "Your fingerprint is unique! God gave you a fingerprint that no one else has, so you can leave an imprint no one else can." This statement is powerful because it encourages me to own my own unique design in being able to transform and change this world.

So, sis, you are uniquely designed and wonderfully made. You are a gift to this Earth and to the world. You have a purpose on this Earth, and there is a place where your fingerprint is needed so you can gain access to change this world for the betterment of everyone else.

Your upbringing and your experiences, good and bad, make you uniquely prepared and designed to change the world. You may see yourself as being a mere copy of someone else, but remember, even twins are different, and so are you! Before you tell yourself you are not any different, ask yourself: how are you different? How do your experiences allow you to have a different imprint or perspective on a situation? How will you make an imprint that will uniquely transform and change the world for the better? You got this! Be You! Become You! And make a mark on this world with Your Fingerprint!

The dynamic you!

"No guilt, no shame"

There is a common phrase we learn as children that says, "Sticks and stones may break my bones, but words will never hurt me." Words may not hurt physically; however, they can be very damaging mentally and emotionally. I remember one day when I heard words that cut so deep I could not breathe from a family caregiver. I told myself it was just words and to not let it get to me, but I still carried the weight of those, which created a heaviness that almost became unbearable. As I processed the words, I had to determine why they cut me so deep. Then, I realized it was tied to the shame I carried with me as a working mother, wife, and graduate student. I realized the heaviest weight we carry as working mothers is not the balance of responsibilities but the shame that accompanies the choice of being a mother and working professional.

Separately these roles are celebrated, but often when it is combined, an amount of shame joins the party, which says the following things:

"You are not cut out to be a good mother because you chose to work too."

"You have to choose work or family life, but you cannot have it all."

"You cannot be effective in the workplace if you're navigating motherhood."

Oh, and "you are deciding to have children and be a mother; it is going to be sad to lose you."

This shame weighs us down as we aim to give 100% in every area of our lives, leaving us to wonder why we have nothing left. So, do we change our goals, dreams, and aspirations because we desire to live full lives by tapping into the blessings of what each role offers? Or do we navigate the balance and release the shame that holds us hostage from being able to fully manifest our full capacity to grow and nurture inside as well as outside the womb? To do this, we must take a hard look at the shame that binds us.

Now this entry has not been created to shame those who may say those very things to working mothers, but as a declaration to say we "working mothers" will no longer hold YOUR shame.

We have often struggled with misplaced shame and called it "mom guilt." You know that guilt you may feel when you miss a pivotal event in your child's life when they catch a fly ball or hit a home run in a softball or baseball game due to having to work late. Or the feeling of wanting to lay with a sick child and comfort them, but you cannot miss any more workdays because you were never given enough workdays to include your child being sick anyway. The issue I have with mom guilt is that it focuses too much on a single event that makes mothers feel inadequate, and it never fully highlights the broader contribution of a working mother's capacity to cultivate nurturing work environments at home and in the workplace. This mom guilt is also an assumption that one did something bad when they handled an obligation for work or vice versa when a mother handled an obligation to meet a need for their child.

As working mothers, we are often shamed into thinking our decisions and choices to be mothers and working professionals are bad things. In fact, the term "mom guilt" is a common feeling many working mothers feel as we try to navigate the balance of life. If we can be honest with ourselves, some of us never feel bad for working, which is at the center of the word guilt.

Rene Brown emphasizes the difference between shame and guilt in one of her TED Talks. She identifies guilt as a feeling of conviction for doing something bad and shame as a feeling of being something wrong. As working mothers, we must be intentional to remove the shame of being wrong and the guilt that we are doing something bad.

We must cling to our reasons for deciding to be both a mother and a worker outside of the home. We must know that the balance we advocate for creates a better work-life balance for everyone. We must know that our insights, cares, and concerns make us an asset to the organization. Our ability to do both makes us relatable, compassionate, forgiving, productive, and forward-focused. We understand the power of sustaining humankind as well as creating opportunities for our children to have a space in the workplace to meet the demands of their own families someday.

Working Mother, thank you for all that you do! Thank you for choosing to raise a Nation as well as an organization. You are not doing anything wrong, so remove the guilt, remove the shame, and move forward in the purpose for which you were designed to fulfill. When you begin to feel shame and guilt, graciously or fervently give it back to the one who is trying to get you to take it on. You are not doing anything wrong, so do not hold that shame or guilt any longer.

The Emotional You!

The Angry Black Woman

I recently sent a message with this statement, "I am not an angry Black woman ☺ but concerned." I felt as though I needed to justify the words and questions I was proposing in my email. I wanted so badly for the words to come across as concerns versus anger. But why? Why must I cover up this God-given emotion called anger?

As human beings in leadership, we are often taught not to cry and not to be angry. So what emotions are left? Happiness, fear, disgust, and surprise. It's funny how these emotions are allowed full reign when it's under the authority of someone else's comfort level.

Anyhow, one day I decided to get to happy by way of surprise and removed my fear to speak about my disgust. I spoke about my concerns with not being treated as a full human person with a hierarchy of needs who aims to reach that point of self-actualization once basic needs are met. The place where one's full potential is manifested, intellectual capacity met, and one's creative nature has a chance to flourish. It is here, at this place of longing, where my anger was discovered. The emotion I was taught to suppress was now bursting out for a chance to be heard.

It is an anger that cries out for justice for all, not just for some. It is an anger that aims to help the oppressed, afflicted, abused, and used. It is often an emotion that is misunderstood and misrepresented. However, when it is girded in love, not hate, it is the most powerful emotion to bring about the change that is needed on this Earth.

So as an angry Black woman, I am learning to respect the journey of emotions that have led me to anger because it's never really just raw, uncontrollable emotion. It's an evolution of all the other emotions. For instance, it may start with happiness. Once happiness is removed due to a force of nature, someone else's neglect/abuse, or one's personal choices, it may evolve into fear as one grapples with anxiety faced by the removal of their happiness. Not wanting to be surprised by this removal of happiness that has now turned to fear, one may enter a state of disgust against the very thing that stole their happiness, ultimately resulting in anger.

Now, let's pause and realize again anger is not just a simple emotion. It's a process. It's a journey. The angry Black woman is not expressing this anger as a first emotional response. Please respect her enough to know that she has gone through the full range of emotions to express her deepest sentiment on how to gain happiness back for herself and for others. So don't be fearful of the angry Black woman; you will be surprised by what you will find if you only take the time to understand the disgust that led to the anger inside.

If you're still afraid of the angry Black woman, picture Sojourner Truth, Harriet Tubman, Rosa Parks, Shirley Chisolm, Michelle Obama, Kamala Harris, and many more who may have been perceived as the angry Black woman at some point in time. Without these angry Black women, slaves would not have been freed, laws would not have been changed, Black leaders would not exist, a nation would not have been saved, and hope would not have been sustained.

It's insulting to label Black women with one emotion, but if we are going to be perceived by it, one should know it's an emotion manifested by the culmination of all the other emotions to bring about righteous indignation for ourselves and others. This righteous indignation was seen from our Biblical characters, whom some picture as white women, but we know the truth. The women were angry … women too! From Ruth, Naomi, Esther, Mary, the woman with the issue of blood, and others. All women who experienced "a strong feeling of annoyance, displeasure or hostility." It pushed them to have a baby born into a broken world and allowed him to be crucified on the cross. It pushed them to stay united with one another when life gave them some hard blows. It pushed them to press into Jesus to be healed of their issues.

So, I don't know about you, but I love the justified, redeemed angry Black woman in me, in my momma, in my grandmamma, and my grandmama's mama. It's the anger of redemption, it's the anger of betterment, and it's an anger filled with righteous love. Now, I must rewrite my message to say, "This Black woman is angry because …"

The called you!

Navigating calling; purpose while being a helpmate

My husband and I met in seminary. We both knew we had a calling in our lives to do ministry. My ministry was to college students/young adults while my husband was pursuing his calling in youth ministry. We both ended up graduating with a master's in theological studies with different concentrations. A year after graduating, we got married, and I left my church to serve with him at the church he worked at. This transition was difficult for me because I could not find a way to fit my calling into his calling while also being his helpmate. I tried my best to help him in the ministry, but I still felt a void and lots of disconnect because I could not find a way to fulfill my calling while supporting his. I remember reaching out to a minister's wife to talk about how to navigate calling while being a spouse. I asked this pivotal question, "Am I now called to my husband since we are married? Has my calling changed now that I am married?"

It took me years to flesh out this very question. I noticed many women around me put their dreams on hold to raise their children and support their husband's calling. Now, I am not against this if it is what God has directed a woman to do. As for me, I could not understand the double standard of one spouse being able to pursue their calling while the other spouse would have to align their fulfillment with the needs of their husband's call. I began to more deeply analyze my situation and discovered the call of the wife is to submit to their husband, not serve their husband. Let me clarify; the wife is to serve God and submit to their husband to be a helpmate. This revelation completely shifted the burden I felt with pondering whether I should forfeit my calling for my husband's calling.

As Black women, we are unique, dynamic, rational, and emotional beings who may desire to be a helpmate to a spouse and raise a family. We are called to serve God and God's calling for our lives. Some of us do have a separate calling from our spouse. We have a unique mark that only we can make in this world. We can submit to our husbands while also serving God with our whole hearts, mind, and strength.

As we continue to be helpmates for our spouses, we must identify what it means to help versus serve. The definition of help is to "make it easier for (someone) to do something by offering one's services or resources." The definition of serve is "perform duties or services for (another person or organization)." Are you making it easier for someone to do something, or are you performing duties and services for your helpmate or for God? Both spouses are equipped to give 100% of themselves to the service of God, family, and work. This balance takes agreement, sacrifice, and understanding that each partner was created to do the fullness of God's work to help make the world a better place. Black woman, you have a unique God-given calling to transform and change societies.

The transformed you!

Leadership that develops a healthy sense of community

My first career job shaped my life by asking two fundamental questions in an interview process: "How do you build a sense of community?" and "What is your leadership style?" The answers to these questions have been an evolutionary journey of homage and self-discovery.

How do you build a sense of community? I pondered that question. I had to pull from all the areas where I had seen and noticed community. I looked at my community and my house. I looked at my community that involved my grandparents. I looked at organizations I was a part of, especially the youth groups. I reflected on my church community and the groups I was a part of in college. I came up with six factors that helped establish a healthy sense of community. Fellowship /gatherings, leadership, ownership, resources, awareness, and education. These factors were part of my outward journey of practices for leading; however, as a Black woman in leadership, I struggled with how to describe an authentic leadership style that resonated with my strengths and gifting. I knew servanthood was a style that I was good at, but I also knew my style was much more developmental and transforming.

As I studied leadership, I discovered that Black women's experience of leading is very different than other leadership styles due to the various levels of oppression one is often up against; however, they still seem to survive to help others. As I reflected upon the leadership traits in my mother, my grandmothers, and my great-grandmothers, I realized their leadership style was to build a sense of healthy community. And that, for me, is what Black female leadership is.

It's a leadership style that desires to see a healthy sense of community. These women in my life always made others in their community feel loved, nourished, encouraged, and redeemed. The six traits of building a healthy sense of community remind me of the movie *Big Mama's House*. The movie shows the six traits of cultivating a healthy sense of community in various ways.

The factors have been made into an acronym, F.L.O.R.A.E., to reflect the notion of being a habitat where various plants and flowers grow together. These F.L.O.R.A.E. factors are character traits of the role of the Big Mama in the African American community.

Factor 1: Fellowships – A key character trait in the depicted Black image of female leadership through the *Big Mama* movies involves fellowships and gathering with food. Not just any type of food, but food that tastes so good it soothes a weary soul. It is the food that releases chemical endorphins while creating nostalgia filled with childhood memories of laughter, games, and safety. As bellies are filled, discussion happens, and Big Mama rejoices in seeing those in her community satisfied and safe.

Factor 2: Leadership – The leadership of Big Mama is close to none that I have ever seen. Big Mama had a leadership style of speaking to all her children in the ways they needed that were unique to them. Sometimes these conversations came through discussions, sometimes, through an analogy, and other times it just came as a question for one to ponder over. Big Mama had a keen ability to bring loving correction when needed while also exercising grace and compassion. The style of Big Mama also had to work with Big Papa's style of leading as they worked together to raise others in the family community.

Factor 3: Ownership – Big Mama also had the ability to make sure others felt as though they belonged in her house. A sense of belonging is often lacking from other types of leadership styles. Big Mama would always ensure people had a place to sit, something to eat, and that they were comfortable. Many people would just call this good hospitality, but this is a leadership gift that helps others feel loved, secure, safe, and valued.

Factor 4: Resources – Somehow, Big Mama always had what was needed to help her community. Big Mama always knew how to stretch a meal, provide connections, and give a stash of money if needed to help others in their situations. Big Mama worked hard to make sure her community had what it needed. She sewed clothes, made the meals, cleaned the house, listened to others when they needed it, took them places, and checked in on them. Big Mama always tried her best to handle physical needs as well as one's spiritual and emotional needs.

Factor 5: Awareness – Big Mama always displayed a keen awareness of knowing something when she looked into your eyes as though she was getting a download into your life. This awareness would often come with a critique, comment, or wisdom in parable form that may have been hard to understand initially. The intention in these moments was to bring awareness to a situation that she observed and something she wanted to be changed, corrected, or addressed. At the heart of these moments of correction were love and a desire for her community to be better. Big Mama was self-aware, others aware, and Christ-aware as she trusted in a higher power to carry out her soul's desire for her community.

Factor 6: Education – Big Mama was always an educator of some sort. She may not have held many degrees, but she had a wisdom that was so unique some would have thought she went through the highest levels of formal education. Big Mama was brilliant even though she may have only finished high school or a couple of years in college. Big Mama's wisdom taught us how much we can grow into being great people, how we can grow to have great communities, and how we can impact the world for the better. Big Mama was educated not only on what was going on in our lives but also educated on what was going on in others' lives. She understood how the influences outside her community would impact her community, and she tried her best to protect her community from toxic things.

Various traits of Big Mama are manifested in all the powerful Black women in my life, and I am grateful for their journey. I am grateful for their sacrifices, and most importantly, I am grateful for the loving wisdom that they have passed down to me and my community. To all the representatives who are characteristic of the Big Mama image, thank you so much! And I love you!

CHAPTER EIGHTEEN
Severina Ware, CVA

"Names matter; labels matter. We should always pursue the highest title available and fight for the labels that reflect our clout."

–Stacey Abrams

"First of all, check your tone."

Three lessons for my sisters with the job that has got them messed up

Growing up, I skirted the line when it came to playing with my mom. I knew exactly how far I could go without getting into too much trouble. My mom and I are both hard-headed Libras. She's sharp-witted and loud, curses like a sailor, and never backs down from a fight. I can honestly attribute a few of my traits to her, but we differ in many ways. My traits are more along the lines of balance, deliberate but quick-witted, and direct. While she is quick to jump in, I am slow and methodical in my approach. One of my favorite phrases I can recall my mom using on me while growing up is, "First, check your tone; I ain't one of your little friends."

It would make me laugh because I didn't want her to be one of my friends (she was my momma for a reason), but more importantly, I knew at that point I had flown too close to the sun and needed to pull back. It was then I realized I had a few different options at hand. Keep walking a treacherous line and cross the wrong one (my mom had a paddle she delivered her whooping with) or be logical in my next move (close my mouth) and live to see another day. That was a different time, and it took me a few years to notice that, as I got older, I lost a bit of that fire for the wrong reasons. The sharpness to dare to fly a little too close to the sun and recognize that I was ready to shift to my next play or move became a thing of the past as I navigated new waters that threatened me in very different ways.

*****

I vividly remember receiving the email from Handshake regarding a part-time job fair at a nearby university in the middle of the pandemic. I didn't pay the email much attention as my role focused on volunteer engagement and management. When I came to the organization, I knew the volunteer program needed work – this was communicated to me. I quickly realized that the work the program required easily took up 85 to 90% of my job description. I attended several job fairs in my role prior to the pandemic, but time spent away from the office and my workload was never justified; it seemed a waste of time. While ideally, college job fairs are great for exposure, more than likely, these students are looking for part-time/paid work. Passing this one up seemed fine since we weren't in the market for an influx of volunteers to come back into our programs as we gauged our pandemic reopening measures.

Then, the same email was forwarded to my inbox from my executive director stating it may be a good idea to attend to recruit for a particular program we seemingly needed more individuals to participate with. I agreed with her that it could indeed be a potentially decent recruitment pool for exposure for paid tutors seeing as they would be paid. I followed up on her request to register our organization to attend the event. I had an unspoken hesitancy as I was listed as the main contact to attend:

1. Our offices weren't fully open, yet we were planning to attend a college fair.

2. This was slated as a part-time job fair.

I can openly admit that my downfall is always myself. My top three strength finders are wooing, positivity, and communication. In short, I'm a people pleaser. There isn't anything I won't do to make others comfortable, even if it's a detriment to my well-being or, as in this case, my job. For days after agreeing to this event, a part of me felt this job fair wasn't critical to my role within the organization of managing volunteers and taking me away from the 4,682 things that I was juggling at the time.

With a lot of help from my therapist and executive coach, I learned that I didn't necessarily need this to reflect so heavily on me.

It was my moment to lean in, and I reached back out to my executive director.

The cliff notes version was that I didn't feel comfortable attending the part-time job fair and not just for the two reasons above. As a team of one, I frequently found myself stretched thin and knew these recruited individuals would potentially be managed by another team. To mitigate this, I suggested a better fit to make this benefit everyone in the long run. I offered a solution of sending a staff member from the education team who shared more knowledge on the needs of these essentially part-time employees they would be recruiting and managing. What I received back involved the following statements:

"at the end of the day, tutors are volunteers, paid or unpaid ... we clock their hours as volunteer hours"

"only reason tutors are paid is to help recruitment and retention"

My apprehension increased. I tracked all the volunteer data and had yet to keep track of any of these hours in my volunteer database, meaning, in my eyes, they did not count as volunteers. Also, I had never met a volunteer who was paid for their services. There was an offer to discuss this further, and I appropriately requested we speak on this topic in my next one on one.

I didn't follow through. I know you're probably reading this like, "SIS, COME ON! You got this in the bag!" Well, we went through the motions of my one-on-one discussing everything coming down the pipeline and my upcoming week-long vacation, but I couldn't bring myself to commit to this conversation. There was a lot to unpack from the previous email communication, and I knew I needed more time. This was on track with what the last year reflected professionally. After a few organizational developments, I took a step back in voicing my disfavor with situations or expressing my direct needs. There's nothing like feeling questioned, undervalued, and diminished to take the wind out of your sails.

During the pandemic and working from home, I could allow for some freedom to step back into my own with a healthy work-life balance and clear boundaries. I am a fully developed individual who can encompass the care, compassion, and love for the work I do but not have it take over every aspect of my life. Leaning into effectively doing my job and allowing for exploration to where I saw my career going became fuel in the long run. I was building a network of connections that were great soundboards to ensure that I was thinking and speaking when it came to my wants and needs.

A blessing was that every month I was able to attend different professional development meetings that gave me insight into growing personally and professionally. In one of these sessions with Jarie Bradley of Sound & Sable, she highlighted three key questions: *"Do I mean it?"* *"Can I defend it?"* and *"Can I say it thoughtfully?"* These subconsciously unlocked all the thoughts to tap into the much-needed conversation with my executive director.

The light bulb was shining bright, and I remember connecting with Jarie following this session to thank her for the enlightenment. The weekend came, and I sat down with a printed copy of the email plus those key questions and went to work. The copious amount of notes I took to prepare for this meeting and set a clear path of tangible goals and outcomes that would benefit the organization was a work of art. I took a photo of my notes to post on my social media with a general comment about "leaning into much-needed conversations." Shortly after, I found myself thrust into the conversation, unexpectedly prepared to defend my initial reasoning as to why this was not the ideal event to attend.

My social media post was mentioned in passing by an unknown coworker who was following me. They had seen the unblurred subject line and part of my boss' name and took it upon themselves to let her know I had shared it. Essentially, I had flown too close to the sun with this one. For the first time, after a long time, it was different. I was ready.

As an in-depth discussion regarding the part-time job fair started, I embraced and tapped into three critical lessons I want to share with my fellow sisters right now. These are not one size fits for every situation, but you'll understand as we start to talk about them why they are each incredibly important.

1. Don't question or compromise your knowledge and expertise.

I've been in volunteer management and engagement for nearly a decade. Not only have I been doing the work every day, but I also sit

256

on a professional board and was recruited for a planning committee for a large conference specifically geared toward volunteer engagement professionals.

Upon the explanation of the part-time paid tutors' hours being tracked as volunteers, I knew I needed to tap into my network and knowledge. I questioned colleagues on their experience with part-time job fairs and the benefits of attendance. I also leaned into pulling out my old college textbooks on volunteers and notes from previous seminars to justify my uneasy feelings. The best help came from the internet, and a plethora of groups I belong to provided me with advice and gems to support my stance. According to Cornell Law School, the legal definition of a volunteer is as follows:

An individual who performs hours of service for a public agency for civic, charitable, or humanitarian reasons without promise, expectation, or receipt of compensation for services rendered is considered to be a volunteer during such hours.

At this point, I could easily justify my expertise on this matter. There was no reason for me to question my years of experience. It also stood true that there is never a reason to compromise one's knowledge and expertise. Having all the facts to support any stance is vital. Being able to substantiate your stance and increase your validity in proving your point may sound scary at first. As Black women, we are often overlooked, and our thoughts and suggestions don't carry the same worth as our white peers. Hence, we find ourselves often stepping back from offering even valid, well-researched opinions for consideration.

It is vital to take stock in understanding you can be the subject matter expert and can support any logical decisions ahead of you. Use that knowledge and expertise to your advantage to make your stance and prove your point. In my situation, I could effectively establish from my expertise regarding volunteers that:

1. Part-time tutors cannot be volunteers.
2. These hours shouldn't have been tracked as "volunteer hours."
3. In most cases, from peers in my field, attending these part-time job fairs didn't yield the best results, especially when your job is only offering three to five hours a week of paid work.

Explaining and defending my knowledge/expertise with facts is always nice but leaning into it helped me realize my next point more than ever.

2. Stand up for yourself.

For three years, I found myself working early in the morning and late into the night to prove I deserved this job. Not only was I accomplishing the role that I had to create over the years since starting, but I also took on tasks that were bigger than me. Over the course of this time in the role, I had given so much of myself up to something that didn't require the attention or level of detail I put in. The role became an extension of me, and I would often put my life on hold in fear of my dedication to the mission being questioned.

Black women shouldn't feel obligated to go in and save people/organizations, especially if they don't want to be saved and are willing to cut corners to bring new people into the organization.

If you remember from earlier, I initially opted not to have the conversation regarding my apprehension around this part-time job fair. My emotions and drive tend to get wrapped in the bigger picture of the good that I am achieving while ignoring the red flags. I knew that I wasn't in the right headspace to have a clear, concise, and logical conversation. I was too wrapped up in what could go wrong and a lot of anger.

After the clarity of the session with Jarie, I first realized that I needed to stand up for myself. The red flags for this event were apparent, and this was not the time to be timid. Standing up for yourself means more than just speaking on the issue at hand. This need to stand up for me in this moment was reclaiming my time and reminding people what I brought to the table within this role.

When you take the time to really lean into what it means to take a stand, you look at several different factors. You are learning to communicate more effectively on tough subjects, which in turn makes it easier on several items. The confidence and respect you build in yourself and with others while exploring standing tall in your beliefs and goals is critical in decision-making.

Don't take for granted that nobody else will if you don't stand up for yourself. Nobody else can't until you find it in your own core to look at the bigger picture and understand that you deserve to be heard.

We are often afraid to take a stand and tend to do our own tone checks to avoid looking like angry Black women. There is nothing to fear in staying true to what you believe and can prove as right. This is your time to be unapologetically you, and sometimes, that means you have to know when to cut your ties.

3. Know when to exit and be intentional in your decision.

The conversation was successful, and I did not attend the part-time job fair. I was able to prove that it wasn't beneficial for my role, and the conversation led to several issues that required further attention. In my three years in the role, it was one of the most beneficial and exhausting hours and a half I have ever sat through. The biggest insight from the conversation led to my intentional decision to exit from this role.

I knew it was time, and several other factors in play had prepared me for this exact moment. Little did I truly know that in just a few short weeks, I would be sitting in yet another meeting with my executive director. A conversation would involve her informing me that my position might be changing and that the board was looking at a few roles to revamp the organization to serve the community better. This change meant that the role that I would likely have more interest in would come with a significant pay cut from what I currently made and possibly working weekends. In the blur of the moment, I remember her telling me she wanted to give me a heads-up since I am a planner and had my little girl to think about.

She was right about one thing; I am a planner. Plans were already in place to search for a role to transition into that would allow me to explore new avenues and tap into a higher potential.

While I didn't have a new job yet, I was making intentional goals and moved to find a place to explore the skills I had built upon in the last three years in my role. This step is so critical because many of us aren't equipped to just up and leave our jobs at any given time, nor do we want to put ourselves in a role that isn't going to provide us with any satisfaction in the long run. One of the most important things I can share with you is that you absolutely do not want to rush yourself into another role that could land you in the same predicament.

In the past, I've always been in dire situations in my job searches. Every job transition felt like a do-or-die situation. Ideally, it is not a situation you ever want to find yourself in, but life happens.

First, it was moving from California after graduating college to support a husband while he went back to school after military service on the pay of a seasonal job. Next, it was finding a full-time job to continue that support and be an adult with a real salary and health insurance. The story continues with a few more job transitions and always being happy that the next job offered better pay or flexible hours. Not once did I think to myself that maybe I deserve both and much more.

Several times, I questioned if I still belonged and chose to stay because I was so worried that the organization would fall apart if I wasn't around. Over the years, I had never truly been intentional with my career planning, even with a bachelor's and master's degree. Putting that amount of stock into your role will only hinder you from recognizing when it's time to resign and look for new opportunities. Understand your why and make an effective plan that will allow you to depart on your own terms.

*****

Queen, always remind these folks to check their tone and realize that you aren't one of their friends, pawns, or playthings. You are a whole woman with knowledge, expertise, and logical contributions to provide in any room that you enter. You have proven that you not only belong in the room but can build the table that everyone sits at. There are conversations and projects that you deserve to be a part of, even when people are intimidated or scared for you to show up as your full authentic self. Go and seize the day!

I promised my executive coach that I would no longer speak about this position, and if she is reading this, I'm sorry. This is really the last time because, as we discussed in one of our last meetings, we are operating at a higher level now. I'm going to make it up to her; stick with me. Even with all the hard lessons I learned from this previous role, I'm grateful for the experience this organization allowed me to grow.

My contributions during my tenure there allowed me to realize what to seek within my next role and what I wanted from my career in the long run and allowed me to spread my wings to be a leader in ways I never imagined I could. The knowledge I gained in seeking and understanding what is for me will eventually find me when it is supposed to resonates deeply, and I am glad that I am here now. Before I finish, I have one quicker note for you, sis: don't let your coworkers find your social media channels. They aren't trying to see you win, and I can guarantee someone is a snitch. These people don't need to be on your socials trying to keep tabs or pretend they care about what is happening in your life. Keep your personal circle tight and your professional network wide. Trust me on this; they ain't your little friends …

Acknowledgment:

This is dedicated to all the little Black girls with unusual names; make them choke on it. To my precious Doll, Bear, Preston, Soul Family, 2021 BWNPL sisterhood, Ixchel, Ale, Hunny, and Pops, friends, family, and the one and only Momma Keva - thank you all for believing in me.

CHAPTER NINETEEN

Shane Woods

"I am convinced that the women of the world, united without any regard for national or racial dimensions, can become a most powerful force for international peace and brotherhood."

- Coretta Scott King

Be the narrator of your own story.

Stuart Scott said, "Life consists of two dates with a dash in between. Make the dash count."

In October of 2021, I was tasked with writing the obituary of my mother, Beverly Ann Foster, one day after I returned from a much-needed retreat to Costa Rica with 50 ladies from my alma mater, Xavier University of Louisiana. I had just landed in Miami and was walking to customs when my sisters called to tell me the news that Mom was no longer with us. They apologized for calling, but they knew they had to get me before I started reading texts from family members who didn't know I was returning to the States. Mom had passed in her sleep at the age of 67, just eight months after burying her mother in January.

I stood in line surrounded by strangers feeling utterly alone. You know your parents will one day no longer walk the Earth with you. However, when that understanding becomes a reality, it initiates you immediately into a new club with kids who have lost a parent. As I made my way through the long lines to re-enter America, I tried to recall the last time I spoke with her. Had I told her I loved her? Did I hug her? Did I leave with the promise of seeing her soon? Why didn't I call her the night before? Should I have sent pictures of my trip so she could see the beauty I had seen? Had I been a good daughter?

How do you summarize a lifetime when you are still trying to figure out if you properly said goodbye? There is no class that can prepare you for the task of memorializing your parents. Where to start? I spoke with her favorite cousins and smiled through tears as they let me know how she reveled in being a mother. I called her closest friends and heard how much she loved her girls. I then turned to her two brothers, who both said her girls were her pride and joy. I asked my dad who had remained her soulmate even after divorcing when we were young. He reiterated that she always thanked him for her greatest gifts, her three daughters, Shane Nicole, Kimberly, and Cory, along with her three grandchildren. I reluctantly turned to my sisters and let them know that I was struggling to fill in the dash between March 16, 1954, and October 3, 2021, for our mother.

My youngest sister gave me Mom's phone. She said, "I think what you need is in here." In the notes, I found a document titled

"To my girls" that had been written at 11:27 am on May 21, 2021. Mom had written her own obituary on her phone. It had everything I was looking for. She always reminded us that she had taken care of everything, and we would not have to worry about what to do when she left this life behind. For some reason, I had forgotten this promise. Beverly Ann Foster understood the assignment and narrated her own story, and I was able to share the highlights of how she filled in the dash with the world. This last message from my mom encouraged me to take a more active role in narrating my own story.

"Never give up on what you really want to do. The person with big dreams is more powerful than one with the facts."

- Albert Einstein

As I begin thinking about what I can share about how I have navigated this world to land in nonprofit leadership, I can specifically recall when I had a dream to become more than what was expected of me. Early on, I knew that I had to believe in myself and rally others to help me achieve my dream as I traversed disappointments along the way.

The summer before 5th grade, mom moved us from Houston to small town TX to be nearer to her and my dad's kinfolks to assist in taking care of three girls, and I am the only one with a middle name. A tender issue amongst my sisters that gives me great satisfaction to leverage in familial teasing from time to time. Everyone in my family and at school at that time called me Nikki vs Shane Nicole.

The halls of my intermediate school in Sherman were lined with those lockers that seemed to go from the floor to almost the ceiling, their domination only halted by windows at the top that allowed teachers to place student work on the seals to display what the kids inside were learning and producing. Now across from the room where I easily and eagerly mastered mathematics and science, I always noticed awe-inspiring projects on display.

Each month brought a new batch of artifacts that kids in my same grade made to demonstrate their understanding of natural phenomena. Meanwhile, I noticed a pattern that did not sit well in my 6th-grade soul. We were not doing what I saw in those windows. Our day-to-day consisted of worksheets and … more worksheets. This was in no way equivalent to what I saw being assigned to those in the glorious class.

The tipping point came when I saw the body system models being constructed almost daily. These 6th graders were doing what I had only known up until then as something God had done – which was to have built the human form. I had had enough, and I wanted to know if my teacher could explain this dissonance I was experiencing. So, I let the teacher get through the lecture and start us on individual work. Then I raised my hand and asked for permission to approach her desk. She obliged, and let me tell you, that is when the inquisition began.

"When will we start on the body system? Will we build the same models? Do we all get our own model? Can we take them home?"

She took a breath and began her response. "Nikki, we will not be doing that in this class." She saw the question, "Why?" flash across my face and continued, "Those students are in the gifted and talented program. They follow a different scope and sequence than we do here."

I asked, "How do I get in there? I want to do what they are doing."

"They were tested in elementary school and have been on that track for years."

I let that sink in, and she probably assumed I was done, so she looked down at whatever task I had interrupted her from completing prior to this little chat.

To my 6th-grade mind, I figured that meant that I had not had the opportunity to take the smart kid test because I was a transplant which also meant there was a chance that I could demonstrate what I could do. I summarized my thoughts quickly and said, "Oh. So, if you move to the area in middle school, then you must be able to request a test, or does everyone think your gifts can only be identified in elementary school?"

At this point, I received the widely known teacher's look asking me to sit my tail down, but instead, she managed to say, "Nikki, I am not quite sure about the process of testing into gifted and talented in middle school, but I know that those kids are smart and capable of doing the work. In this class, we do what everyone is capable of doing." I finally took the hint that the conversation had reached its end, and I nodded and returned to my seat.

Now please believe me when I say I was not done because those body models were calling me to greatness. As the day progressed, the voice in my head asked, "Did she not think anyone in the class was smart? Did she think I was not smart or capable of doing more than what she assigned?"

On the ride home on the bus, I remembered my mom telling me the story of how when I was a toddler, I took one of those large orange TI Speak and Spell learning machines apart and put it back together. When she asked why I did this, I replied, "I wanted to see where the voice came from." From stories like this, I knew I was more than capable. I knew I was gifted and talented, but I never knew it had a title that had to be earned via testing.

My dad's parents had engrained in each of us to take our education very seriously. My grandmother worked in the Sherman library, and my grandfather was a retired educator and coach with a master's degree. I was fortunate enough to spend time with my paternal grandparents just about every day after school. When I got off that bus with a plan, my Papa spotted me from his perch under the carport, strutting into the yard. He must have read my face knowing something was brewing.

"What plan are you hatching now, Nikki?" he asked. I immediately knew I had an audience, and I let loose.

I yelled, "HOW DO I GET IN THE SMART CLASS?" He smiled, patted the steps next to him, and asked me to sit. In between taking bites of my pb & j sandwich and large gulps of sun-brewed sweet tea, I caught him up on what happened in class and how I felt that I needed to be in the class with the smart kids making body models that would put DaVinci to shame, or so I thought. Kid confidence is like nothing else.

Our conversation spilled over into dinner because we had to pause a few times as there were other grandkids present who had the nerve to also need assistance with frivolous things like homework or household first aid (running barefoot meant stubbed toes had to be addressed). Ridiculous. Anyways, the solution was that he would take me to school as soon as he could get a meeting with the counselor.

When the day came, he picked me up in his freshly washed Cadillac, wearing a quite dapper suit with shined-to-mirror perfection shoes. It was a far cry from the day-to-day uniform, consisting of his tan Member's Only jacket, polo shirt, and heavily starched jeans with tennis shoes. However, the importance of the day must have been communicated to my granny as she had me dressed in my Sunday best with perfectly combed ponytails, greased face, and a new coat.

We meant business and dressed the part. Once we arrived at the school, we waited in the main office, which, as we all know, is usually the sign that someone was in trouble, so my friends who saw me mouthed questions asking about my general safety. I assured them that I was fine and able to remain seated.

271

They understood and went to class, knowing their friend was not being sentenced to hard labor. After morning announcements, we were escorted to the counselor's office. My Papa said, "My granddaughter, Shane Nicole, has questions. You may have the answers. I am here as a service to her. She needed to know that adults listen and believe kids. I give the floor to her." He turned to me and said, "Nikki, this is your meeting."

I again retold my story as to what I saw and what I believed was an urgent issue; getting me into the gifted and talented program so I could be with my people. After several minutes of me talking and her asking a few questions about my interests and current grades, she, to my dismay, told me that I would not be able to make the transition as quickly as I wanted, which was that same day.

However, there was a path to greatness for me. It came in the form of a course selection for grade 7. No test was needed to select honor classes. All that was needed was consent from an adult guardian, and I for sure had my grandpa. After we finished the course selection process and thanked her for her time, he looked me in the eyes and said two words, "Now, shine."

That same year, I went on to win the Invention Convention, a competition that challenges young minds to create a device to assist with accomplishing a common task in a new way. That win let me know that I didn't have to operate within the limitations of the public education system that felt that kids were fixed in their potential. I was going to let my brilliance shine. I didn't let go of my dream of being

272

in the smart class even when told the facts of why I wasn't in that class. I carried that same determination with me as I matriculated through public education.

Even as I went on to college, I graduated with honors in biology, history, and English, thanks to knowing I needed to believe in my intelligence and ask for help as needed to reach my next goal.

"You're never too old to set another goal or to dream a new dream."

- C.S. Lewis

In the classic horror story *The Shining*, Dick Halloran tells the young boy, "Some places are like people; some shine and some don't." For me, to SHINE means one must:

(S)elect the path you want to take

(H)ave a plan to reach the end

(I)nitiate the plan

(N)avigate the "Nos" that will happen and

(E)ncourage yourself and enjoy your walk on this path.

Nothing says seize the opportunity to start again like leaving medical school in your third year to become a middle school science teacher. Talk about karma. I had entered medical school with the intention of becoming an academic in medicine. I wanted to act as a gateway in the pipeline for getting more women of color into medicine because I recognized that Black women need to talk to doctors that look like them and understand how we live, feel, and heal. However, I lost the passion needed and took another route to empowering young women.

With a one-year-old daughter and husband, I knew I had to find a job that would allow me to use my biology degree to the fullest. My sister-in-law had just moved to Fort Worth and said they needed more science teachers. It was heaven sent. Teachers can ignite the passion of discovering the world through science. I quickly sent a resume and received a call the next day asking if I could come to the administration building to discuss openings. I drove to the appointment, was given the address to J.P. Elder middle school, and headed off to an interview. I got the job on sight. I again heard my grandfather's voice telling me to shine.

At the beginning of my first school year and every year afterward, I gave the caregivers an assignment. I asked them to share with me what made their 8th-grade student special and how I could help them shine as a student in my class. They then sent the letters back in sealed envelopes. I would then call them up to my desk one by one to hear them read what their loved ones wrote and felt and believed they were great at. Many experienced big emotions, as it may have been the first time they realized their family sees them shining.

Throughout the school year, I would recall those conversations and even have them reread the letter to course correct as needed for those who were not living up to not only my expectations but those of their families as well.

I would always bring my students back to the idea of finding what makes them shine during the space science unit. I would ask, "How is a star measured?" I would remind them that the sun we see or feel daily is the closest star in this solar system. They would also inform me that when they went outside on a clear night and looked up at the vast sky we all share, they saw stars appear as points of light. They would let me know that we cannot simply find out how big a star is with a tape measure. I would press on and ask if there was another way to figure out how to distinguish the stars from one another other than their position in the sky.

Inevitably, someone would point out that some stars are brighter, and some are considerably fainter. I would then lead a discussion about how astronomers use indirect means to categorize stars by measuring their temperature and their luminosity or how bright they shine. I wanted my students to own their shine and see how it is a way they can choose to make others aware of their presence. For me, the world I operate in does indeed revolve around me like our planet revolves around the Sun. To succeed, everything I need is within me or within my reach. My shine allows others experiencing seasons of darkness to find their path by showing them what can be until they find their own shine.

I heard the son of America's beloved landscape artist, Bob Ross, say in a Netflix special, "... the first step of accomplishing anything is to believe that you can do it ..." I ask that you all take that spark within you and become a fully formed radiant star. Be the center of your solar system. Create the life you want while you walk on the Earth's surface. Seek progress over perfection. Visualize yourself achieving and living beyond your potential. This is your time to shine.

"Start now. Start where you are. Start with fear. Start with pain. Start with doubt. Start with hands shaking. Start with voice trembling, but start. Start and don't stop. Start where you are, with what you have. Just ... start."

- Ijeoma Umebinyuo

I visited my dad in 2018, and I remember him telling me on my way out of the house, "Nikki, you don't have to look like what you have been through." Although it stung at the time, I got in the car and looked in the rearview mirror. I was not living my passion anymore. I wasn't living. I was simply surviving. I was eating and weighed nearly 250 lbs. I had just filed for divorce after being married for 18 years. I was in the midst of bankruptcy and struggling to maintain the bills alone. I was navigating single parenthood while working as an assistant principal at a campus nearly an hour away from my house, which meant I rarely saw my daughter for no more than a few hours each day. This was not where I thought I would be in my 40s.

My dad's words rattled around in my head, and I couldn't shake them. I looked like I belonged in a Tyler Perry movie, and that was unacceptable. I was living as a victim in this story, and that was not the Nikki who had believed in herself in 6th grade. That was not the Shane Nicole who led the district's science department for over 88,000 students and mentored young teachers to become true educators. I no longer wanted to look like a walking Lifetime story.

Coincidentally, I received a message on Twitter from a colleague about a possible new job. I updated my resume and sent it off with no hope of hearing from them. In the meantime, I downloaded an exercise app, bought some walking shoes, and made a plan to get healthy. My sister acted as my accountability partner. To my surprise, I was asked to interview for the job. Three interviews later, I asked to take on a role as a STEM director for a world-renowned girl-serving nonprofit. They said I was the unicorn they were looking for and that I shined in all phases of the interview process. I had taken my life back, welcomed a new season, and found my shine again.

A few years later, I began receiving messages from friends saying I was an inspiration to them. Coming out on the other side of divorce, bankruptcy, and significant weight gain was not going unnoticed, and I had no idea. I had taken a break from social media as I healed myself through walking, hiking, meditation, and spending time with my family, especially my daughter. When I returned to Instagram and, later, Facebook, I shared pictures of what made me happy, which was life. I was shining, and that was helping others who were meandering in life as I had done in silence. Some would ask how I did it, and I said I simply chose a day one and started.

"Don't be afraid to start over. This time you're not starting from scratch, you're starting from experience."

- Biggs Burke

What goal have you been sitting on? What dream have you categorized as not for you because of your current circumstances?

One of my favorite narrators, my uncle, Julius Thompson Sr, who passed away suddenly in May 2020, spoke these words to a class of future lawyers, "Each of you is uniquely made, and your authentic self is enough. Don't change you; just continue to refine you. Protect your most valuable assets, your physical and mental health."

What I want you to do, my sister in nonprofit leadership, is to simplify your life by doing only the things that you can do and do them well. It's not too late to take over the story, your story, and narrate the most exciting dash ever.

- Shane Woods

CHAPTER TWENTY

Shawana O. Carter

"Never set limits, go after your dreams, don't be afraid to push the boundaries. And laugh a lot - it's good for you!"

- Paula Radcliffe

Hell no, you can't put limits on me!

Webster's dictionary defines limit as "a restriction on the size or amount of something permissible or possible." Well, since I operate in a space where I ask for forgiveness instead of permission, I am good. When was the first time someone told you, you couldn't achieve something because you looked different, started late, or were uncertain about how to do something?

At 17 years old, I found myself a mom. I heard the people I loved - at church, in my family, and in my school - begin to whisper about how my life would be over and that I was limited to the number of things I would accomplish. I lived in that space for many years, and now I can tell you that those thoughts were complete and utter

279

bullshit. I know I was placed on this Earth to make waves, and I am having a great time doing that! I have learned to live life without limits.

So, how do you learn to live life without limits? Listen, I don't have all the answers but know that it is a process. It has taken me many years to be comfortable living how I want to live and working how I want to work. I am sure that placing limits on myself will slow me down. So, let's talk about removing the limits.

<u>Don't believe you are limited because of past mistakes</u>:

You can't because you screwed up. Listen, as we go through life, "playas fuck up." That's my favorite line from the movie *Friday After Next*. It simply means that as we go through life, we will all screw up at some point. But just because we messed up this one time doesn't mean it's over for everything. Often, we live in households or communities that continuously remind us of the mess-ups we make, and they make us feel these limits, either self-imposed or placed on us by others, are accurate. They aren't. Our past is just that - the past. It was either a lesson learned or repeated. We must remind ourselves that we can achieve anything, no matter what time we get there or how long it takes. If I want it, I can have it, but I must put in the work.

I was 18 years old, had one child, and it was time for graduation. Let me tell you how hard I had to fight. I literally did work until the day before graduation. I wasn't always sure if I was doing this single-parent thing right, but I did my best. I knew that I was destined for greatness; I just hadn't figured it out yet. I think I took the long road to get where I was going; I am reminded that there are always some ups and downs on this road. I'm navigating adult and parenthood, and I have come upon an excellent government job. Yes, ma'am! I thought I had arrived. And then you come home in the lights are off, or you go to cook dinner, and there is only enough for your kid. You keep telling yourself, "I know you, and I know you created me for more. What is it?"

Don't believe you are limited because you don't fit in:

Hey, I know it can be lonely at the top, but you have to be okay with that. Your calling or destiny wasn't told to you via conference call. This is you and your Higher Power. You have to walk in it. The decisions you make about your life won't always seem practical or easy to implement, but they are necessary stepping stones to your getting to the top. F that box you think you need to fit in to make moves. You only need to be you! Do the work, and the rest will come. I have had the pleasure of meeting some beautiful people who didn't fit into the boxes placed on them, and they are mad successful. You just have to believe in yourself.

Limits are for suckas!

I dare you to believe that limits don't apply to you. Listen, I have spent many nights trying to figure out why I haven't accomplished what my circle has, but I now know that what I allowed myself to believe held me back from getting where I was supposed to be. Oh, I got here on time because it was God's timing, but think if I - if you - hadn't held on to those limits. Where would you be? I am not telling you to rush anything but to remind yourself that unless God says stop, you keep going. I am here to tell you that the moment you stop being concerned about them, you will begin to see yourself in a new light and see that anything is possible.

Moving past the limits you imposed on yourself.

The stories we tell ourselves are the worst kind, yet they are the easiest to believe! Stop it! Be kind to yourself. Think back to when you were a child and remember knowing that you were the fastest kid on the block. Until you got beat by a quicker kid, but that beatdown didn't stop you! It forced you to level up to be better. Do the same thing with the limit you give yourself. Tell yourself that you can do it! Regardless of what the world says or the people around you think. YOU CAN DO IT! Whatever it is, do that! I stand here today as a teen mom, a divorced mom, a grandmother of one, an owner of three businesses, a nonprofit founder, an award winner, a giver of hope to many, and a survivor of what would have made most quit. But I am still standing with both feet planted on the ground and ready for whatever is next!

CHAPTER TWENTY-ONE

Stephanie Epps

"You don't become what you want, you become what you believe."

- Oprah Winfrey

Unapologetically DO YOU!

Dear Black Woman in Nonprofit Leadership - Unapologetically DO YOU!

"Do You" is a phrase I have used my whole adulthood - as a response to certain questions, as a thought to myself, and as a declaration to others. Some people ask what it means, and my thought is that it means whatever you want it to mean. What it means for me, particularly in the space of being a Black Woman in Nonprofit Leadership, is to be uncompromising in the authenticity I unapologetically bring to every table I build, take a seat at or walk away from.

In navigating white supremacy culture daily, doing mission-based work that is either fighting or dismantling oppressive systems, circumventing structures that were built to ensure I don't succeed, or navigating culture points that exasperate the already difficult nature of working in this space, I like to think that me doing me is my own form of protest against it all. It is not the sole reason I show up how I do, but it is definitely a factor. In a world and space where assimilation reigns, my energy goes toward modeling big and small aspects of resistance – self-care, upholding boundaries, and embracing unique qualities, approaches, and lens – all in the name of productive progress.

And unapologetically, for me, that means without compromise, guilt, or permission. Given that the spaces I occupy, along with other Black women who do nonprofit work, do not create space for me to exist, asking for permission to create space for my needs seems pointless, so that is not a part of my process. I find no reason to feel guilty for existing, given that space is created for others to exist without compromise, so I do the same for myself. All I want for my fellow Black women in the nonprofit sector is to be seen, be heard, and for space to be created for us to exist. So, in short, I am out here unapologetically doing me, and I invite you to do the same.

A question I have often heard asked of Black women in nonprofit spaces but not nearly as often of our counterparts is, "Who are you to do this work?" That is an interesting one for me because we are usually the most qualified for a number of reasons - not just because we are often educated and experienced but also, given the focus of mission-based work, the likelihood that a Black woman is a part of or adjacent to whatever population and/or mission that is being served is pretty high. It often feels that there is a template - either implicit or explicit - that people feel the need to fit into that I either can't or haven't given any real energy to. I choose not to entertain it because it's usually rooted in something problematic. I have seen people get caught up in the titles, the degrees, the accolades, etc., and I can't help but question it a little. *Are you doing all this to build your skill set? Or to gain confidence/knowledge in a given area? Or because this is what you were told is the path? Or because you want to be a competitive candidate for roles? Or because it will be cute on your resume? Or because you want to be perceived a certain way? Or ensure that you're not perceived in a specific way? Is this meant to be an equalizer? Or a number of other possibilities.* I am a proponent of education and self-elevation, so I am not knocking this concept by any means; however, I think a lot can come from asking a few questions around intentionality.

What I have seen too often and what Black women in these spaces can get caught up in is placing their value solely on those things. I think it is important to understand what you offer without the other things, so they just serve as a supplement or enhancement, not the foundation. The foundation is you; it is your lens, your experience, your life, no matter how many ways white supremacy culture attempts to diminish that through gaslighting, impostor syndrome, perfectionism, or anything else. I find there is an incongruence between collecting accolades and simultaneously not wanting to give into the structures that make them necessary in the first place, but like all things, it requires balance. Whether to fight to liberate ourselves from these expectations or play the game is something I go back and forth on, but that's a different conversation for a different time. And that is not to say that people should not be proud of their accomplishments or even boast about them - but I think it's important to understand the balance as well as what it looks like to leverage those to reduce barriers rather than to uphold them.

All that said - in the spirit of "Doing You" and being unapologetic about it, I encourage everyone, particularly Black Women in the nonprofit space, to assess what they uniquely bring and embrace that. Your specific life trajectory and the unique set of experiences you've been through give you a lens different than anyone else that is meant to be leveraged and is needed in this work. I encourage you to find it, explore that and run with it. I know that sounds easier said than done, especially when so much of what it means to Black in any space is to dilute yourself, often to coddle white discomfort. But it's not about them. At all. It's about the mission. It's about who you serve. It's about you. Unapologetically. I mentioned equalizers earlier, and I think knowing what you uniquely bring and being able to communicate that with confidence is inherently an equalizer. Some of you might read this, and audacity will be the first word that comes to mind, and I agree. I dare you to have the audacity to have confidence in your lens and approach to your work, being informed by your life experiences.

This started as a dare to myself and hasn't stopped since. This has manifested in a few ways in my life, particularly in my approach as a Black woman in nonprofit leadership. The work I do requires me to be a people manager, project manager, and program manager. There are myriad ways to approach all those things, and my approach is to be inherently inclusive, which requires persistence and resistance given the oppressive systems always at play. For example, a lot of work culture is focused on the dominant culture, like centering practices around extroverts. Meeting culture centers around being in person, sharing on the spot, processing real-time, etc. Many people are slower processors and need information ahead of time to be able to actively share thoughts during meetings or are better with written than verbal communication. I try to make sure meetings that could be emails or docs don't get on the calendar, end meetings early when needed, and gauge when pre-work for meetings is needed to maximize our time together. Using these meetings to create space where people can share a variety of thoughts and provide input into the decisions that affect their work and roles is also a big part of what it looks like for me to focus on creating an inclusive environment. I dared myself to challenge the norms, and now it's just a habit, one that I'd say is a good habit that started small but makes a notable impact on team dynamics. Little success led me to explore what bigger successes could look like so I could create space for those who not only process how I do but come from a similar background as I do.

For me, "Do You?" has manifested in a multitude of ways, including new skills, talents, personality traits, human characteristics, frameworks, and more. I am proudest of my naturally disruptive nature. I grew up not being allowed to question many things around me; now, I question almost everything all the time. Not only do I ask a lot of questions, but I also probe for intentionality, rationale, effectiveness, and more. My brand of disruption comes from a lens of working toward necessary change and/or evolution. Depending on the original state of things, it is sometimes embraced but is often met with pushback and/or gaslighting. I am a naturally confrontational person, especially in a way I know not many other people are in the spaces I have worked in and navigated, so disruption is easy for me. Like being disruptive, being confrontational gets a bad rep and has a negative connotation, but like being constructively disruptive, being confrontational can also be constructive. For example, I don't feel uncomfortable giving pushback to or calling those out who attempt to gaslight me and minimize my voice. I approach it in a firm but non-argumentative way because, at the end of the day, I need the message to be received, and going in to argue or pick a fight reduces the likelihood of that. However, that doesn't mean being overly amicable or letting things slide. Again, it's about balance. While this often calls for me to say things that might make the recipient uncomfortable, I enjoy it because there is usually some kind of benefit or progression at the other end of the conversation. Whether that is gaining new insight on a situation, resolving an issue, learning something more about the person, or collecting intel to help in creating a path forward, in my experience, it is worth it (almost) every time, so I embrace it.

My unapologetic nature also manifests itself through empathy. I'm a Cancer, so I'm a natural empath, which I have found to have pros and cons in the nature of the nonprofit world. Being an empath sometimes makes it hard to set/enforce boundaries or makes it easier to ignore red flags that should instead be a priority to address. On the other hand, it can make the relational aspect that many roles and organizations require come more naturally. However, what I do not enjoy about the nonprofit space is that it is often predicated on conflating niceness and niceties with kindness. For me, the former is rooted in fragility, white supremacy, and a facade, while the latter is rooted in respect and empathy. I do not need to like you to treat you with respect and empathy. As I create space for your humanness, it does not have a prerequisite of liking or feeling a specific connection to you; you get that because you are human, not because of how I feel about you. I feel like these concepts get jumbled and make things become personal when creating space for humanness shouldn't be personal; it should be human, and given that we are all humans, a default.

But that is also another conversation for another time, as I digress. I show up as an empath that embraces boundaries AND accountability as they are not mutually exclusive as the nonprofit space often tries to paint the picture. For example, based on how I navigate relationships, I am intentionally not friends with anyone I work with. That doesn't mean we can't/won't/don't connect on a human level because I do with most people, at work or not. It means I won't let personal feelings become the basis for navigating humanness. Giving people that you know better or more unfair advantages is inherently not equitable, and as someone who strives to battle white supremacy culture in as many ways as I can, I strive to be as equitable as possible.

Back to the topic at hand, I am a human of action, as acts of service are my top love/appreciation language, so modeling is a big part of my process. I could tell stories for days, but I think it might be helpful to share some guidelines I live by to ensure I maintain my unapologetic "doing me" attitude. I have shared a few examples of how that has come up in my journey, and given that I have experienced a lot and from that and more, here are five keys to unapologetically doing me that create space for me to be seen, heard, and exist in the nonprofit world:

1. ***Understanding still vs. stagnant:*** For me, it is important not to fall into the trap of being nonstop busy like I have in my past. For me, complacency is something that I try to avoid, and the way I would do that is by always being busy. I have many passions, interests, and skills, and it took me a while to figure out that they don't all need to be addressed at the same time and at the same level. To find that balance, I have to schedule a time to be still and literally do nothing and/or do something that is focused solely on decompression or rejuvenation because when left to my own devices, I will run myself ragged. I used to be

worried that being still meant that I would become stagnant (the gateway to complacency), but I was conflating the two. Stillness and pausing from the busy or reducing it where I can is one of the biggest factors of my self-care journey.

Ask yourself: *How many responsibilities can/ should I juggle at once? What would it look like for me to say "No" or "Not now" to this request/opportunity? What do I miss out on if I say "No" or "Not now" to this request/opportunity? What is the right amount of momentum and balance to avoid getting into a rut?* There is no better way to create space for someone than to allow them to rest and pace themselves, and this achieves that for me.

2. ***Using my voice:*** As I'm sure you can imagine, this one focuses on being heard. I have a voice that needs to be heard. Period. If I am embracing what only I can bring to a position, team, or organization, then I have to share my thoughts. Sometimes it has been a popular opinion, and sometimes it feels like I'm the only one in the room with that view, but either way, it is mine to share. Black women in leadership positions in nonprofit, in my experience, have been few and far between, but they provide an unmatched perspective. Whether it is met with accolades, awkwardness, anger, or a number of other feelings/thoughts, the likelihood is that I am providing a necessary lens that otherwise is not coming from somewhere else, so I make sure to bring it.

Ask yourself: *If I don't say this, who else will? If someone else usually says this, how can I support them in their message? Who or what is worse off if I say this? Who or what is better off if I say this?*

3. **_Boundaries:_** I am the queen of boundaries; they are key to creating space for someone to take up space how they see fit. I have navigated different stages of my life and careers without them and would NOT recommend that. It is so easy to get caught up doing so much for other people that it is even easier to lose yourself and your needs in that mix. Having a solid understanding of what you need to be true in a situation to consent to it or actively say no to it is the basis of how I set my boundaries. Whether it is being firm about my hours of availability for work matters, not being friends with people who I work with, and not taking on tasks, responsibilities, etc., at my own expense, to name a few. Now, I think everyone has their own thresholds of what they can withstand or exceptions they are willing to make, but only you know what that looks like for you. It often feels like in the nonprofit space, we should be ride or die for our causes, but we are no good to anyone if we die, so figure out what it looks like for you to be able to continue to ride - take breaks and detours, stop for gas, etc. as needed!

Ask yourself: *Who am I helping, and who am I hurting if I do this? Is there a way I can do this that minimizes harm to me and/or others? Am I doing this for your reasons or for other people's reasons? What are my capacity/limits/thresholds for navigating this situation?*

4. ***Know what is worth my time and what isn't:*** People often talk about choosing your battles so that you can win the war. In the nonprofit world, it feels like there are many battles and many wars, some of which are worthy of my time and some that must be deprioritized. I think strategy from a self-care standpoint is important but also from the lens of effectiveness. I don't have the bandwidth to fight every fight that exists, and I'm not positioned to do so, to be honest, so compromising my peace and joy by trying to attack everything at the same time isn't helping me or anybody else. On the other hand, if I go full force on every topic all the time, it minimizes the effect and impact. We cannot do everything at once, so deciding what is or isn't worth my time before I invest my energy is a default part of my approach. Being intentional about this is key to being seen in these spaces because you can easily be taken for granted without it and/or fade into the background.

Ask yourself: *Is this a battle or a war? Is this something I should be dedicating my energy to? What should I trade-off to maintain this as a priority? Will pursuing this compromise my quality of life?*

5. ***Check myself:*** The onus of keeping me in check is on me. I will create space for others to be able to give me feedback, and I will be intentional about how I receive it, AND no one is in control of me but me. Unapologetic does not need to be reckless - quite the opposite, it should be very intentional. Being intentional about what I do and why and how ensures that I can keep myself

293

in check and check others if needed. I do not want to uphold the problematic structures and culture points that run rampant in the nonprofit world, so it is important that I embrace "doing me" as well as understand that if I don't want to uphold these things, unlearning is necessary and that starts with me making that choice to be better.

Ask yourself: *What equalizers need to be addressed? Am I upholding white supremacy culture with this action or approach? Am I creating the space to receive feedback? Am I doing the work to unlearn what is necessary so that I can do better?*

Now, this is a good list, but I'm only human, so there are definitely things I still need to work on. Such as all things, even being unapologetic and "doing me" is imperfect. I also have a whole list of things that I have struggled with in the past or continue to struggle with today. These are the things that keep from being seen, heard, or being able to take up space that should be. I would like to note that I believe in duality as a human, so personal me and professional me are one and the same and overlap, so the examples I give will be professional and personal because they are symbiotic, at least for me. Some of my personal traits bleed into my professional life, and some of my professional traits bleed into my personal life because I am the same person and don't feel the need to compartmentalize in that way. That said, there are some warnings I think would've been helpful to have sooner, so I will use those to share some caution in a few areas:

6. ***Knowing when to part ways:*** Now, this is universal - it can apply to work, relationships, passion projects, etc. The empath in me used to have a propensity for ignoring red flags. For example, in a past relationship, after three years of being together, my partner told me they didn't know what love really meant, if they believed in it, regardless of whether they loved me. That is a red flag. There is nothing wrong with being on the human journey of self-exploration and not knowing how you feel about love (although three years is a long time to be going with the flow, but I digress). However, there is something wrong with ignoring this is a clear sign that the person had a good amount of self-exploration to do before they could show up as a healthy partner. I saw this as something we could work through since, no matter how I show up, I can't affect how a person processes love. I kept myself in a process that needed to be absent of me because I wanted to be a recipient of that love. Choosing to say and support that person's journey without considering my needs and perspective was doing myself a disservice. I stayed with this person for two-plus more years, and I learned a lot in that time, so I don't regret it by any means. I eventually broke it off for several reasons, but it could've saved us a lot of time and learned different lessons, avoided mess, etc., by seeing the red flags for what they were and not what I wanted them to be. This also applies to previous organizations I have worked for. Similarly, about three years into working at a given organization, a fair

amount of drama and toxic-predicting things had transpired, and I was faced with a choice to stay or go. I decided to stay. Again, I stayed for two more years, and while I learned a lot, it was at the cost of trauma that I have since processed and moved on from, but it took a six-month work hiatus and moving to a whole new state to really work past. I could have learned a whole different set of lessons had I decided to part ways before things got toxic. So, something I continue to work through is to create space for human mistakes but not let things get toxic and drag out longer than they need to. I have been trying to be more intentional about trusting and listening to my intuition but not letting it make me paranoid or make rash decisions. Balance is key!

7. ***Removing myself from messy reality:*** When things get a little messy, I tend to create an insular bubble and prioritize that and turn a blind eye. I mentioned before that I am confrontational, so my default reaction is to address things head-on. I bring it to whoever it involves because that is how I handle conflict. HOWEVER, if they don't match that energy, I take that as a sign they are not about to put in equal action to address said issue, so I create a bubble that I can control where I know things will go well because I am the biggest factor in it, and then I don't care about the rest of the reality surrounding the situation. For example, in my personal life, I have relationships with relatives where I have shared explicitly what I take issue with and what it

would take to resolve said issues. The response in some situations has been, this is me/I am who I am/it is what it is/I can't do anything about the past, so get over it. I read all of those as cop-outs to taking real action, and I can't work on a relationship on my own, so I just don't communicate with them. My bubble becomes a world where they don't exist, whereas, in reality, they do, and so, is that really helping? Well, yes, it helps me, but does it help the situation? - that could go either way. For a work example, I have worked on the program side of every nonprofit I have worked with/for. If/when a time comes that I don't agree with leadership and the direction they want to take things with the org, I let them do what they do because it's their organization. I have some amount of control/autonomy over what is going on in the program, how we run, etc., so I create my ideal scenario in my space and deprioritize whatever else is happening in the rest of the organization. Not in a way that excludes the rest of the organization but in a way that creates a false sense of things going well because it is in my area; that doesn't change the fact that if things are going bad in any other part of the organization, it ultimately can/will affect my team so I shouldn't turn a blind eye to it. I have attempted to address this by trying to use the approach with my team as a model of what things could look like - not to shame leadership or other departments or other sites or other orgs, but to lead by example, which hopefully is a stepping stone to finding a happy medium or common middle ground.

8. ***Balancing equity, authenticity, and expertise*** - Inequities show up all over the place in the nonprofit world in my experience, and one of them is in positionality alone. I don't want our accomplishments to be minimized, and I want people, especially Black women, to gas themselves up AND if liberation is the key, what else can we focus on that's not upholding white supremacy culture? I want to figure out what it looks like to NOT over-romanticize titles, awards, clout, etc., but still find value in achievement and make sure it is recognized with comparable positionality in each organization. I struggle with what that balance looks like or if it can even exist. They feel at odds with each other, and adding in that mix, the dissonance I feel about how "expertise" is navigated, particularly in the nonprofit space, makes this even more complex. In my opinion, the term expert is thrown around relatively loosely in this space and is often used in a condensing, patronizing, or begrudging way when it comes to Black women in the nonprofit world. It has often felt like other parties will yield reluctantly or use "expertise" to get it off their plate and shift ownership but still try to indirectly control the narrative in some way. Instead of yielding because we likely are the best lens to address a given issue, it feels like they feel they are doing us a favor. It's another way that equity is imbalanced in the nonprofit world from my perspective. I don't want to have to be the Moral Matriarch all the time - I want to be able to show up authentically and know that I am an expert in some ways but

still don't and won't know everything - and that is okay. I want to be able to model what it looks like to know what you know as well as know what you don't know coming from the authentic lens of life and work experience. In an ideal world, the titles, awards, etc., aren't the basis for my knowledge and the work I produce, but by-products that we can all take or leave that could be nice to have but aren't necessary. Transparently, I'm still flushing this out the more that I navigate the nonprofit space and juxtapose it to my past work experiences in tech, etc., but it is definitely on my radar to continue to explore.

Getting back to unapologetically doing you - authenticity and transparency is my main target when I say the phrase. That is my ultimate dream for any and all Black women in nonprofit leadership. Most people just want to be seen and heard or, at the very least, have the space to exist, and that is what I want for Black women in nonprofit leadership. Not just because it's equitable, not just because our experience is often the root of success in several organizations, and not just because it's long overdue, but because it is what we have earned and deserve. I don't know how long it will take for the nonprofit industry to catch up to where we are and make room for us, but that's for them to figure out, not us and not me. In the meantime, I will continue to do me and take up all the space I can when I can because that is what is best for me and the work I am committed to. In the timeless words of my favorite Cardi B song *Get Up 10,* "I ain't tellin' y'all to do it, I'm just tellin' my story." I am not one to try to lecture or tell people how they should live, but instead to just model my humanness - the good, the bad, the accurate. Hopefully, it creates space for that to catch on, but even if it doesn't, it creates space for me to continue to do what no one else can do ... ME!

CHAPTER TWENTY-TWO

Tamika Sanders

"I got my start by giving myself a start."

- Madam CJ Walker

O ne day, about a year ago, I found myself sitting in front of my work laptop, at home, after wrapping up what felt like the millionth Zoom meeting of the day and feeling drained. I just knew I was over the day. No more emails or work-related texts would be written or read. Not another follow-up phone call would be made that afternoon because I was done. Or so I thought. I opened my personal email, skimming and deleting and stopping for one very interesting subject line, which read, *"Black Women in Nonprofit Leadership Deadline."*

We had been living in "unprecedented times" for about seven months, as many would describe living through a pandemic. My new normal consisted of a workspace that had gone from a physical office of three at a busy family center in Northwest Dallas to an office corner in Bishop Arts where no one would steal my pens or my peace, and I could listen to Beyonce OR Jay-Z exclusively, even *explicitly*. Notice I said office corner, not corner office because my desk setup was nestled in a corner of my living room in my small soft loft apartment, surrounded by my growing plant collection; a Monstera deliciosa behind me, a fiddle leaf fig tree to the right, and, among others, my prized Golden Pothos stunningly trailing nearby.

I loved being at home for work, even if the work itself wasn't very exciting. Each morning was, in fact, a new day because I wasn't very good at routines, though I tried them so I wouldn't lose my sense of responsibility and, of course, my employment. Some days, I could manage to get out for a short walk to the coffee shop before starting the day, and it would feel like a win, while the day before, I may have struggled to even get out of bed in time for a meeting that I would not have to leave home for. Life wasn't all that exciting for me, but it was my life.

I knew I wanted more, but I wasn't quite sure what I wanted more of. I had a nice small circle of friends, some of whom I have known since childhood and others I have held close over the years. I didn't get out much other than the occasional brunch or happy hour here and there. I was also single. My social life wasn't very exciting. I always felt that I would figure out a way to change things around one day, and I was planning to move to Georgia to be closer to my mom until I could figure out exactly what I wanted to do. I just wanted change by any means necessary. I was not happy, and I really had no idea how or where to begin to create change in my life. As it turned out, November 12th, 2020, was that day for me.

I opened the email around 3:30 pm on that Thursday afternoon, and it read:

"Today is the day, the day you submit your application to participate in the Black Women in Nonprofit Leadership cohort. The cohort is ready to support your professional, personal, and healing goals through our 12-month curriculum. You do not want to miss out on 12 months of professional and personal development curriculum and healing practices, 11 months of Executive Coaching, six months of honing your skills to amplify your voice in the sector, plus so much more that leads to your leaving legacy. Start your journey. We begin January 2021, virtually, with a goal to graduate to in-person meetings by Summer 2021. We hope to see you there."

Just reading that introduction excited me! I had so many questions, and I am pretty sure I asked them aloud even though there was no one around to clarify anything for me. *What was this? Why had I not heard about this before? Who are these women? How can I get involved? And finally, oh shit, what about Georgia?*

I had a very loose plan to move in February, at the end of my lease. Of course, if I had been more proactive – which I tend not to be, I may have been applying for work in Georgia, beginning the packing process, and setting money aside for my actual move, yet I hadn't thought about any of these things. Something about the very thought of the move itself felt like I was just giving up on Tamika and clinging to my mom for some sort of redirection that wasn't up to her to decide. My mom was a huge advocate for allowing me the time and space to figure things out at my own pace, and she and her husband were ready to welcome me into their mountain home and would allow me almost any amount of time I would need to get on my feet. But just reading the email gave me life!

Not long ago, I decided I simply was not fulfilled. I felt stuck, even if others who knew me would not agree that I was. At 36 and depending on who you ask, one might say this paradigm shift could be connected to my age — perhaps this sudden issue with complacency was due to hormonal changes and the frequent reminders of the ticking clock that is the woman's body – particularly in terms of the women's reproductive system.

I don't know what it was, how it happened, or why, but the shift was intrinsic, and it couldn't have happened at a more perfect time. Even though I wasn't totally sure of how to turn my life around, I sensed this opportunity was the start of just what I needed, so it seemed well worth postponing the move. I had spent enough time feeling sorry for myself and fighting my anxiety and depressive episodes alone. I needed change, and now, but sometimes, the problem with recognizing the need for change is that one doesn't always know what steps to begin with and that alone can be quite daunting. Intuitively, this email felt like a sign – I mean, it mentioned a

deadline for something I had never heard of before.

Still, I knew that I needed to seize this opportunity; the time was about 3:30 pm, and the submission deadline was at 5:00 pm that very same evening. I spent the rest of that afternoon, that evening, and past midnight working on the lengthy application, submitting it well past the cut-off time of 1:30 am. I said a little prayer before I submitted the application because just missing the submission time may have been enough to disqualify me from exploring this cohort any further.

The wait for the email announcing who had been selected for the cohort had me on edge. Only 20 applicants would be selected. Throughout the wait, I would constantly talk myself out of expecting to hear back. Instead, I rehearsed thoughts like, *this cohort isn't for me because I am not a leader. There will be so many other women much more qualified than me. Do I deserve this? What are my professional, personal, and healing goals, anyway? I am not even all Black.*

Being a person of mixed race, an Afro-Latina as I learned to identify in my adult life, there were times I felt I wasn't Black enough, but then I also wasn't Latina enough. You see, I've always lived in my head, judging myself harshly and doubting myself consistently. And to be frank, I lacked confidence in owning my identity and showing up authentically.

If I am not careful, I could spend hours reliving moments of fear, guilt, or shame over things that I cannot change. I can even imagine what the alternate version of myself looks and lives like in a utopian, parallel universe. Her curls are always defined and poppin', and her ends are never split. She loves her fupa, she can make it rain,

305

and best of all, she feels seen, loved, and valued by her peers, her family, and her lover. These kinds of thoughts are predictable and reliable; they always come through, and for a long time, have seemed the only thoughts that made sense; *I don't belong, I don't have what it takes to be successful, I am too this, not of enough of that, and worst of all everyone sees it. Why should I take up space where I don't belong?*

I could sure as hell think myself out of almost any opportunity, no matter how great if I obsessed over these types of thoughts long enough. Some days, I'm pretty impressed with how far my thoughts can go. On other days, they've gone so far that it's hard to get back to center. Those days often feel like a full-frontal assault on who I am altogether.

Have you ever thought or felt that way? Have you ever prematurely counted yourself out because you heard a persistent little voice in the very back of your mind, pulling at the hem of your confidence, egging you over the edge of self-doubt, and throwing you into a state of anxiety that seems to paralyze you?

This isn't a chapter about mental health, although, of course, the thoughts were anxious, and the concept of "getting back to center" can be rather exhausting, I dare to say even depressive. I won't focus on impostor syndrome either, but for the sake of clarity, impostor syndrome can be explained simply as doubting your abilities and feeling like a complete fraud. And if you're a woman of color, particularly a Black woman, you probably know just what that's like.

I finally received the exciting welcome email on December 8th. I must note that this was not what I was expecting; the timeline for the application process, per the initial email, was to include interviews for applicants that passed the application process, and those were to be scheduled during the week of November 23rd and November 30th. So, you can imagine that after all the negative thinking and doubting myself, I almost wished I hadn't applied. I didn't want to get my hopes up. When I still hadn't heard back about an interview, I decided that previous week that I just had not been selected for the cohort. But this was not the case! In fact, I learned later that so many women had applied for the cohort they ended up extending it to an additional 15 women.

We held our first session on January 21st, 2021, and then every third Thursday of the month that year. These sessions were the highlight of my month; we'd explore topics like Black women and mental health, personal and business branding, building social capital, the art of negotiation, and more. I met amazing, talented, passionate women who embraced and mentored me. These women were responsible for change in the very organizations they worked in; some of them had created the spaces they were in, while others were reviving dead situations and elevating their teams because of their tenacity.

I would be lying if I didn't admit that I initially felt so small next to them. They were educated, decorated, and successful. I did not see myself in that way. Many of them were confident; I was not. They all knew that they were Black women through and through, and they owned it. I, on the other hand, struggling with my identity, was wondering where I would fit in. *Would they see me as one of their own?* That didn't last long, though. They always uplifted me. Included me and checked in on me when I got too quiet in the group chats we had between sessions. We created and curated a safe space for healing, accountability, and learning. We had many opportunities to affirm and comfort one another, and we did at any chance we could. We also connected outside of the sessions over coffee, lunch, or drinks. We volunteered and worked on assignments together.

These women became my safe space. Until the cohort, I had never imagined I would be so connected to so many new people who were eager and willing to support one another because it turned out we had been facing many of the same challenges in the workplace. This is what helped me see that I was not alone.

Being part of the Black Women in Nonprofit Leadership cohort was necessary for me. It truly impacted my life in many ways. Throughout my journey and as part of the cohort, I also participated in executive coaching. Together, my coach and I set goals for my professional and personal development and tracked my progress, and the results were nothing short of transformational. My coach met me right where I was, and her mentorship helped me navigate some challenges in my professional life, which in turn helped me improve my overall situation. Since our coaching journey, I have completed the cohort, broadened my social and professional networks, and taken on new opportunities for growth.

Being part of this experience helped me to see the areas of my life that I needed to focus on. And as I mentioned earlier, though I wanted change, I did not know how to facilitate the process. When I thought about the personal and healing goals that I mentioned earlier, I knew that I wanted to be healed, happy, and whole. So, to help gain some traction, I decided on three things that I needed to do to help me get there and ultimately help me lead what I believed would be a fulfilling life. Those three things became my focus throughout the cohort, and they helped guide my journey.

I will share those three things next, but first, I would ask you to consider the last time you allowed yourself the opportunity to identify your needs and desires without connecting them to someone else's actions or opinions. When was the last time you took a chance on yourself, doubted your fears, and gave imposter syndrome a run for its money? Personally, I realized that prior to being in the cohort, I had never actually done that for myself. So, I'd like to encourage you to put yourself up for these three challenges:

Go deeper - I wanted to be healed from trauma so that I could experience the full spectrum of life and not just the glimmers. Trauma arrests you, stagnates you, and if left unattended for too long, trauma can alter your perception of the world around you, making it difficult to trust others and maybe even your own judgment. As Black women, we are seen as strong, and in the face of adversity, we still rise to the occasion, often in spite of what we truly feel. During my time in the cohort, I realized how necessary it was for us to be in therapy. We are constantly being traumatized and retraumatized by the systems we live in, even though the framework didn't include us from the beginning. I sought therapy because I knew I could no longer go at it alone. I had great friends, but I needed to figure out what was really going on deep inside of me that held me back in areas like relationships and owning my identity. Finally, connecting with a Black therapist, who I don't have to code-switch for, really helped me see that caring for others while neglecting my own healing was a trauma response. I needed to redirect that energy and turn it inward so I could nurture myself and simply just be.

Don't tap out - You must make genuine connections with others. And I hate to break it to you, sis, but those connections aren't always going to be family or the forever childhood friends who knew you back when. When I thought about what I wanted and needed to be happy, I thought about new connections and opportunities. Yet I was always pretty timid and wouldn't challenge myself to meet new people or go out alone. I remember praying for strong Black women to connect with because as an Afro-Latina – yes, a Black woman – I still did not have very many Black friends.

Participating in the cohort helped me learn that there is protection AND accountability when we have a circle of sisters we identify with and can safely unpack our own internalized oppression with. Getting to know and learn from these wonderful Black women has brought joy to my life, mending pieces of me I didn't even know were torn and affirming my identity in ways I didn't know I needed. And you know what? I think I'm finally beginning to see in me some of the great things they see in me. I love it here. Tap into your sister circle, and if you don't have one, start by affirming a Black woman or inviting them for coffee or lunch.

Look back at it - How we tell the story of our life is crucial. More important than how we tell it to others is how we retell it to ourselves. I was over the narrative of my brokenness. Repeatedly rehearsing and counting my flaws just really made me feel less deserving than the next person, and that just wasn't going to work for me any longer.

I could look at my life as a mosaic, a piece of art made of broken pieces, and that is nice. But I desire the ability to shift and recreate when ready, altering the patterns to make it all more mesmerizing, and that makes me think of a kaleidoscope. Similar in the sense that there's fragmented beauty in both, but one is still while the other will shift if you move it. So, take a look back over your life and reconsider that even the ugly parts still contributed to the beauty that is now and what is to come. Although I still have a long journey ahead; because healing isn't linear and happiness is essentially a currency, I know that choosing a holistic approach to help facilitate these changes is what will ultimately yield this sense of wholeness I crave.

Look, I know I said I had *three* challenges for you, but who doesn't love a bonus? Here's one last thing to consider.

Wrap it up - I know there are days when even getting out of bed can be difficult. When those days threaten your current state of wellbeing, I want to challenge you to get up anyway. Protect your peace and envelop yourself with self-regard and forgiveness, and give yourself grace. We are still the authors of our own stories, and we are worth every single page we turn.

Go after the things you want, trust yourself and that inner voice that doubts your doubts.

CHAPTER TWENTY-THREE

Taylor Hall

"Start unknown, finish unforgettable."

- Misty Copeland

Dear Black Women in Nonprofit Leadership,

Spoiler alert: I don't have a life-changing epiphany to reveal to you in this chapter. Quite honestly, this chapter is less about the nonprofit sector and my professional learning and more about my personal learnings. I am confident that they will have a deep impact on my holistic life, including my professional one. I can't promise you some profound takeaway that will forever change your life or your approach to life. What I can promise are transparency and honesty, probably too much of both; an overshare, if you will. A wise friend (and cohort peer) said that we don't often enough "deprioritize the destination" in efforts to prioritize and appreciate the journey. Wow! Isn't that the truth? Shout out to Stephanie Epps for that brilliant revelation.

So, mama didn't raise no fool. I'm a quick learner, and that's what we'll do here, together, in this chapter. I'll share and reflect on my journey because I'm hyper-aware that I'm still very much processing this experience. This cohort and season of my life have been deeply revealing. I'm aware that I have much more to process before I feel like I'm beginning to tread water and before I can truly share the full impact of this experience. So, in the meantime, here's a look inside my journey (thus far) that you did not ask for, but that I hope you find helpful. Even if that means it gives you the perspective that you're not alone or we're all just trying to figure it out. Let's be human together and shed light on the work that it takes to get to the best version of ourselves. So, let's start at the turning point.

Frustrated. Exhausted – Physically and Mentally. Sad. Lost. All descriptors that hit me over the head in 2020. Life hit me HARD. The pandemic forced life to halt. We had no choice but to reflect and become more aware. The constraints of this crisis debilitated my ability to cloud my life with busyness to topically treat my lack of joy and contentment. I realized I was hiding in the busyness; overworking, shopping, concerts, trying every new restaurant my city has to offer, volunteering (virtually), drowning in social media, TV, and movies, and packing every free moment with *something*. But when the world slowed down, I was forced to slow down, too. The lack of stimulating distraction brought into plain view that I was a convoluted mess of feelings and emotions. I had been stuffing them down and not dealing with them. Desperate for change, but not sure how to make it happen. These feelings culminated in seeking. Seeking an out. Seeking a revelation. Seeking a solution. *Something* needed to give!

Through a series of events, I stumbled upon Dallas TRHT in 2020. Shortly after I started following the organization, I saw the announcement for the Black Women in Nonprofit Leadership (BWNPL) Cohort.

The Cohort purpose read "to provide an intentional space for Black women in the nonprofit sector. BWNPL is designed to support Black women with self-care, community-care, healing, personal and professional development and crafted to the specific needs of Black women leaders."

I read the words "healing and development," and I knew I needed to apply them. I applied and was accepted. It was a Godsend! I decided I was going to inundate my challenges with solutions: the cohort, an executive coach (actually two, but we'll get to that later), and therapy. Not to sound cliché, but I felt like God brought all these things together for my good.

So fast forward to the first cohort session, where we were prompted to answer the question, "What am I hoping to get out of this cohort?" My response was:

1. Connectedness! I want to be in relationships with more Black women in nonprofit.
2. Tools to work through stress and anxiety.
3. Affirmation/Confidence – I want to be more sure of myself

and the things I have to contribute.

Looking back, I definitely received everything I hoped for and so much more. The cohort increased my awareness and consciousness. It became my mirror, showing me my reflection and things I had been avoiding, missing, and or neglecting. It helped me put a name to the challenging things I was experiencing. The cohort helped me call them by name so I could begin to combat them and deal with them. So, to make a long story less long (but not short), here are a few things I learned related to the things I hoped for.

Connectedness is important!

We weren't meant to live this life alone, and that's for a reason. We need relationships. Not only do we need to be in relationships, but we need to communicate. I know this isn't news but bear with me. The connection I found through this cohort made me realize I was isolating myself and suffering in silence. I used to feel that everyone – my parents, my friends, my village – had enough going on in their own lives, and I didn't want to be a burden by weighing them down with my challenges. Especially because, on paper, my life seemed great! Great job, a great apartment, a decent car, and a great social life. I truly thought I shouldn't have any complaints. But still, something wasn't right. Each cohort session topic facilitated substantive conversations that forced me to do some much-needed self-reflection. This experience helped me to put words to the things I was feeling and experiencing. The sessions also helped me to open up to my cohort peers. In return, my peers were generous and vulnerable with me by sharing their experiences. Their willingness to share helped me realize I wasn't alone. I was not the only one experiencing these challenges, professionally or personally. Additionally, they helped me realize that some of my challenges weren't my fault. I would never wish for anyone to share my troubles, but it lifted a weight, knowing that some of these challenges were more commonplace than I thought. Not only were they generous enough to be vulnerable, but they were also generous with their time and their wisdom. Some reached out, checked on me, and sent notes of kindness. Because of them, I felt a little less lonely. Because of them, my village has grown. I'm so grateful to have met these brilliant, innovative, inspiring, gorgeous women. They've done so much for me personally; I can only imagine where we'll go professionally together.

Professional advice should be a proactive solution.

I waited until I was at a dire point to seek out therapy, the cohort, and executive coaching. I desperately needed some tools to help with the stress and anxiety that had built up over time. I hired an executive coach, Chiedozie Okafor of the Nelo Effect, at the same time I applied for the cohort.

Chiedozie helped me realize that I needed boundaries, not just personally but professionally; this would ensure that I honored my needs. I was pouring myself into my work and relationships, and I was burned out. I needed to prioritize my work-life balance. So, I adjusted my environment and started pushing toward balance. And by balance, I mean eating lunch, sleeping more, working fewer nights, and no weekends. Unbeknownst to me, when I applied for the cohort, we were gifted the opportunity to work with an executive coach.

My second coach, Catherine Wheeler, completely shifted my perspective on work by saying, "It's not what you do; it's how you do the work." She helped me realize that I was placing my value in the work I was doing but not in my approach to the work – the gifts and strengths I bring to the work. Catherine also provided me with a multitude of tools and resources that helped me identify my values, create a routine for staying connected with my network, prep for the first 90 days of my new role, and so much more. These two coaches helped me work through my internal and external challenges. I learned that my mental and emotional health play a vital role in helping me do my job well.

Before, I was so busy striving to collect achievements and accomplish goals that I put all my value into it, which heightened my fear of failure. I was so afraid that failure meant I wouldn't be valuable anymore. But I'm learning that failure doesn't detract from my value. It's just a learning lesson that is a part of my journey. And it is my responsibility to use those lessons to get better at how I do my work. The combination of the coaching, therapy, and the cohort helped me pause; it gave me the opportunity to understand my triggers and patterns that weren't serving me. Unfortunately, it took me getting to a desperate place before I sought help. Moving forward, I want to be proactive versus reactive.

I now personally understand the need to treat my mental and emotional health as I do my physical health. The same way I go in for an annual emotional is the same way I need to routinely check in on my mental and emotional health with a professional. The objectivity of a professional empowers me to step outside of my challenges so I can see the whole picture. I can only imagine what would happen if I was continuously looking at the picture as more detail is added. This is just a working theory. TBD.

Additionally, these professionals gave me tools that I'll continue to shape into a routine and a rhythm to destress and decompress. For now, what I can say is that professional advice, whether proactive or reactive, works! Seek it out if you are able. I'm sure I'm preaching to the choir, but it needed to be said, just in case.

Know or learn your value

As I mentioned earlier, I set out on this journey for affirmation to increase my confidence. All my life, I've been a rule follower. I'd only really known success from graduating high school and attaining two degrees. I didn't really have to face failure until five years into my career when I entered management, and the responsibility and accountability were heightened.

For so long, I let myself be defined by following the rules, getting good grades and degrees, and doing a great job at work. I thought my value was in what I did — checking all the right boxes and meeting every goal whether I set it or someone else did. That revelation my coach Catherine shared about "it's not what you do, it's how you do the work" flipped everything upside down and inside out. I realized I'd been defining my value in a way that wasn't serving me. During one of our cohort sessions, one of the facilitators asked us to share what value we provide. I was praying not to be called on, but of course, when you pray those kinds of prayers, God is on a lunch break. Just kidding, God (hopefully you laughed up there). Anyhoo, I got called on to answer, and of course, I froze. And these words tumbled out of my mouth "I don't really know. I know I'm valuable; I'm just not really sure how I'm valuable." Then, I proceeded to turn off my camera and sob. So, my mentor (cohort peer and guardian angel), Benaye Wadkins Chambers, gave me an assignment — write down the good things your loved ones say about you and google how they can be useful in the workplace. I won't get into the details of my assignment, but I will share the prompt with you in case you're in the same place I was. I'm learning to find the good in myself without a qualifier — a degree, a job title, or a marital status (that I don't have). I'm just learning to love me deeper as I am.

Before this cohort, it was always about ticking the next checkbox, the next goal, and the next accomplishment. Now, I realize that's why I felt this mounting pressure closing in on me. I keep waiting to become this aspirational version of myself. I guess I felt like once I became "HER," I could finally rest and be content. But I realize now, that isn't really living. I'll probably always be striving for more and better, and I can't hold my breath while I do it. And it's definitely not fair. I wouldn't tell my loved ones, or anyone for that matter, that they would be so awesome when they become "x" versions of themselves. I'm always preaching that we should meet people where they are and try to understand their context. We should love them as is. So, why wouldn't I give myself the same treatment? And honestly, literally, as I type this, I realize I've approached a lot of my life with this harsh treatment. "They'll really respect me professionally if I accomplish what no one else has or if I make my mark in this very specific way." "The next guy will stay if I'm this version of me." "I'll feel worthy of God's love when I'm a more disciplined Christian who knows the bible forward and backward." This thinking caused me to discount my strengths and my accomplishments, and how people might perceive me or feel about me. So, now I'm working on loving this version of me because she is already worthy. She has already earned it. She is already valuable. (Or at least that's what I'm going to keep telling myself until I believe it. Ha!) Please don't take this the wrong way. I've never been completely void of self-confidence or self-esteem. I have absolutely amazing parents that made sure to shape me into a confident person. But life definitely has a way of testing your confidence and your fortitude. It can make you question so many things which connect back to those annual (or multi-annual) holistic check-ups. I have to work constantly to reinforce the things I know while continuously discovering the value in myself. I don't have it all figured out. But this cohort and all the things God brought together on my behalf changed my life for the better.

Honestly, this is really just a new beginning. A new beginning of discovery and understanding. A new beginning of grace. If you don't leave this chapter with anything else, please leave with this. Dear Black Woman, take care of yourself. Take care of all of you because all of you shows up professionally. You can't show up as your best self in any environment, even more specifically in an environment that requires perpetual giving, like the nonprofit sector, without taking care of yourself. You know that old saying, "You can't pour from an empty cup." Yes, here I am again with the clichés, but it's so, so true. Get to know yourself, rediscover yourself, understand your value, but also understand what fills your cup. It's okay, and you should seek professional help. We all could use a little objective help, right? And don't forget to connect. Lean into your relationships, personal and professional. You need the village not just for the laughs but for the camaraderie, to be seen, and to feel a little less alone. One last thing, please be generous with your learnings and your wisdom. Share the good stuff with the next Black woman. We need each other. I didn't realize how much until this cohort, but I'm so glad God knew for me. The generosity of the ladies in this cohort and our fearless, brilliant cohort director, Errika Y. Flood-Moultrie, has been invaluable. I'm forever indebted.

Thanks for allowing me to share a piece of my story with you.

It's definitely to be continued.

Sincerely,

Taylor Hall

CHAPTER TWENTY-FOUR
Tina L. Robertson

"I am still in progress, and I hope that I always will be."

- Michelle Obama

The wisdom of the rocks

Proverbs 4:7 New Century Version, The Holy Bible

"Wisdom is the most important thing; so get wisdom. If it costs everything you have, get understanding."

Dear Black woman in the nonprofit sector, you are positioned in this sector, placed here by God who, before you were even born, designed you to do good works within this ripe field where need, loss, oppression, and great challenge are prevalent. You are not haphazardly doing this work. You have a purpose and will be on multiple assignments, desirable and not, until your purpose is fulfilled. My greatest lessons throughout my nonprofit career have guided me back to this premise which has served as my anchor. Knowing this in my heart and soul keeps me grounded. It keeps me focused. It keeps me committed. It

325

keeps me encouraged and hopeful. It keeps me tethered to the calling that is upon me to be a light and changemaker in the hardest of spaces, times, and places. Yet, in it all, it is a good work! And I believe that knowing this will also support you throughout your nonprofit career.

I know you are continually thinking about your success. We all do ... and should. Who doesn't want to be successful in their career at every phase? As I think about what has made my career successful in this sector so far, it is not what others may define as success.

When I define success for myself, it is this: *being who I am to be, doing what I am put here to do with intentionality so that others will be inspired and driven toward their greater good, now and after I am gone.* This is my legacy. This is the measure of my success. And that means this could look a million different ways. It doesn't box me into a narrow view of success, particularly "climbing the ladder." This focus allows me to flow in the freedom of God's plan for me. If the proverbial "next level" is around the corner, great! If the promotion takes two to three years longer than I might have planned, can I still see myself as successful and purposeful where I am and in what I'm doing? Yes! More importantly, am I becoming who I am to be in all the steps and turns in my career? Yes!

What about you? What does success look like for you? What compelled you to a career in this sector? What is/are your anchor(s)? What do you hope to contribute? To gain? How are you focused on not just doing but being? What do you hope is your defining legacy in this sector?

We live in a time and society where a priority for living and working is more individualistically focused. "What's in it for me?" "I've got to get mine now. You better get yours!" "Do. You. because they are going to do them!" "You have worked way too hard. They owe you." These are just a few of the narratives we have likely internalized and, sometimes, actualized in our career paths. The reality is that our success doesn't always happen in this way or based on these expressions. And honestly, the nonprofit sector is not necessarily inclined to be faithful to us and our dreams. Yes, you are valuable, Sis! Yes, you do have to take care of yourself and advocate for yourself. Yes, you have to stand on principles and keep strong boundaries. And yet, you also need to be aware of other significant influences at play if you want to have a successful career in this sector.

I want to share with you why I believe so strongly in all of this. Some of the most valuable lessons I learned about being successful in this sector came from a specific experience I had in my childhood years. During the summer months when I was in elementary school when most kids were sleeping in and watching cartoons – for the first few weeks of the break from school—my six siblings and I were awakened each morning by my mom, around 6 am for about two to three weeks, to get out of bed to work in the garden. My mom decided to utilize the space on the reasonably large lot of land we owned on the side of our house to create a garden. What was so peculiar about this is that we lived in the heart of the city, in the hood. This wasn't country life or wide-open spaces, but my mom didn't care. She had plans in mind. My mother was "all goals," even back then.

A few things become very clear to me early on during that time. One, I knew I never wanted to plant a garden of my own when I got older. And two, I was definitely not a morning person. But the early part of the morning was the coolest part of the day in the summer months in Indianapolis, where I grew up. To avoid the heat and especially not having air conditioning (which wasn't uncommon in that part of the country), early risings made the most sense in my mom's mind.

The lot on the side of our house transformed from a play area to a planting area. We used every type of garden tool you can think of coupled with all our combined strength to complete the entire process of removing the grassy top from the surface across the wide span of the lot to get it to the point where the ground was ready for planting. The process was lengthy and challenging. However, my mom (all goals, remember?) had a plan and a methodical way of helping us prepare the ground for planting food that we would eventually harvest and that she would "can" (a food preservation process) so we would have enough to eat during the cold winter months of the year.

My mom was (is) a genius, innovative, and a brilliant leader and manager. She organized, equipped, and skillfully directed seven children of multiple ages in this enormous effort every year for

328

several years. I credit her for the "wisdom of the rocks."

You see, after we removed the top layer of grass from the dirt, we couldn't just start planting. We noticed that just underneath the top layer, there were multiple rocks, large and small, embedded deep within the layers of dirt. They had to be removed before the dirt could be prepared to lay down seed. Clearing out the rocks was the most grueling, undesirable, and time-consuming part of the garden work for us. It required a lot of patience and perseverance. It took the most time of all the efforts. And it was this process that yielded the hardcore wisdom that I've cherished over the years. **I learned that there are critical parts of any work that can't be wished away or pushed away.** If we had avoided the rock-moving work and just started putting the seed down because it was easier, less demanding, and took less of our time, it would have allowed for fewer days with the 6 am wake-ups, but it wouldn't have returned the harvest we were working so hard to get.

I learned that no matter what phase of the work you're in, it's all valuable and needed work. From all my memories during those "garden years," what is most salient and impactful to me is not the times we planted down the seeds. It was not when we watered the seeds or even looked for the sprouts, not even the harvesting. It was the work we did to clear the rocks. That remains front and center for me when I think back to the garden experience, as I call it. I have often wondered why that stands out to me. Was it because it was the most difficult part of the work? Was it because I sometimes dreaded getting up those mornings to do the rock clearing? The truth is, I don't know why. But I do know this: to put seeds down without moving them first would have been an exercise in futility. Apart from the rock-clearing, the growth and transformation of that lot would not have been possible. And ultimately, the larger goal would not have been achieved. It was all necessary to get to the end goal … to get to success.

My mom imparted her gardening wisdom while we were children. And that wisdom translated into life lessons. For me, specifically, those lessons became valuable best practices and the framework that ultimately helped me see and achieve success in my nonprofit career. My mom's wisdom became rock wisdom. As I learned from her, I learned from the rocks. My mom knew a few things that only wisdom could teach you. **She knew her landscape.** While I'm sure my mom likely wished she had the option of another lot to work, one with a different and more ready type of dirt—softer, more pliable, and better prepared for planting—that wasn't the lot she had (no pun intended). She worked within the context where she was positioned and saw purpose in it.

She accepted the condition of this lot on the side of our house and wisely, patiently, and methodically did what was required to produce in that space. **She knew herself,** her capabilities, and her limitations. She couldn't do it all by herself, nor should she have. Because of this, she also knew how to tap into and utilize the abilities of her children—to work as a team—to get the outcomes she knew were needed for her purpose. She also knew how to pray and depend on God for the harvest that only he could give. But her faith in the process, without her works, would have produced little or nothing. **She knew her purpose and assignment,** why she was even gardening in the first place (so her family could _successfully_ eat in the winter months, remember?). That is what drove her commitment through it all. **She knew the season** she was in and that the season wouldn't last. The summer months of getting up early and managing seven children to help in the garden wouldn't last forever. _This_ work was for _that_ time. What had to be done during the summer could not be done in another season.

She didn't expect the preparing and planting season to look the same as the harvest season. She was patient, hopeful, and expectant—knowing that even if she couldn't see the end result when _she_ wanted to, her labor was not in vain. Each season has its important purpose. What she was investing into the summer season was not any less a measurement for success than what would be required in other seasons.

I have remembered my mom's example and the wisdom of the rocks over the course of the many years of my career, particularly the last several spent in the nonprofit sector. I share them with you because I know that the "lots" you will find yourselves in to do this work will not always be desirable or easy. You might feel like giving up at times, question whether you are in the right profession, become jaded or disillusioned, or simply just lose your hope along the way and wonder about your success. I want to remind you that you are positioned. Don't give up on it. Don't give up in it. Be encouraged and grab hold of my momma's wisdom of the rocks!

Rock #1: Know your landscape.

Galatians 6:9 New Living Translation, The Holy Bible

"So let's not get tired of doing what is good. At just the right time we will reap a harvest of blessing if we don't give up."

We are wired and trained within the nonprofit sector to seek out and produce change. We are tasked with producing outcomes and, generally, pretty quickly, and many times, without all the needed resources to do so. We often enter our workspaces with our hearts set on the vision we have for the role-at-hand and goals for what we hope to achieve as part of our career path. We create expectations of ourselves and others, armed with all our marketable goodness defined in our resumes that include our skills, training, education, and experience. We are hope-filled with the essence of our transformational energy—that "Black Girl Magic." All well-intentioned and composed of our own plans and ambition. And yet, at times—not so far down the line—we can encounter resistance to our goals, barriers to our progress, and minimization of our abilities and potential.

This described me in the early years of my nonprofit career. I was so excited—always—about what I could bring and what I would do toward change. What I didn't realize until I tapped into the wisdom of the rocks from my momma's guidance is that the first and necessary step in guiding success in every workspace is knowing and understanding your landscape. All the gifts, talents, passion, potential, and planned accomplishments won't matter if you don't assess the landscape and the context in which you are working.

Steven Covey coined the phrase "Begin with the end in mind." This has incredible value. I would add this statement from the garden experience, "Begin with the landscape in mind." This looks like knowing the history of the organization as well as the city and community in which it exists. Knowing the organization's climate, culture, and life stage/cycle. Knowing its foundational structure and governance model. How has change happened traditionally? Has change happened at all? Is it stagnant or are there some signs of life and growth? Who holds the power? Is that power being shared? What are the values, and how are those exemplified?

In a nutshell, what is the reality and not what you want it to look like or feel like for you? These are just a few questions to help you assess the landscape and context in which you're working. Sure, some of these answers may take time to identify and understand, but much can be known if you just ask the questions and keep your eyes open to the truth in the answers. **Once you have assessed appropriately, you can accept and access accordingly.** In other words, when you know what's in front of you, then you can show up in that space with the wisest plan and goals for *that* particular landscape. You won't waste your energy trying to make that landscape something that it is not. It doesn't matter what your colleagues are doing where they are and how it looks in their "lot." Yours is yours. Remember … you are positioned. Purpose-minded. And desirability is not a requirement for success.

I love how my mom knew to make use of what was directly in front of her. She took note of the context and then got to work doing the next thing, then the next thing, then the next. Her larger vision hadn't shifted at all, but the way she approached the work did. So, if your landscape still has many rocks to clear before it is ready to move forward in the way you had hoped, adjust and help clear the rocks … or don't. But know that the frustration and challenge feel very weighty if you're in a rock-clearing context but are trying to put down seed where the ground is not ready—or trying to see sprouts and harvest before it is possible. Just do the thing that your context needs right now to the best of your ability. And simultaneously be a voice for what is needed next. All of this is part of the work and part of your success.

Reflection Questions:

Describe the landscape that lies before you. How have you assessed the context? What do you know and what is still yet to learn? What do you need to accept so that you can do the work you are positioned to do in this workspace?

Rock #2: Know yourself.

Romans 12:3 New Living Translation, The Holy Bible

"... I would ask each of you to be emptied of self-promotion ... Instead, honestly assess your worth by using your God-given faith as the standard of measurement and then you will see your true value with an appropriate self-esteem."

We tend to look externally first and think about what others need to shift, grow, and develop. We administer all kinds of assessments, different measures, and surveys and review applications for service provision and employment. These tools provide us with the necessary information to adequately assist and guide those with whom we are partnered for their next steps. Yet, it is easy, and even more so tempting, to minimize a needed and continued focus on learning and understanding ourselves in the various career stages and life cycles we move through as Black women and professionals.

Self-awareness, self-understanding, and self-acceptance are critical skills to practice that will serve you well as you engage in the work of serving others. Self-awareness includes being mindful of who you are (your identity) and who you are becoming. It also includes having an accurate sense of what you bring to the table as well as what you don't—what you will need from the support and input of others. This reflective practice helps you recognize and evaluate your assets, strengths, and your growth edges. Self-understanding is when you can connect and align who you are and what you possess to different contexts and relationships. Self-acceptance is self-love. It is a true and authentic combination of owning up to and being okay with who you are and where you are at any moment in time—

knowing that you have inherent value and worth even as you are in the process of being processed.

Also, it is so important to have an accurate view of yourself. While your inherent worth and value are never in question, it is possible to be unauthentic in life and in your career. If you overestimate your abilities, capacity, and readiness, you will not operate within the reality and necessity of who you are and need to be in this time and space. And consequently, the growth and development that is necessary to navigate and sustain future experiences and interactions will be lost. We live in a time when building brands and creating optics is the preferred way of doing life and business. Social media often offers the vision of a thing rather than the truth of it, painting the perfect picture when the reality behind it hasn't quite caught up with the illusion being offered. This can create a false impression about success and minimizes what is actually required to achieve it.

Worse yet, illusions are a false reality. You can't afford to subconsciously believe the hype. You are purposefully positioned ... a proud Black woman who understands that others' success is tied to ours. Choose to use the branding and other resources available to you to represent the truth of who you are and to uplift the truth of others.

On the other hand, underestimating your abilities, capacity, and readiness is equally as problematic as overestimating. Having an accurate view of yourself obligates you to stand up for all that you are, all your accomplishments, accolades, hard work, and achievements. It requires you to own and display all your shine and make no apologies for it. And do so with gratitude, grace, and humility. That shine hits different!

As Black women, we are susceptible to subtle messaging that tells us to either change to play up ourselves to the point where we can't be real with ourselves or others or dumb ourselves down so we don't offend anyone and make spaces feel comfortable for others. But we cannot abandon ourselves to fit into either of these binary narratives. We can choose to be successful in the authenticity of who we are … but first, we must know who we are and resist the temptation to be anything other than that.

What I appreciated so much about my mom when I think about the garden experience was that she didn't overrate or underrate herself. She was solid in being okay with who she was, where she was, and what was in her hand to do. She had strengths, and she played those up and used them, and she knew to ground herself in the truth of her growth-reality. She accepted when others (her children) offered to do the work.

As for me, learning about myself has been the most challenging yet rewarding life and career experience I have engaged in. This past year, I learned that I lean toward underestimating myself, and that has caused me to play down who I am and have become, particularly professionally. I admit to having bouts with imposter syndrome. What I love about life is that often, it will offer us unique opportunities to press into our growth edges.

As a result, I took on three new professional experiences, and I am so pleased with how they turned out. I am stretching and challenging myself more and more to be fully and boldly in my shine. I am so grateful that even after 30-plus years of working professionally, I am constantly learning something new about myself. I've realized that the more I learn about myself, the better I show up in all aspects of my personal life and career. And that extends to everyone around me. My best service to anyone in this sector is to be in process with myself, and I believe the same will be true for you.

Reflection Questions:

What is more challenging for you to practice, self-awareness, self-understanding, or self-acceptance? What seems to get in your way? What is new that you have learned about yourself in this last year? How is that new learning useful for you at this phase of your career? How are you accessing resources to learn more about who you are and what skills you possess?

Rock #3: Know your purpose and your assignment.

Proverbs 19:21 New Living Translation, The Holy Bible

"You can make many plans, but the LORD's purpose will prevail."

I have met with many people over the course of my career for different reasons. Some were for leadership development and mentoring; some were because they were dubbed "a good move for your career." With others, it was to help me learn how to mentally and emotionally navigate the terrain of the mostly white nonprofit sector. Through those connections, I received a multiplicity and diversity of input, guidance, and feedback on why I should take on a particular job. Some of it was conflicting. Some of it was extremely valuable and helpful. I am still so very appreciative of all who have poured into me. But how could I figure out what made the most sense for me? Was I supposed to be climbing the ladder to success? What did that mean, really? What should I be doing and when?

It became clear that I needed to take the time to truly sit with God and understand my 'why.' Why was I even in the nonprofit sector? I had a plan, yes. I had both short and long term visions. Check. But the more I spent time seeking out my purpose and praying about it, God's voice became clear. Then, I realized that climbing the proverbial career ladder wasn't my purpose. Lots of people "climb ladders" but don't live in their destined purpose. I knew that God placed me here to fulfill his purposes and destiny for my life, and my nonprofit career was one way He wanted to accomplish that. My purpose is to be successful in God's way. I shared earlier what that means to me.

Purpose is actualized through the assignments God gives us in various work roles and opportunities. In one place, it looked like me leading and managing a younger, maturing team who needed specific support, growth, and encouragement the way I would give it. In another place, it was to be the listening ear of the executive director who trusted me to guard their heart and struggles in that season. In another place, while sharing an office with a 25-year veteran therapist, my assignment was to soak up her wisdom and care and to learn as much as I could from her while seeing the most overwhelming client cases I have ever known.

When you know you're on assignment in your purpose, the work situations become a bit more manageable every day. Not always easy, but doable.

Several years ago, I had a conversation with a pastor friend when I was job hunting after making a difficult decision to abruptly leave a workplace when the work culture had deteriorated so significantly it had begun to affect my health. After taking a few days to settle into the change, I began to look for employment. In less than a week, I received four callbacks and had three interviews scheduled. One workplace, in particular, was very interested in me, and I was in them. However, it was going to be close to a $20,000 salary and benefits decrease from what I was earning, and the position title was a step-down. I wondered what this would mean for my longer-term career aspirations. This friend said these words I have never forgotten. "Sis, God operates on assignments, not on ladders." He encouraged me to know that God may move me up, back, over, down, or around. My career path didn't have to be a straight line up; it just needed to be purposeful. He encouraged me to remember that as long as I was living out God's purpose for me, I would never regret it.

You know what happened? I accepted that position. I worked at that place for two years, and because of the generosity of the executive director, I obtained 95% of my clinical licensing hours

340

toward my clinical social work designation in a split opportunity with another organization. This was not nor would it have been possible in the previous workplace or even the ones before that. The executive director left just short of my two-year tenure to work for another organization, and unbeknownst to me, she had recommended me to the board to serve as interim executive director. I accepted that new role, and my salary and benefits increased during those months by almost $40,000. If you do the math, that is double what I lost in income when I arrived at the organization two years before.

I think back to my mom and how she modeled purpose and assignment. Her purpose was to take care of her family. Her assignment in that time was to do it by planting the garden for food. I'm sure she would have chosen something different if given another choice, maybe something a little more glamorous and far less taxing. But whenever we gather as a family and reminisce, as it relates to the garden experience, we can't help but have so much gratitude for the provision it was and the bonding we shared.

Your purpose and assignment may not make sense to you but do it anyway. If God calls you to it, whether it feels like you're moving up, back, down, on the side or around, it will be fruitful and make a difference in your life and the lives of others.

Reflection Questions:

How have you determined your purpose? What assignment is yours presently? What is the hardest part of the assignment? Most rewarding? How will knowing your purpose and assignment help you be successful in the various stages of your nonprofit career? How will you keep from comparing your assignment to others?

Rock #4: Know your season.

Ecclesiastes 3:1 New Living Translation, The Holy Bible

"For everything there is a season, a time for every activity under heaven."

Ambition is a heck of a powerful driver. Yet, without wisdom, understanding, and discernment, it can recklessly take you off the road of your purpose and God's timing for different stages and steps in your career. In large part, your success will be tied to your ability to accept and patiently and strategically navigate the varied seasons of your career. I am the first to tell you that this has been the biggest challenge for me. Identifying the season I am in and working with the assurance that seasons will change has kept me encouraged and motivated in these recent years. It has also helped me get to a place of contentment in the latter seasons of my career. Knowing my purpose is my "why." Knowing my assignment is my "what." And knowing my season is my "when." Timing is everything!

If what we dream and hope for happens too soon, we may not be ready for or capable of what the moment calls us to. If we wait too long in comfort zones or become jaded, stagnant, or stuck, we may miss out on a perfect opportunity to do something new and grow in ways that are needed for our own development and for that of others.

In one workplace, I was in a leadership role where I was comfortable with my salary, job duties, and the flexibility it offered me to come and go as I wanted and to create programming as extensively as I wanted. It was ideal for me, and I had planned to ride it out in that role for as long as I could. Why change anything? It was working for me!

However, when an opportunity became available to move to the next level of leadership in that workplace, I thought about all the reasons I didn't want to leave the role I had. It was chill. After multiple contacts from colleagues and other leaders in that workspace encouraging me to apply for the position, I began to pray about it and consider it. What I realized was that I had grown complacent and stagnant in the position I was in. It felt good to me, but it was not the continued space for me. My season was changing, and I knew it and felt it. It was time for me to push out of that comfort zone and press into the next level of growth for me and embrace the purpose and assignment that would come with what was ahead.

Different seasons have different reasons. That is why you really need to know your purpose and assignment. They will correspond with your seasons. I think about how focused my mom was in those planting seasons. She knew the hard work had to be put in before any signs of growth could occur. She sacrificed so many mornings and her own time to ensure we put in the effort in the summer season to get to the harvest. If we didn't spend the energy to do the hard work and make investments into the soil, we could expect nothing in the harvest season. Operating on the wisdom of seasons means patience is an absolute virtue. My timing and what is timed for me by God are not always in alignment. That's why it's important to know your purpose and assignment and then tap into the wisdom of seasons.

And with that, try to enjoy and appreciate the season you are in (believe me, this is still my work in progress!). A quote by Lucy Pretorius speaks to this, "Borrowing from tomorrow will only rob you of all the blessings that you can enjoy today." We are consumed with the next in this society. We are enamored with what we do not have and what we are planning to get or be next. We want Fall to come because Summer is too hot. Then we get tired of raking the leaves and hope for a little colder air so the trees will stop shedding them. We are ready for the cold days and early dark evenings of winter to go in exchange for the bird-chirping mornings and once-again dewy, green grass lawns of springtime. Then it starts all over again. In our careers, we can exist the same way. Constantly working toward the next instead of making the most of the season we are in and letting the purposefully timed intervals of life guide our way. This is not easy. But to be purposefully successful throughout our careers, we will need to know the season we are in and make the best of it until the next one comes … in its time.

Reflections Questions:

What season are you in at this phase of your career? What is hardest for you in this season? What is the best part of this season? What is this season showing you or teaching you? What is most helpful for you to practice patience during this time while keeping your dreams alive?

Amazing, powerful, and gifted Black woman … I am so proud of you! I am grateful for you and what you are bringing into this space. I am excited for all that is in store for you and for others through you. Remember, you are positioned, and to be purposefully successful, you will need many resources along your career path. Most of all, *"Wisdom is the most important thing; so get wisdom. If it costs everything you have, get understanding." -Proverbs 4:7.* It is my hope and prayer that the wisdom of the rocks will help you do just that.

Blessings,

Tina

CHAPTER TWENTY-FIVE
Yasmine "YaYa" Lockett

"Don't try to lessen yourself for the world; let the world catch up to you."

- Beyoncé Knowles

The YAYA Method: when you aim, you achieve

L et's have a conversation. I need you to do me a favor and pretend to be someone else. I want you to pretend to be my dad because, well, that's who I am talking to in this conversation. I feel like my authentic self when I am talking to him. Okay.

Dear Dad,

Did you know I only had $44? I'm pretty sure you did because you know me. Thank you for not asking me to spend any of it on my journey to adulthood. It was enough to move into life and not too much to distract from the building process. Listen to this.

WHAT IS A BURGER? Oh, right, it's all I could afford with my $44 but DO NOT worry because, within the next three building

347

seasons, I could afford Applebee's! You're probably wondering exactly how I pulled it all off, right? Well, I prayed, shook the right hands, AND the wrong hands. I know you remember some of those wrong hands. Yeah, unfortunately, they are necessary on this path. Remember the man who followed me around without my permission? Still trying to figure out if he really enjoyed my stage presence and perfectly arched feet or not! Anyhoo, those experiences enhanced my cravings to set realistic life goals. Okay, back to the $44 that moved me into life because I still have not spent it all. I did think about sharing it with my building partners, but I needed to stay prepared for rainy days, and they were plenty! It rains a lot in this place, but it's never wet! Trust me, this place is NOTHING like home, so why did I stay?

Everyone keeps asking me that question, but by building season number five, I had a better understanding when I helped one of my former students, Churchill, enroll in a better-suited middle school. You heard me right, dad, I found my purpose! It was nothing to go outside of my comfort zone, go the extra mile, to help this young man further achieve his goals. Can you believe they force our students to attend schools based on their addresses? Okay, I am being a little dramatic because no one is forced, but I learned that our nation's school districts ACTUALLY make decisions over youth education without their input!

Daddy, I know things about the educational system because my passion has driven me to my purpose. Yep, I said it. Those leather

348

ballet and tap shoes took me on a path of self-discovery that I wasn't even aware of. Those blisters from my point shoes were a gift, a blessing. I mean, I'm surrounded by young people who cannot imagine walking in my shoes as a child. The interesting thing is, we NEVER had it all, and we worked hard for EVERYTHING! By the way, thank you and Mama for using most of your financial resources to feed my passion but MAN, if I knew what I know now, I would have saved you the trouble by simply bringing you the registration packets for free and reduced costs community programs that offered the same training and development.

This is why I helped Churchill. He did not deserve to be placed in an environment based on an assignment created by people he didn't know. His talents deserved to be nurtured in a place fitting of his desire. You taught me that! This is work, this is progress, so why are people so pressed about my credibility because I am not from here? Is it a crime to leave home to build a new home? There are members in my circle that say it is, but I am not ready to come home, and I do not agree. Purpose is still calling! Time to navigate disappointment. Folks will have to look at me as I reach for them. There is a specific language that I now know how to interpret for these realistic goals I mentioned earlier.

Building seasons six through 11 showed me that language. Guess what, 'I am the language," but I still needed to figure me out. The arts of networking, leadership, community, engagement, and outreach became near and dear to me. Oh, shoot, here come those titles. Titles! Why must they be of any importance? I thought this space was exempt from TITLES! Where on earth did I get that from? They usually get in the way, delay progression, and needs do not get met! MOVE, GET OUT THE WAY! Rest assured; I'm still navigating disappointment in my purpose. Remember, I had to give the engagement ring back, but we dodged some MAJOR disappointment. See, daddy, I am growing. Learning how to grow more efficiently. The ring was the wrong size anyway, and maybe it was a beautiful distraction.

That distraction may have interfered with me sticking to my $44 plan! Yes, the $44. Whataburger and Applebee's can have that because humble beginnings have transpired to purpose driven high-level professional priorities in spaces that penny-pinching, or pinching penny created. It's time to fine tune because I have a ton of Churchills to support and a million grown people to paint the bigger pictures to. Daddy, I am in season 13 and I got this! Your baby girl has as many answers as she does questions! I also have more tools for navigation AND I have a TITLE LOL. Do not worry, I am using this title and all future titles with PURPOSE and PASSION. Now before I go, I need you to answer my question. Did you know I only had $44?

Now I have your attention, let's talk about everything! The nonprofit space was the furthest thing from my mind since the beginning of time. This was not a plan or a goal of mine growing up. As a matter of fact, I didn't begin to understand the nonprofit sector until after graduating college. To me, all these Salvation Armies were the same. These are the organizations that raise money to give back, blah, blah, blah. There's no money in it and they are led by wealthy white people who need to fulfill their philanthropic obligations. Yes, obligations! Crazy right? Here I am thinking all nonprofits were founded by people who have deeply-embedded desires to give back to the less fortunate.

Nevertheless, before learning the truth, I was always convinced that it wasn't for me. No one in my family ever spoke about nonprofit work or even described it as a profession. The funny thing is I was practically raised in a nonprofit if we want to talk about church; I know, it's not the same (but it is). Think about it, tithes and offering are basically fundraisers. That money is essentially used to pay salaries and put money back into the church for expenses and community outreach. Participants (members) receive faith-based knowledge and spiritual guidance (professional development) to become stewards in the community (outreach). Let's go to church, hallelujah! Who knew? The preface was being set for years and I didn't even catch that nonprofit vibe because it's always just been CHURCH for me!

Wow, all those years choir singing, praise dancing, bible study, and Sunday school was preparation for a life I currently live. Interestingly enough, this work is more rewarding to me than singing in the choir at church. I'll explain that statement a little more later but for now, just flow with me.

At age three, my mother signed me up for ballet classes at a Young Women's Christian Association (YWCA), somewhere in Pittsburgh. Wait, what? The YWCA is a nonprofit. Okay, back to my story. Taking dance lessons was not my idea, but my parents knew what they were doing, right? Although, I've heard the stories of me screaming and crying when mommy leaves the room, I only remember the adrenaline I felt pumping at dance competitions by the age of six. Competitive dance was my thing, and those trophies were my vice! Being a professional dancer became my dream, and from that point on, every resource I could acquire was to feed that dream.

However, we didn't really take advantage of resources to feed this dream of mine. After the YWCA phase, we moved into the fee-for-service model. This model is expensive! Both of my parents worked to provide income to our household and could not afford dance tuition or private school, but they figured it out. If I had my way back then, I would have dropped private school in the third grade and used all my mother's money to feed my dream, dance. I couldn't even fathom going to a community center or a free program. How can quality be associated to free programs? It was definitely unheard of plus, I had to keep up with proper training like my peers to get where I was going.

Here's where I insert my first brief pause in this story to say, "Thank you parental units and hope I didn't break your bank too much!"

Dancing was the dream, the goal, and my first job! "Oklahoma!" was the first musical I choreographed and my first job. Most kids were only a year or two younger than me, but I was the CHOREOGRAPHER and I got paid! Now, here I am still feeding my dream and slowly climbing into the profession at 15 years old. I also had a regular job which included asking people, "How many?" and telling them, "It will be a 15-minute wait. Name please?" All additional pennies to pinch for the dream was the aim of the game.

High school was a piece of cake, right? All teenagers have jobs, play sports, are involved in the arts full time, and can maintain good grades with ease! Oh yes, did I mention that I was also helping my parents raise a toddler? Those years yielded fears and tears but above all the passion for my dream grew even more. You could not tell this tap dancing, hurdle jumping girl NOTHING and according to me, I had it all figured out.

College was not an option for me because my parents would not have it any other way. The decision to major in dance was the "my way or the highway" approach. Why weren't they excited about that decision at first? All I could think about was the crying in a dance class at age three! Hello, mother and father, this was pre-destined! Since I had to make college a priority, I would major in a field of my choice. If only the grades and test scores aligned with my talent, I needed a full ride! Countless auditions, low acceptance letters, and partial financial assistance were the only things rolling my way. We needed MONEY! Were we out of money due to years of paying dance tuition or private school? Surely those three years in public school and my getting jobs helped reduce stress on my parents' finances? Nope, that's not how it works, but college was still on me. I had to figure out how to get in, and this challenge felt like competing on the big stage.

University choice number three was a pivotal moment for my career, I just did not know it at the time. My mindset was still at the place of getting it over and done with. You do not need a degree to become a professional dancer. My goal was to perform and travel until my body gave out! I needed to be at auditions and looking for gigs! Going to college was a waste of time, plus, you will be old when you graduate, auditioning next to 18-year-olds! Let me repeat myself for a second, "I did not want to go to college!" The thought of disappointing my parents and family drove my thoughts in a positive direction and having a degree in dance seemed pretty cool now.

In four years, I could get back to chasing my dream. There were opportunities to come about that increased my appetite for college as well as expanded my network. Walking into the Greek life was one of them. This arena included maintaining an acceptable GPA, lots of public service, and an inherited network of amazing women all over the world. Of course, I was more excited about other details at the time so, imagine if I was excited about expanding my network? Sidenote, sometimes tunnel vision can delay progress. Be careful.

Having a full load all four years of my undergraduate career was crazy! I am not quite sure how I was able to join a sorority. Where did I find the time? Between classes, rehearsals, student teaching, work study, and gigs, it almost seemed impossible. Additional to all that, my ballet professor thought I was a joke, we were a joke. Or was it the issue of relatability? How many Black dancers had my professors trained? It wasn't making any sense because I made the audition! I was good and talented. Why were the best dancers on this campus so fragile in this new environment? I am referring to the seven percent of Black women who got accepted into this prestigious institution at the same time. My PWI (predominately white institution) needed Black women to build a diverse and inclusive environment. When will this freaking pattern end? I needed a release back then, too.

Partying was my release, nothing to be ashamed of here. Social entertainment can be a form of networking. The gift of gab is my thing especially with some music and libations! How to finesse the doorman or promoter can be another chapter in this book however, there is an art to networking in social environments. We were young with light pockets, sorority girls, and looking for normalcy outside of school. We needed to meet our sisters and brothers all over the city at various campuses to expand our network. Seriously, that is what we were doing whether directly or indirectly. To this day, I am still connected to individuals associated to my social endeavors who play an integral part in the manifestation that is today! With, all these proponents made a great recipe for this prequel of this story, my story, her story.

Privileged middle- and upper-class kids are the worst! I dreaded all of my teaching practicum hours which were spent at a local studio near campus. These little brats gave me anxiety like no other. Take me back to my high school student teaching days where I was allowed to be creative in my own way while working with kids who not only looked like me but also enjoyed a passion for dance. Maybe it was a different type of thrill that made the difference.

In high school, I needed to student teach to pay dance tuition. Here in college, I am now teaching for a degree with no immediate compensation. I get it now, but listen, as a 19-something-year-old, this was lame! The difference was in the pressure of achievement. Teaching in my home studio was familiar and gave me a sense of pride. Aging out as a student into a position of leadership while in pursuit of a professional dancer career hit different for me. While we found the means to support an expensive hobby, I did not grow up as a middle-class child, yet my family lived in a middle-class world.

The hustle was always real in my family, and we were good at figuring things out. The degree of separation for me in comparison to these whining brats I had to teach is privilege. Privilege was not a constant in my life, and I usually had to fight for it.

Everything seemed to come easy to all my private school friends as a kid. Slumber party and shopping weekend invitations were endless, but I couldn't always go. When I was in attendance, relationships I had with my peers were solid enough to overshadow my lack of. All my friends and their parents loved me! I'm talking about the "play in my hair and offer to pay for everything" love. Brown skin, that was the difference. Or was it? I believe my skin color started the additional recognition, but my personality and talent were the true front runners. At an early age, I believed that no one saw color if you gave them something else to focus on. Was I just trying to belong or fit in? Was I being my authentic self or was it performative?

I wonder if the students I trained in college took up careers in dance or was it just a hobby? Why did it matter so much to me? Those children had nothing to do with me or my desires, right? I thought so and couldn't quite put my finger on it. I used to always get that feeling, anxiety about connecting all the dots to every endeavor I embarked on. The longing to have everything make sense to validate a reason why. I believe I was still trying to prove myself. Entering college as a dance major seemed foreign to everyone and I was determined to prove them wrong so everything needed to have purpose and make sense. All things should have been aligned by my senior year until my professors said, "if you don't have a gig by graduation, good luck." Good luck? What does that mean? I am about to obtain a degree and that doesn't count? You mean college isn't going to give me a job? Where is the internal system of favoritism for the educated dancers? We should have a seat at the table! Panic! This panic was toxic, complimented by many half-baked ideas. Standing in line at D.C. audition for 14 hours in below freezing weather was one of them. Rejection and hypothermia became the outcome of that audition. When I went back to the drawing board, I made the decision to stay in Atlanta and audition until anything came about.

Graduating and celebrating the completion of that phase should have been motivation enough to launch into a dance career, my dream! Why was I still bussing tables and getting cut from auditions? A degree should equate to TSA pre-check (still feel that way) but it didn't. Here I am in a mild depressive state not because of failure but I want to prove my success to my family! Where are the gigs?

Right when I began to buckle down and resort to a plan of teaching in studios until I found a decent nine-to-five, my network began to knock on my door. "Have you heard of Dallas Black Dance Theatre?," says my childhood studio director. At this point, I didn't care if she asked me about a company in the pits of Idaho, I was there! Of course, I knew about one of the six historically Black founded professional dance companies in the nation! Why on earth is she asking me about that? She asked me because she knew me. She asked me because she knew my dream. She asked me because she knew my drive. Remember the student teaching to pay for tuition and associated fees of competitive dance? This woman was there for 12 years supporting those efforts while providing opportunities for me to succeed. How did I rise to the occasion over other amazing students under her leadership? Let's just say it was my time. No need to mention us sharing the same sorority … All I had to do now was make the cut! It was all on me, no pressure at all. AND FIVE, SIX, SEVEN, EIGHT!

I had only three weeks to figure out a complete life transition from Atlanta Georgia to Dallas Texas with no money or plan, other than dancing in the company. It was time to tap into that network again and this time I solidified a plan for transition with a place to stay, a job, and a mechanic! The mechanic was for my car ladies and gentlemen. That 1998 Chevrolet Malibu needed some tender loving care before making a 14-hour drive across the country. All those boxes were checked just days before my departure! "Look at me mommy, I made it! No need to be sad or uncertain, we've been planning for this. I got this because this is the dream. I must leave because this space doesn't compliment what I want. You can always visit and remember, I'm only a phone call away."

This plan was solid until it wasn't. My acceptance into this dynasty came with a few caveats. There was fame and no fortune, monetary fortune that is. Freedom of choice or speech was prohibited. They owned us. However, I was living my dream! College was not so bad after all so, how dare I complain! This beast, being a grown woman on her own as a professional dancer was ferocious! What am I doing? It's one thing to be prepared for something and adjusting but I made a 180-degree switch in three weeks and now I am by myself. Staying busy was the key. I needed to compliment my progress with a little cushion so, it was no problem for me to balance several jobs while training nonstop and performing all over the nation. The urge to prove myself was ongoing. There was no way I was going to fail.

In my efforts to continue to support my dream, I seemingly slid back into teaching. Now, I am in Dallas working with kids again but this time, it was the side hustle and not THE hustle. These little humans in Dallas were receiving training from a professional dancer now! The paychecks reflected that as well. Let's take this to another level and demand more. Within three years, I was coordinating outreach programs on behalf of the organization. Sounds good, right? Wrong! I had no clue what I was doing and here I was again with these KIDS! The only resources I had to pull on were my experiences with the different spaces of teaching dance to kids since high school.

How can I figure out how to connect those experiences with this work? Improvisation 101 kicked in. This is a college course I hated but now it's time to put it to use. First step was to ask these young people about their world. I needed to know their thoughts and what they wanted. After all, this group of kids were aspiring to be professional dancers like myself. Here was my opportunity to introduce them to a side of their desired field that included outreach which enhanced exposure. This party girl – I mean socialite – called every promoter, event planner, DJ, and friend she knew in her efforts to book unconventional shows for them to perform in. We shook things up a lot and I enjoyed every bit of it! My kids weren't just performing in schools; they were performing everywhere. Parents were excited and this youth ensemble felt good and made the organization look good!

Everything seemed to always circle back to this point but this time, something was different. The organization took on contracts with the school district that involved the integration of arts enrichment and education. Everywhere I was sent to teach came in the form of an afterschool or summer program. Children were receiving art classes for free through these programs. You mean to tell me that I can be a kid at a regular school and when the bell rings, I can stay and participate in a dance class for free? Everything I could recall from my childhood to now as I was pursuing my dreams in performing arts was starting to get together.

At this phase in my life, it seemed very simple to me. I knew every angle of this play because I participated in all these components one at a time. Seemed like I had a knack for this type of work and when I left the company, I knew what I wanted to do but wait, was this temporary or permanent? Was I pausing my dream or starting a new one? Here comes the mild depression again! Torn between getting back out there on that stage and moving on to build a sustainable life.

Should I be tapping into other talents or moving to a different lane on the same track? Is it time to go back to graduate school? As I was in limbo trying to sort things out, these contracts from different nonprofits kept coming. It was nice to have them, and Lord knows I needed them, but I also needed more.

I felt like I drove around the world each week because of all the campuses in high demand! Where is everyone? Am I the only one willing to provide enrichment services to kids afterschool? This pool had some shallow water which is probably due to the low compensation without benefits. The hours are weird as well so, how do I make this work for me? What do I need to do? I knew I couldn't live on contracts full time, I had STUDENT LOANS. Hello! I wonder if I can make this a full-time endeavor with a BFA in dance performance/pedagogy? There are some educational credits in there. Technically, those aren't needed for this career if you ask me, but we all know how that goes.

My expertise was needed in this field anyway. People who were running these programs held degrees in administration, business, and education but couldn't relate enough to supplement academics for kid's afterschool. Kids shouldn't be forced to go to a class because it's 4.15 pm and fourth grade is scheduled for theatre. Imagine having a room full of 20 or so fourth graders and only five of them actually want to be there. Guess what the other 15 kids are doing? Federal dollars come with unreasonable stipulations so, how do we conform to satisfy all parties?

Rise to the occasion and apply! I can run programs like this with my eyes closed. This is nonprofit like the Salvation Army, United Way, and the American Red Cross. The younger me saw it that way. The younger me was turned off by this sector. I was too focused on my dream but the passion for that dream had driven me to my purpose. A full-time salary with benefits position fell into my lap without warning! I was officially a nonprofit professional. Aside from unnerving data collection for reporting and compliance, this was my jam! Working for kids didn't bother me anymore. Did you catch that? I said working "for" kids and not "with." When you look at it that way, it changes everything.

There were many nuances in this work. The term "frontline" wasn't a title but it sure was used like one. This word describes people who directly work with participants in programs served. Frontline isn't considered a leadership position. Let's take a moment to chuckle right here. All my hard work, dedication, sweat, stress, etc. is discredited to being just frontline. This word needed a new definition to me however, I'll bite for now. I am at the bottom of this nonprofit totem pole, right? (wrong). I need to continue studying and researching.

You see, I had a boss, who had a boss, who had a boss, who had THE boss. All the bosses above me took the meetings and set the strategic plans. Frontline implemented the work, collected feedback from participants, and built the relationships within the programs and at the schools. I enjoyed this work. I enjoyed learning about the kids, their families, their communities, and their desires. I enjoyed bringing their ideas to life on these campuses. The rewards outweighed the politics of dealing with ignorant and/or unwavering decisions made by people in higher up positions, "the boss's boss."

However, the money would often stop or run out, which usually causes professionals like me to make ongoing adjustments. How could Annabelle and Sally to keep their positions amid all this inconsistency with funding and grant cycles? Why is Mark a campus manager for a predominately African American school? Things weren't really adding up and unfortunately, it's survival of the fittest for me, for us. When I say "us," I am referring to Black people and more specifically, Black women! We were killing it out here in these streets!

However, climbing the ladder into a rightful position was challenging. I don't know what took me so long to get annoyed with the words "you need a little bit more experience and have you thought about going back to school?" The more I got involved in this work it didn't make sense to go back and get another degree for what it is that needed to be done. I mean, this work was about creativity, expression, passion, and determination and I mean what were we all doing here. I felt like we were just collecting a bunch of data and turning it in so we could continue keeping our funding so, where we actually getting any work done for these families that we were supposed to be serving. Oh, times up, the funding has run out!

So, what's next, where do I go? Remember when we talked about this, I said that the funding is inconsistent and often ends abruptly. Nonprofit feels like gambling. It feels like professional gambling to provide resources for people in need. It can really cause anxiety if you let it and I wasn't quite sure why I had so much anxiety about this work. I guess I really was living my purpose. Everything began to align, and now it was time for me to figure out how to navigate so I could get to a place in this space where I could make some calls, call the shots, make the decisions, and have that seat at the table. How would I get there? What was the right channel for me? By the time this grant cycle had run out in this position that I had obtained, I knew it was time for me to move. Moving up or out was the question. Thankfully, that networking came knocking on my door again. This time it was internal networking! Can you believe that the organization that I was currently thinking of transitioning out of is the sole reason I moved into the next space of my career?

Respect the process, no matter what it is. I have to say it took me a minute to respect the process, but now I know, I'm so glad I figured it out! The next phase of this nonprofit career, purpose, included having the opportunity to travel around the city of Dallas observing and assessing other out-of-school time programs for children. Some of these organizations were partners from my previous place of employment and now I get to share my field of expertise with them in their endeavors for their program needs and desires.

Here I am now, traveling from program to program, seeing every individual, unique program thinking, "we're sitting on a goldmine here." I'm also looking at myself in a way that I can recognize I'm experienced now! I have a wealth of experience. As a matter of fact, I've been doing this since I was 15 years old! I should be writing a book about this (no pun intended).

However, the irony is that most of the programs I engaged with were predominantly white-led, yet provided services to populations of minorities, people of color, you know, Black and Hispanic people. In this space, I consult with the organizations' executive white leaders. Did you catch that? I am meeting with CEOs and directors, consulting them on program quality initiatives, so they can, in return, provide effective programming to the population they are trying to serve. Am I still frontline? Frontline now had a new meaning to me it can be more than just providing hands on services directly to participants. The definition of this word is evolving so it basically depends on the mission. I still considered myself to be frontline in a different capacity.

Be yourself because the original is always worth more than a copy! Authenticity is very important to this work and to me. Often, people surrounding me will say, "don't take it personally, it's just work." I disagree, which is why I have been able to single-handedly create an entire program from the ground up. Put all your background experience, networking, and professional development together, and brand it! My brand brought me to a chapter in my life that I was not expecting to see for a while. This TITLE feels good! I am now encouraged to use it in a manner in which necessary progress of change will be brought to the forefront.

FOR ME, ADVOCACY IS THE ABILITY TO RECOGNIZE AND REVEAL THE TRUTHS THAT WILL BENEFIT OTHERS. TO COMFORT THE AFFLICTED AND AFFLICT THE COMFORTABLE IS MY METHOD TO ENSURE EXCELLENCE AND EQUITABLE FOR ALL STUDENTS IN THE COMMUNITY.

Yasmine Lockett

I am using this title to show off unconventional pathways to success. I am a nonprofit educator, and I am a Black woman in nonprofit leadership. I will no longer feel subjected to feeling inferior to those in power but instead, I will have my seat at the table.

CONCLUSION

You are done reading this book. All these pains you have gone through as a Black woman may be engulfing your mind, yet you are feeling motivated to restart your journey. But where are you standing today?

Are you the girl feeling separated from others in the classroom? Are you the one feeling insecure because of your dark color and kinky hair? Or are you the worker sensing segregation in your workplace?

No matter where you stand, this book can relate to you. It is about the stories of women who lived through the notion of being inferior in early childhood, while others learned about being discriminated against during studies.

Ultimately, they joined a nonprofit organization. They sought to bring progressive changes to the structure and policies, but they were ignored or blamed repeatedly, and they decided to quit the job.

The consequent realization was that their races are a stumbling block to the persuasion of nonprofit services. Many fell into the pit of imposter syndrome, i.e., doubting their abilities. They started believing in white superiority as they had a monopoly over the nonprofit sector.

In the end, they all succeeded in breaking the cycles and systems created to keep them marginalized. But how did they succeed? By finding solutions like discovering one's support system or believing in one's strengths.

This book is full of lessons, but the question is when will you apply them in your life? Chin up, as *it's time to dare to live your way.*

ABOUT THE ORGANIZER

Errika Y. Flood-Moultrie is the leader of Black Women in Non-Profit Leadership (BWNPL) programming, Executive Director and Founder of Connections Multiplied, and most recently, her nonprofit organization Connections Multiplied, Too. An experienced consultant and coach with extensive knowledge in nonprofit management, program and fund development, capacity building, and leadership development, she holds a Master's in Organizational Management from Dallas Baptist University. BWNPL and Connections Multiplied - formerly recognized as Connect Three was founded out of her experience, proven executive skills, and passion for empowering nonprofit leaders to pursue personal purpose while leading with visionary excellence.

Having held positions as National Field Director for the American Diabetes Association, Director of Community Engagement for the Dallas Symphony Orchestra, Senior Director of Marketing & Public Relations for the Dallas Black Theatre, and most recently, Director of Strategy and Operations for Dallas Truth, Racial Healing and Transformation (TRHT).

Errika is best known as "the connection catalyst," able to strategically guide and facilitate leaders and organizations in the development, implementation, and funding for exciting and innovative new initiatives.

As a consultant with over ten years of experience in providing facilitation, project management, and strategic counseling for moving organizations through their organizational equity planning and implementation, Errika led the grant development and project implementation of the W.W. Kellogg Foundation-funded TRHT efforts in Dallas. As the lead consultant for the local initiative, she was responsible for facilitating the donor collaboration seeking support, writing the grant for support from Kellogg, and led the project direction for the $1.5 million effort in Dallas. She leveraged her experience, passion, and connection in this role in the nonprofit sector to lead infrastructure development, community engagement, and facilitation and training for the Racial Equity Now cohort.

Over the years, her work with various agencies also motivated her to develop a new generation of leaders who think critically, act courageously, and work collaboratively in the ever-changing and highly competitive nonprofit arena. Consequently, Connect Three provides not only innovative strategies for agencies but also professional networks that produce high-performing professionals who reflect the communities that they serve.

Errika is fully engaged in her community and serves on various boards and within her church. She is the proud mom of a beautiful daughter, Sydney, and a vivacious 100-pound Rottweiler puppy, Orion, and resides in the Desoto, Texas.

Made in the USA
Monee, IL
24 April 2024

57416863R00207